Journey to Kars

Philip Glazebrook was born in 1937 and has travelled in many parts of the world. He has written four novels, *Try Pleasure* (1968), *The Eye of the Beholder* (1974), *The Burr Wood* (1976) and *Byzantine Honeymoon* (1979). He lives in Dorset with his wife and four children.

Intrigued by nineteenth-century accounts of adventurous journeys through the Ottoman Empire, Philip Glazebrook became fascinated by the heroic characters which the travellers developed for themselves in their writings. With this interest and many questions in mind, he planned a journey of his own, which took him through the old Serbian and Greek provinces and islands, through the ruined cities of Asia Minor as far as Turkey's eastern frontier with Russia at the fortress of Kars, then back by Trebizond, Istanbul and the Balkan capitals. He travelled alone for months at a time when Turkey was under martial law. Out of his journey grew this remarkable book, of which Paul Theroux said, 'It is a rare travel book that combines the personal and the scholarly with a good rough trip, but *Journey to Kars*, is just such a book – I think it a considerable achievement.'

D0594862

PHILIP GLAZEBROOK

Journey to Kars

PENGUIN BOOKS

Penguin Books Ltd, Harmondsworth, Middlesex, England
Viking Penguin Inc., 40 West 23rd Street, New York, New York 10010, U.S.A.
Penguin Books Australia Ltd, Ringwood, Victoria, Australia
Penguin Books Canada Ltd, 2801 John Street, Markham, Ontario, Canada L3R 1B4
Penguin Books (N.Z.) Ltd, 182–190 Wairau Road, Auckland 10, New Zealand

First published by Viking 1984
Published in Penguin Books 1985

Copyright © Philip Glazebrook, 1984
All rights reserved

Printed and bound in Great Britain by
Hazell Watson & Viney Limited,
Member of the BPCC Group,
Aylesbury, Bucks
Typeset in VIP Bembo

Journey to Kars

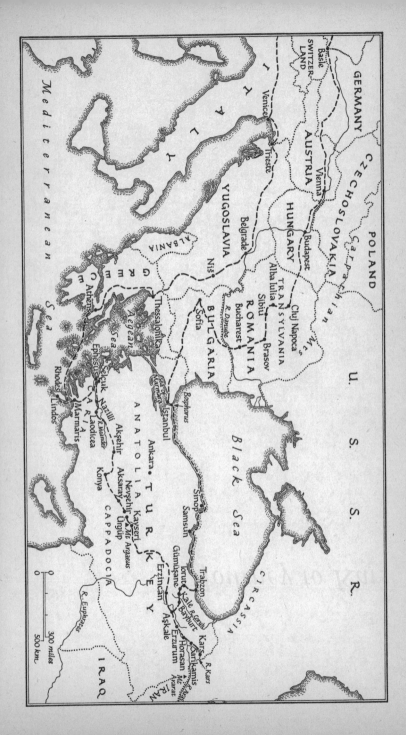

I

※※※※※※※※※※※※※※※※※※※※※※※※※※※※※※※※※※※※※

I

I had stopped at Belgrade for the sake of one view, nothing else, so in the morning I walked up through the town, under tolling bells and a wet sky, towards the dark old fortress which I knew would command the prospect I wanted to look out upon.

It was a cloudy warm morning in September threatening rain. Soon I reached a park, gravel walks, benches, plenty of strollers, pleasant if shabby grass, well stocked with busts of patriot and philosopher. Groups of old men sat about as if discussing their part in the War; or perhaps a military flavour seemed to infect them from the fosse filled with artillery, mementoes of both wars, which surrounds the fortress I was approaching. From a hut labelled FOREST MUSEUM there trilled the recording of a nightingale's song, such famous music warbling amongst the rusty guns that I was reminded of one of those allegorical Great War poems which you need a classical dictionary to understand. I hadn't forgotten that it was here, upon this Serbian fortress of Belgrade, that the first shells of the Great War exploded.

But it was on account of Belgrade's significance sixty or so years before 1914 that I had left the train from Paris the night before and had climbed this morning to the fortress. Now, by way of a bridge over the grassy ditch, and tunnels through many a stout wall, I emerged under an immense sky on the highest rampart, and took in the view I had come for. The Danube! The Danube at its confluence with the Sava lay below. From my feet walls and hillside fell rapidly away to that vast pool below the fortress where the two rivers rolled their tides together, and from which the Danube rolled on, flowing southward brimful through forest, flowing under a low wet sky, its broad unhurried waters showing in whirlpools, or against labouring boats, the suck and swirl of its power. Here, between Semlin on the Sava's Austrian bank and this fortress of Belgrade under Turkish suzerainty, lay the frontier between Christendom and Islam for much of the nineteenth century. Whoever pushed off in a boat from Semlin in those days, with their baggage and servants and English saddles and English guns, to approach the crescent-crowned mosques glittering above the dark water, here began their Eastern travels. 'There was something solemn in the ceremony of departure,' wrote James Fraser of his crossing in 1836, 'for once gone there was no returning; it was like quitting the living for the dead; and as I shook hands with my last two friends, and got into the frail punt-like boat, I could not help thinking of Charon and the river Styx.'

This was the view I had come for, and these were the travellers I had hoped to glimpse as they pushed off on their adventures. I meant to meet them again and again, between here and Turkey's eastern frontier with Russia, where I intended to go, and to understand, if possible – by seeing some of the scenes they travelled through – something of what was in their minds; why they came, what they wanted of the East, who they thought in their hearts they really were, these Englishmen of the middle years of the nineteenth century, who travelled restlessly about the realms of Sultan and Shah in a spirit of adventure which seemed to be inherited, or imitated, from the knights-errant of Malory and Tennyson.

The threat of plague, which entailed quarantine in a lazaretto for anyone emerging from the Turkish Empire, was what Fraser fixed on to make return 'impossible' once embarked at Semlin; but plague, and the gloomy bastions of Belgrade above the water, stand in that extract (and in the traveller's mind) for dread of all manner of menaces and dangers in the East which lay ahead. What gave them the appetite for such dangers? Did the false-tongued pasha and the robber chieftain do duty for the Sorcerers and Black Knights of Gothick romances? I had thought about these strange individuals, and their motives for Eastern travel, at odd times whilst reading their *Travels* in the library at home, or working in the garden or woods; now I wanted to see whether the ideas and theories I had evolved seemed watertight away from such quiet scenes, when tested against experience of lands they had travelled through. I formulated to myself this question:

What was the impulse which drove middle-class Victorians to leave the country they loved so chauvinistically, and the company of the race they considered God's last word in breeding, to travel in discomfort, danger, illness, filth and misery amongst Asiatics whose morals and habits they despised, in lands which, at best, reminded them of Scotland?

That was the question I had set out from Victoria Station the day before to answer, and this is the account of my journey. I have been nowhere unusual. I have done nothing reckless, made no discoveries. But the scheme of my travels is this: that besides going myself as far as the valley in Armenia where the Araxes flows into Persia, besides looking through my own eyes for a glimpse of the snows of Ararat, I have been there, and to Konya and Trebizond and many another haunted city, in the company of ghosts, the shades of real travellers, whose voices I have tried to overhear, and whose thoughts I have tried to understand. I have heard Seneca quoted to the effect that, in order to make a delightful book of travels, you must first make yourself a delightful companion. There is no chance of that. Anyone who has travelled with me two stops on the Underground advises me to travel alone. But if I could communicate a one-hundredth part of the interest and high spirits which sustained me without flagging almost every mile of the seven thousand or so that I travelled, by bus and boat and train, in the months I was away, the book would be worth reading.

2

An evening or two before I left Dorset I described to a neighbour (who has been all over the world) my intention of travelling to eastern Turkey by boat and train and bus without a move planned beyond the possession of a single ticket for the train to Athens which I had in my pocket. He thought for a bit and shook his head (like the eldest oyster who did not choose to leave the oyster-bed): 'No, I should worry about my next night's lodging too much.' Those are the words of a realist. Objections raised by others – thirty people a day murdered in Turkey that summer, for instance – show them not to be practical travellers. What is most essential, in reality, for peace of mind on a journey is a watertight attitude towards your next night's lodging. You either book ahead, and don't go if you can't get a booking; or you don't book and don't worry. My trouble is that I'm a booker-ahead trying to squeeze into the other category because I admire it more. Belgrade, my first stop, found out my weakness.

Worse than the moment when the aeroplane tilts downward to point at the sparkling lights of a city where I haven't got a bed for the night was the recognition through wet dark windows that the long khaki-coloured train was clanking into the suburbs of Belgrade. With all its faults the train had become my home on the twenty-six-hour journey from Paris. In the past I have often seen these drab East European coaches attached to French trains, destinations behind the Iron Curtain stencilled on their plates – BEOGRAD, PRAHA, BUCUREŞTI – a grimness and even a menace about them, but I had never before clambered up into that part of the train. At the Gare de Lyon I did. In corridors crowded with refugee-like persons clutching bundles or sobbing at windows I recognized that this, not Victoria Station at nine-thirty that morning – not even Dover Castle receding from the deck of the Channel boat – was my real departure. My dread of the whole journey crystallized: and my exhilaration and buoyancy increased.

Why I dreaded Turkey I don't know, but I did. This was the anniversary – 23 September – of my first being sent away to school thirty-three years ago, and I felt that what I faced now was just as hostile: severance from family and from all that is familiar; non-comprehension of the language and customs of those I must live amongst; uneasiness, and uncertainty, and discomfort. But I felt too, as the train gathered speed through the flare of sunset south of Paris, the buoyancy of a boat the tide floats, and the tug of the wind in its sail.

> There lies the port: the vessel puffs her sail;
> There gloom the dark broad seas . . .

The train went through a metamorphosis before leaving the West. I had stayed at the corridor window the night before, watching the vast dark mountains of Switzerland slide against the sky until the Simplon swallowed the train; in the morning, at Mestre, in the wide cool perspectives of early Italian light, Western coaches and Venice-bound passengers were shed. What remained of the train set out very slowly, with a sinking heart, for Belgrade. It was empty, and somehow old-fashioned. As we neared the frontier, the line wound through dream-scenery, a sea-coast of cliffs above aquamarine water, of cypresses and stone castles, such scenery as exiles misremember of a homeland left long ago. The empty train, the scenery, were like a void between two realities.

At Trieste the void was infilled with a rush. Into the train swept a crowd of sturdy, darkish people with a thousand bags and bundles. They pushed into seats, squashed luggage into racks – they overwhelmed the train by settling upon it the way starlings overwhelm trees, a dingy, shrill, wing-rushing crowd dropping to roost on a line of carriages. Now began the waiting, which crowds bring with them. Uniforms tramped up and down the corridors. On platforms, and in sheds, more uniforms passed and repassed. The officials' faces, under peaked caps, were as distinct from the faces of the shabby brownish crowd in the train as gaolers from the gaoled, or the army from the mob it fires on. Between train and sheds, in a rustic corner of dust and weeds against a fence, there squeezed a family of gypsies, complete with babies and fibre suitcases and cooking pots. A girl of about fifteen with a baby at her breast wandered about quite freely on the tracks between train and sheds. From the windows, as they spread meat and bread on handkerchiefs on their knees, and drank from big brown bottles, the imprisoned passengers looked down on her. They didn't envy her. The flash of gaiety about her coloured clothes and streaked hair didn't appeal to them. The officials ignored her as if she didn't exist, and the people in the train watched her wanderings with smug pity. Hours passed. Officials came and barked at us, and went away again. I read one of the little World's Classics I buy whenever I see them, and save up for journeys.

The passengers in my compartment were every one of them smuggling blue jeans into Yugoslavia. The minute the train started, which at last it did, starling chatter burst out anew, and all delved behind seats and curtains for their prizes. Materials were fingered and compared. Trade names ('Cowpunch', 'Regal') were gloated over. I had let one of the women hang her fake-fur coat behind my head, so that it would pass as mine, and now I came in for much congratulation (one of the men spoke Italian) as well as for a presentation bottle of beer and a dip in the salted nuts.

Meanwhile steep pine woods and narrow valleys crept past the window. By some special quality of dullness and slowness the journey now became an immensely long one. The train had become its true self, the self promised by those stencilled plates, BEOGRAD, on the drab coaches at the Gare de Lyon. People relaxed. Buttons were undone. Shoes were removed, and swarthy toes appeared on the seat beside me. Some slept. At the window, on low flat lands which had replaced the mountains, here and there an ancient was out minding the cow, cloaked, leaning on a staff, watching the beast graze a strip of grass amongst the maize. Drizzle came on with the dusk. The snail's pace – the utter change in all one's circumstances – the anticipation, and apprehension, of the slowly approaching destination – these were the very reasons I had come by train.

At Zagreb almost everyone descended. Only the woman whose coat I had helped smuggle remained in my carriage. Under the feeble bulb she lay on the seat opposite me, her prize pulled over her head, coughing when she wasn't snoring. Rain scratched the window. I tried to quiet the agitation I felt about arriving in Belgrade. At last the train, so slow all day through those pine woods and winding valleys, so slow over the plains, crept slowly into the battered surroundings of a station, and stopped with the finality of the terminus.

Outside the building lay wide and desolate wet spaces, and

trucks rushing through gushes of neon spilled in puddles. I put my bag in a taxi at the kerb and told the driver to go to the Palace Hotel, which I knew to be in the high old quarter of the town near the fortress. Up steep streets he sped into leafier, quieter avenues. My hopes rose tentatively. The Palace looked the right sort of hotel, too, when we stopped at its door. In I went. They had no room. The clerk, to his delight, was able to add that I wouldn't find a room in all Belgrade, either, on account of a UNESCO conference which had brought 2,000 delegates to the town.

This was the moment I remembered my Dorset neighbour shaking his head like the eldest oyster. I could have booked so easily; or found out that there was no room, and not come. Three more hotels had no rooms and no suggestions. It was eleven o'clock, raining, the taxi driver losing interest. In India, if you suddenly fall into one of the holes which is apt to appear in general plans of travel, you can go back to the station and sleep on a table in the waiting-room. But the solution in Mysore doesn't answer in Belgrade; and here is the crux of all travelling difficulties, that a problem surmounted in a certain instance in a certain land doesn't help a bit in another case elsewhere: each problem is unique. As I said, I'm a booker-ahead trying to pretend I belong in the other category. I faced several months of looking for a hotel room in a strange town in the evening of most days. I didn't feel up to it, failed the test. What was the use of resolving to subdue the dread I felt of Turkey, if I became demoralized by the lack of hotel rooms in Belgrade? In advance you worry about a boulder in your path, but in practice what you get is a pebble in your shoe.

However, in the end the Hotel Moscva, an island of splendour between roaring boulevards, had a duplex free. It was awful. From a fragile sitting-room a stair spiralled up to a dainty bedroom. Traffic threatened to shake the furniture apart. A bad beginning, to be obliged to pay for unwanted 'luxury' at the outset of a long and maybe hard journey: I wanted to settle down at the right level, which the second-class couchette on the French train last night had been, and to make myself content and comfortable with hard beds and short commons. It was a long way to Kars. 'Be satisfied with little,' David Urquhart advised travellers in the East, 'support the bad without repining, enjoy the good as a gain, be pleased with all things.' And here I was one night from home in a tacky duplex. Still, relief is a kind of ersatz delight, and I was relieved to have a bed of any kind to climb into in Belgrade that night.

3

I remained walking about the ramparts of the fortress of Belgrade until I had pictured many scenes on the pool where Sava and Danube meet below its walls. I imagined the immense barges shaped like Noah's Arks in which herds of swine were dragged upstream by forty horses from Wallachia to German tables; and the early paddle-steamers smoking and clanking down the river from Vienna to the Black Sea; and the barges of pashas fluttering with the silks of veiled Circassians, their slave-pulled oars glancing in the watery light. I remembered an incident, too, a Frenchman's début in the East, which took place in the pasha's palace here, and which displays the English genius for mocking the French under cover of pretended friendship. It was 1850, and the Englishman Edmund Spencer was about to withdraw with his French travelling companion from the pasha's audience chamber, on whose floor rested on every side the pipe-bowls of the Turkish dignitaries' chibouks:

As an old traveller, having learned caution on former occasions, I succeeded in making my retreat without doing any injury; but my friend, this being his début into Oriental society, was somewhat over-anxious to exhibit that politeness for which his nation is celebrated – he, therefore, on rising to depart, bowed to the Pacha and the assembly with great ease and elegance, at the same time, stepping backwards, smash! went one of the pipe-bowls. With a suppressed *sacré* at his own awkwardness, and turning quickly round to the owner, alas!, the crush of another bowl was echoed by another *sacré*, and stepping backwards with still greater alacrity, another and another bowl fell a sacrifice. Mortified and confused beyond measure at his maladroit evolutions, our bewildered friend completely lost his self-possession, and reckless of all

consequences, made a hasty retreat, crushing bowl after bowl in his
passage to the door . . .

'The unwonted tempest of merriment which shook the walls,' he
concludes, 'appeared as if it would never have subsided . . . [at]
the unsuccessful attempt of my friend to impress the grave
Osmanli with an idea of Parisian elegance of manners.' It is not
surprising to learn that after a week or so (during which Spencer
implies that 'my French friend' can't ride, is immoral, and is
thought by the Serbians not to belong to a Christian race on
account of the Revolution of 1789) the Parisian finds himself
'from fatigue, unable to continue his journey'. Though exacerbated by one of them being French and the other English, the
relationship of these two – rivalry, contempt, irritation – seems
to me a type of the stress present between all travelling companions. You see the character of a narrator in a book of travels far
more plainly revealed in conflict with a companion than alone. I
stayed some time on the gusty walls above the Danube, thinking
of the Traveller and his companion I should need to invent – and
of their characteristics and their relationship – if I was to write a
novel of his adventures which would make the most of the
fascination I have felt for years in the type. Then I returned to the
uncertainties of my own trip.

   The Hotel Moscva has a travel desk whose apparatus of
efficiency, and nice clean girls, had fooled me into trying to book
through them a couchette on the Athens train. I failed (they
couldn't do anything except book seats on aeroplanes) but went
to the station, which sent me to an office in the town, where I
was told you couldn't book berths, you just had to get to the
station early. Better not to try to arrange your next step, than to
try and fail. Never be taken in by signs saying TRAVEL DESK!
TOURIST OFFICE! INFORMATION! Rely on yourself alone. I went
to the station early, and there I waited with the crowd crouched
amongst its luggage on shabby platforms. There are no seats.
Because it was the only building nobody else was leaning against,
I leaned against the police station, but a policeman came out and
drove me away. I ate a paste-filled wedge of dusty bread, and
waited some more, sitting at last on the platform like everyone

else. I had started out from London with one bag only, but I had got no further than Dover before the handle began to rip out of the fabric, so in Belgrade I'd bought another smaller bag to distribute the weight, and I sat on the platform fussing my possessions from one bag to another like a hen with its eggs.

At last the Akropolis Express rumbled in under the dirty roof-arch, and I sprang aboard. Money pushed into the attendant's hand secured me the promise of a berth. The waiting, a preliminary to all events in countries where officials can arrange people to their liking, had been quite unnecessary. Another time I would have a decent lunch in the opulent quarter and catch the train precisely; but of course there isn't ever 'another time', there's a different time somewhere new, with changed rules.

The train wasn't at all like yesterday's. Though crowded, it was crowded in a different way. For interest I walked its full length as soon as I'd settled my possessions on to bunk and rack. In a succession of coaches Greek peasants were stacked in layers on their shelves in the darkness, or were crouched over food and cooking stoves on the floor, tatters of cloth screening babies, a gabble of Greek spilling out into the corridor. Glimpses into their compartments were like glimpses you might have got from horseback into the tents of their ancestors migrating with the flocks from summer pastures. And indeed I suppose it was from summer work in Germany that these poor families were returning home.

In other compartments Germany was sending out her young by the score. Rigged out in denim and sneakers, asleep with mouth ajar or lounging vacantly with beer bottle in hand, as mild and downy as young rabbits, these large fair Saxon boys and girls sprawled in hundreds along the train. You can't really describe as 'students' those empty, incurious faces gazing into space. A student is altogether a more active, and focused, individual than any of these creatures appeared to be. Not a single one amongst them was reading a book, or had a book in his hand; nor did I see one pair of eyes looking out with any interest or eagerness at a landscape which must have been new and strange to most. They are more like pilgrims than students. They have that mild listlessness of expression – the nearest an inferior artist can get to depicting Virtue – and the same huge burdens on their backs, which I remember from illustrations of the little band of pilgrims in *The Land of Far Beyond*, by Enid Blyton, in the edition of that work which I read in about 1946. From then on, it was of pilgrims on their way through the pages of a child's book that they reminded me wherever I came across them.

At the end of the train I came to a ramshackle café-on-wheels pulled through the Balkans behind the last coach, in which I ate all there was – bread and cheese – and drank some beer. Then I found an empty compartment for the afternoon, with shiny slippery seats, where I read Tolstoy or looked out at Serbia. It is a most suggestive landscape. At the time of my chief interest in it, the whole of Yugoslavia and Bulgaria (as well as Albania and much of Romania) were provinces of European Turkey. Repression and massacre followed frequent rebellions. At Nis the Turk built a tower of human skulls to overawe the Rayahs, or Christian subject-race. Not far off, on the fort of a Montenegrin chieftain on the summit of a rock, Edward Mitford (travelling with Henry Layard to Persia in 1839) counted 'a horrid array of forty-five Turkish heads stuck on lances and blackening in the sun . . . which was rather calculated to damp our spirit of enterprise'. Through these scenes they rode as through medieval Europe, Layard having thrown up his position in a London solicitor's office, Mitford on his way to join the Civil Service in Ceylon. How did they really react to such barbarous sights? Understatement, and the construction of a somewhat idealized character for himself, muffles the narrator's raw responses; on the next page Mitford is inveighing against English barbarities:

Passing through the streets of London in the early morning I have been moved with shame and indignation on seeing a number of English girls, many of them delicate and gently nurtured, kneeling on their hands and knees in the cold and wet, scouring stone steps. O the pity of it! It cannot be said that they do not suffer, for this drudgery has actually generated a new disease, called 'the house-maid's knee'.

The scenery of a country passing a train window encourages the imagination to play upon it: as with being read aloud to, or with listening to music by firelight, what you take in through the senses feeds the speculative inward eye. When I crossed America by train the character in the book I then planned fattened himself on scraps of America seen from the window. On this trip I hope that characters who only exist in pencil notes and tentative ideas will find the food that will put them on their feet and get their act together. As I've said, the travellers who intrigue me were watchful of incidents and of people encountered, making out of what happened to them a character for themselves – the Hero of a book of travels. There was a good deal of artifice in it. Austen Henry Layard, for instance, famous in later life for his discovery of Nineveh, writes an account of the visit which he and Edward Mitford paid to the Montenegrin chieftain whose fort was decorated with Turks' heads. Under his vigorous pen all the characters spring to life. The chieftain, or *vladika*, he says,

had procured a billiard table from Trieste, and was fond of the game. We played several times together. On one occasion while we were so engaged, a loud noise of shouting and of firing of guns was heard from without. It proceeded from a party of Montenegrin warriors who had returned from a successful raid into Turkish territory, and, accompanied by a crowd of idlers, were making a triumphal entry into the village. They carried in a cloth, held up between them, several heads which they had severed from the bodies of their victims. Amongst these were those apparently of mere children. Covered with gore, they were a hideous and ghastly spectacle. They were duly deposited at the feet of the Prince.

It is the presence of the billiard table, never mentioned by Mitford, which fixes the scene in the mind and raises Layard's account by its art above his companion's.

Meanwhile the train drew slowly south through the landscape of the Morava. Long quiet roads amid maize fields served a solitary bicyclist, or a horse-drawn cart; gentle hills succeeded gentle plains. Only, now and then, a swirling brown river hurried by like a messenger from storm and mountain unseen behind these tranquil scenes. There were few people. There, by a clump of sunflowers at a white gate, stood a child holding her grandfather's hand to see the train pass – on how many Balkan afternoons had they stood at that gate at that hour? When I see a child's hand in a grown-up's I miss the touch of my own children's hands in my palm; and no doubt when they are grown up, and long past holding my hand, the sight will still make me lonely.

The platforms of wayside stations were too short for our train; few boarded or left in any case. We stopped and waited, and then went on. About dusk I got out to walk up an empty platform rather than walking up the train, and hopped in again as the train started, and sat for a while in a wooden-seated compartment watching the onset of dark. At seven o'clock I thought I'd go back to my berth – which I'd kept away from because I'd been put in at Belgrade with a pleasant young German couple whose faces very naturally fell at my incursion – and perhaps eat some sardines and dried fruit. I walked down the train, passing the Greek encampments, passing the Far Beyonders, towards (as I thought) the sleeping cars. I was surprised that the distance was so great. I opened yet another sliding door – and found myself looking through a small round window at the track unreeling behind the hurrying train. I had reached the last coach.

And I had not reached my berth. Or my luggage. The train must have divided at Nis. This part, which I was on, must be heading for Sofia, while my possessions disappeared into the darkness of Macedonia forever. I had my passport, fifteen pounds or so in various currencies, and a copy of *Resurrection*. A very disagreeable sensation hollowed me out inside.

I hurried back along the train, which seemed to be going twice as fast now it was going in the wrong direction, looking for someone in a peaked cap who could understand me. No one did. I had no feeling of excitement or adventure whatsoever, just a dreary sense of the hours and hours of explanation and boredom in police offices and railway stations which lay ahead. I sat unhappily down in the train rushing through the dark. Then I had an idea.

Whilst I had been sitting thinking of Edmund Spencer's description of Nyssa in 1850, instead of attending to Nis in 1980, had the train perhaps come out of the station backwards as they sometimes do? In that case I'd have looked for my sleeper at the wrong end. I was in the corridor in an instant, and hurrying towards the engine, on and on, past Greeks and Far Beyonders, past the compartment I'd spent the afternoon in, hoping, fearing – And there it was! There in the sleeping corridor was the young German smoking his pipe! I greeted him like a brother. I greeted his girl friend like a brother. No sleeper ever looked cosier than that white three-berthed cabin, my bags on the top bunk, rattling through the Balkan night. The train slowed down, became comfortable to me. Amazed at my joviality, the Germans offered me bread – and I offered them sardines – and we shared beer I had bought on the platform I'd walked along – so that soon a dormy feast was in progress, the three of us sitting in a row on the bottom bunk, my blood splashing on to the floor from a cut received from the sardine tin.

Later, before I went to sleep, I couldn't help realizing that the fright I'd had showed me to have the wrong temperament for travel. You have to be able to sustain reversals, upsets, accidents. Things going wrong gives you the chance to show self-reliance; and isn't the assertion of self-reliance one of the chief objects of independent travel? If I'd really been separated from my possessions, a couple of days of dogged ingenuity would have been needed to reunite me with them; but it could have been done, and if I'd achieved it I'd have felt extremely pleased with myself. Perhaps, though, it is in the display of capabilities you weren't born with, but have admired sufficiently to imitate, that you take most satisfaction. You put yourself into situations which test the capabilities you most admire, not those you possess. The lion sets no store by courage. I thought maybe I had a clue here to the traveller's need to construct himself as he would most like to be – the hero of a book of adventurous travel – out of the incidents which befell him. The virtues which the Victorians professed to admire most, and which the classical education dinned into their heads and hearts – resolution, independence, steadiness under stress, courage, endurance of hardship, scholarship – could all be displayed in a book of travels through classical lands inhabited by wild tribes. The traveller had a box of colours with which to paint himself in heroic tints far brighter than a man with the same capabilities who stayed at home.

4

In the morning I first looked out of the train south of Thessalonika after a night more improved than spoiled by being poked awake by Macedonians. Intervals awake – clothes swaying on hooks by torchlight, the rattling train, questions, olive eyes under peaked caps showing the contempt of the uniformed for the pyjama'd – between bouts of peaceful sleep had been exciting. Now I looked out. There were the bony hills of Greece enclosing the train! We were passing through dry valleys burnt by summer. Dwarf oak and pine patched the slopes. Greece hasn't the softness of Italy, its austerity repels affection. I felt as a child that the Greek tongue was a mystery I couldn't unlock, a high cold mystery impending punishment, and the word 'Greek' is spiky with that feeling now. On wound the train through dry gorges. A lightless, misty sky enclosed the heat of the hills. Slowly, as the hours passed, the train descended into the levels loved by classical painters, plains dignified by spaced stands of cypress, and backed by huge and hoary mountains. It is a landscape arranged by grand hands. We passed through stations where I tried to make out from the platform clock what time it was in Greece, and how far we still were from Athens. The heat grew. Still no light – no Hellenic clarity – broke through the misty sky. I didn't want to arrive anywhere, particularly not in Athens; I wanted to stay in the train, where I belonged.

The way Athens clutters up its plain with mean buildings I remembered; coming from the noble order of Rome, where I lived when last I came here twenty years ago, Athens appeared a city without distinction, a muddle, a sprawl. Despite support for the Greeks in their war of independence against Turkey, English travellers were nearly united in their impatience with the base and degraded race who had inherited a country, but little else, from the Greeks of antiquity. 'What is left the poet here?' asked Byron, and answered, 'For Greeks a blush, for Greece a tear.' It's a pity that Hellenists from northern Europe encouraged King Otho to build his German palace and capital on the site of the Athens of Pericles. 'At every step,' said Warburton in 1844, 'there is an annoying, even a painful, sense of incongruity between the present and the past.' Reluctantly I put my things together and got out at Athens station.

I discovered the German couple from my sleeper hoping to escape in a taxi into the dusty town. Since there were no other taxis I jumped sternly into theirs and told the driver to take us to the Plaka quarter. Their spirits were low, their expression apprehensive at the extreme ugliness of it all (as well as with the fear that I was planning to spend the rest of my life in their bedroom). We screeched through white noisy streets till the driver stopped in the square on the Adrianou, whence we lugged our bags through crowds of foreign youths in sneakers and denim to the Hotel Adrian. No rooms: pleasurable shrugs from the management. Off we toiled to Hotel Plaka: no rooms. We left our bags, and hunted that confused quarter of alleys and lanes for a hotel. No room, no room, no room. It was extremely hot, the sun now brilliant above the white streets, the hour three o'clock and the temperature about eighty-five degrees. Our eyes became sharp for the sign HOTEL hung in the dazzle of light above streets and crowds. Cool dark entrances we tried were gates into Paradise we were turned back from into heat and toil. At last, on the edge of the Plaka, a man admitted to an empty room. This the Germans took. To their relief, I went on alone.

Alone, it seemed that the streets were full of people blessed above the angels by their possession of a room behind the town's hostile façade. They continued their lives as I could not; it was like a game where you must throw a six before your counter is allowed on to the board. In one bare upstairs lodging I offered to take an empty double room at full charge for two, but the fat Greek's veins began to bulge, and his voice began to rise, and he began to shout abuse. I told him mildly not to shout, which had the gratifying effect of deflating him. It was as if he was a circus dog, now running wild, who had at one time been trained to the words of command I'd hit on by chance. He rang up several places for me, some of them in distant suburbs, but none of them had a bed. He tried to help. It was no use, but he tried. I left him and walked the streets.

His help was no use because mass tourism has swept away the

old infrastructure which existed in all well-known parts of the world where the single middle-class traveller was likely to drop in. Advance block bookings fill the hotels. The pilfering and scrounging of the package tourist and the 'student' has replaced the traveller's liberality, altering waiters' and shopkeepers' politeness into hostility. Here on the streets of the Plaka, filling the flaking alleys from wall to wall, the full tide of mass tourism washed to and fro, slopping over streets and pavements into cafés and new hotels run up to give them beds. Twice I had stopped since stepping out of England with buoyant expectations of finding the old infrastructure in place underfoot, and twice I had fallen flat on my face. In Belgrade it was UNESCO, in Athens the Enid Blyton pilgrims. On the journey, where they hadn't in the least interfered with the space you need round you to travel pleasantly on your own, I'd still felt cramped by the weight of their numbers on the train, just as you can feel cramped in an empty room, if there are far too many people next door. This is a spoiled view, I know. Now that the threat against me, which I'd been aware of in the train, was fulfilled by the numberless crowd filling the town, the hotels, streets, everything – the softly shuffling, vacant crowd – I wasn't being fastidious or spoilt in my hunt for somewhere to sleep. I kept thinking, 'I'll try one more, then I'll give up and go to the Grande Bretagne.' It would have been 'giving up', especially after my gimcrack duplex in Belgrade; for my self-respect it was vital to screw a room of some kind out of this quarter of Athens, and not to cut and run for the shelter of 'luxury' I didn't want or need at this early stage of the outing.

I would have taken any room. I saw a sign pointing off the street, SILVER HOUSE, STUDENTS CLEAN ROOMS. Up the alley I darted into a courtyard. Up decaying stairs the contemptuous twenty-year-old in charge, unshaven as only the Southern races can be unshaven, pushed his feet into his sneakers and slopped along a dark passage smelling of drains to a door he unlocked and shoved open. Two iron beds, cardboard in the broken window, a dirty tiled floor. The manager leaned on the door jamb chewing a match. I gave him the money in advance and set out happy to retrieve my luggage.

Could I find the hotel where I'd left it? Not a bit. Though a loser of car-keys, and other keystones in life's arch, I don't often lose myself. Worse soon followed. Having found the hotel, and loaded myself with my two bags, I couldn't find Silver House again. You need to know the Plaka, and to remember that I'd criss-crossed that warren of crooked lanes a dozen times in confusion that day, to grasp that such muddling is possible. Pushing through crowds, the sun and my bags both heavy weights, having eaten nothing since the sardines last night, I felt too old and too weary to support such struggles. I would have quit, if quitting had been possible. It is from corners like this, which I've painted myself into by incompetence, that I dodge into the first-class compartment, the best hotel, the passing taxi. No way of quitting offered itself. I seemed locked into a downward spiral.

Such was my arrival in Athens. I didn't object to my room, when at last I found it again. The walls were dirty, but not with squashed bugs; the sheet was grey and crumpled with wear, but free of disquieting stains; the lavatory at the end of the passage was just tolerable, if you thought of worse plumbing further east. From the broken window I looked down through angles of red ridge-tiled roofs into a little courtyard. In a corner of this yard was an old enamel bath with feet, and in the bath, clearing it of leaves with her broom of twigs, was a very old woman in widow's weeds. My spirits rose. I voted to stay, rather than search for a hotel to move to, so long as no bugs bit. I hadn't by any means 'supported the bad without repining', but I determined to count as gain what was good about the Silver House.

The damage inflicted on a town by exploitation for tourists affected my room like all Athens. This district, its only old quarter (and this hardly older than the 1820s, when the workmen building King Otho's new capital lived here), thumps and shakes all night with electronically amplified rock music beating down on your head like iron rain from discos on the slopes of the Acropolis. Knowing that the secret of the thing is not to get angry, I fell asleep smiling as 'Never on Sunday' banged in my ears for the thousandth time that day, as it does every day you pass in tourist Greece. Tourist Greece is a sorry place. I had dinner one night in a cobbled street, pretty enough, where most of the tables were taken by German 'students' whilst two American 'students' sat in the gutter playing guitars to them before touring the tables to beg with menaces. These are children of the two richest nations on earth. They were watched with curiosity by a Greek girl of eight or nine in a party dress, the proprietor's daughter, who stood in the yellow lamplight with a yo-yo she couldn't get to run. I watched her try and try to make it bounce up to her small hand. Then down the street under a cloud of balloons came a pedlar. It was he from whom she'd bought her yo-yo. She ran up to him and showed her broken toy. Yes, he had yo-yos, brilliant as sparks glittering up and down from his hand as he made them dance for the diners, but for hers he showed no concern. Through the restaurant door came her father, the proprietor, cleaning his hands on a white cloth. Under his eye the pedlar at once attended to the child's yo-yo. But no lights flashed, no life danced in it. The child's father had hurried in by the time a German boy snapped his fingers at the pedlar. Over to him the man darted, balloons rustling and squeaking in his wake, to flash a yo-yo humbly up and down before the tableful of youths in blue denim. Sometimes you watch a scene which expresses just what is right about a place, and why you like it; that scene in the street which I've described, though slight enough, expressed like a morality play what I didn't like about Athens.

There was a good deal to dislike, but I wasn't going to let pique spoil what crowds can't really touch, if you shut them out of your head firmly enough and open just the little windows which let the beams from ancient Athens fall into your mind like light from the sun itself. One morning early I started out to climb the Acropolis, passing, as I did whenever I went in or out of Silver House, the old dame sweeping leaves industriously out of the bath she seemed to live in. On the path winding upwards, at first amongst houses, then above their roofs into arid vegetation and gaunt rock, there were only a handful of people walking slowly. At the gates, though, on the steps under the Propylaea, there was a crowd of many hundreds waiting shoulder to shoulder

25

who had come in the ranks of buses packing the car park. The numbers in the crowds surprised me every time. Another day I had gone to the Archaeological Museum. As I walked up the steps twelve buses arrived below and spewed out fresh troops to charge the crowds already besieging the place.

It is hard to reconcile such numbers with the private, even secret, experiment of opening your imagination to the most profound and suggestive objects ever made by the hand and mind of man. For Greek art of the great days of Athens spoke not to crowds but to individuals: I mean that it was not demagogic art, as Egyptian or Assyrian monuments had been, which shouted down from the sky on to the heads of Asiatic multitudes; Greek art seems just to tell you quietly, if you have time to listen, that one man alone, and what he does, is all that counts. The haunting, ironic, indwelling smile of the *kouroi*, which no damage effaces, is the smile of the self-reliant individual who looks out on the crowd. In the countenance of the bronze Zeus in the Archaeological Museum, and in that marvellously balanced figure of his, you see and comprehend the four virtues of the ancient world illustrated for you; there they stand where you can realize what they mean, the words 'courage', 'temperance', 'justice', 'wisdom'. But the difficulty is to find a spot where you can stand long enough to get the message, hear the whisper, catch the smile. The crowd thronging past may not intend to be held up by the statues, but they catch and swirl against them like a current snagging against stones, and you get swept away. Greek art may have been conceived for the individuals comprising a little sea-going city state, but nowadays it is looked at by crowds of Egyptian or Assyrian magnitude.

In the museums and in the streets I couldn't help wondering why these countless thousands of people have chosen Athens to come to. Maybe there's a parallel with the way 'a classical education' was pushed an inch or two into the heads of all public schoolboys until recently: the atmosphere in a crowded museum is rather like the atmosphere of disaffection in a schoolroom where boys with no taste for the classics, and no use for them in later life, were obliged to spend many hours each day blundering unwillingly about Greece and Italy. They were trapped there writing iambics because of the desire of the new middle class to buy for their children a form of education which had been an exclusive preserve of the aristocracy before the Industrial Revolution. In the eighteenth century a handful of noblemen made a footpath for themselves to Rome; in the nineteenth, the middle-class travellers who interest me, broadened the path into a road which ran all round the ancient world; now the numbers pouring out of the North are such that these places are all road, and no scenery.

Earlier visitors to Greece would have thought it an absurd case of cart before horse to hear the name of Leonidas for the first time at Thermopylae, or to look at the bay of Salamis without a good deal of Aeschylus going through your mind. They visited Greece to confirm the topography (so to speak) of a philosophy and a history very well known to them, as you might look with interest at the illustrated edition of a book you know almost by heart. Lord Carlisle, in Athens in 1850, says of the bay of Eleusis, 'I was glad to find that the description of the site I had given a long time ago in my Oxford prize poem was remarkably accurate.'

But to someone without much knowledge of the ancient world, and without the affection for its landscape, almost like nostalgia for the landscape of youth, which that knowledge gives to classicists, what is the appeal of Athens? I've noticed that even amongst nineteenth-century travellers, who all at least professed acquaintance with the classics, the more scholarly they are, the fonder the eye with which they looked on Greece. C. T. Newton, for instance, who was keeper of antiquities at the British Museum (and who turned down the Regius professorship of Greek which Jowett was then offered), said of his first sight of Athens in the 1860s, 'Nothing I had read or seen at all prepared me for the beauty of the Athenian landscape; nor can anyone, without visiting Athens, understand how exquisitely the ancient edifices are designed in relation to this landscape.' Whereas here is Edmund Spencer's view, a traveller's rather than a scholar's:

Our first view of Athens excited a feeling of disappointment, which even the distant prospect of its classic ruins failed to dispel, and it must be confessed that the aspect of the arid plain of Attica, with its groves of ill-grown olive trees, and bare rocky mountains; the broiling sun and the clouds of dust . . . even the far-famed Acropolis, situated on the summit of a naked rock, looked little superior at a distance to a ruined fortress, with its ugly tower built in the rude style of the middle ages.

About the Frankish tower Eliot Warburton differs ('Its effect at a little distance is excellent, and its removal would leave a blank which there is nothing to fill up') and his eye for what is salient and picturesque, which makes his book of travels one of the most delightful ever written, leads him to make this comment, as true in spirit now as then:

Full in sight of the Acropolis, in the same plain with the temple of Theseus, and in the solemn presence of that of Olympian Jove, there stands a huge, white, cubic edifice that would disgrace Trafalgar Square – the palace of King Otho . . . Such are the first and most prominent objects that strike a stranger's eye, and they are characteristic of all modern Greece. No one can blame this people for wishing to become a nation; but their ambition to become *ancient* Greeks is fraught with embarrassment and difficulty.

I thought of Warburton's comments when I was flooded up the steps on a comber of tourists the morning I went to the Acropolis, and looked around me. There is nowhere you can look without the awfulness of modern Athens extending in every direction as far as you can see. There wasn't a corner of the whole summit that didn't have someone standing on it with a camera in his hand. What there is, which would certainly have ravished Newton, if not the others, is the sculptures in the museum up there, taken from 'the Persian layer' which hadn't been excavated in their day. Better the poetic setting, the crumbling marvels rising above a Turkish village in the wide Attic plain; or the wonderful things dug up since those days, displayed to jostling thousands above a hideous city? Only by looking upward into the brilliant dazzle of Greek light can you see stone against sky as travellers in old days saw it. Warburton complained of modern Athens, but he could step out of it: 'When I walked a few hundred paces out of the noisy city, and found myself in a solitude as deep as that of the Desert, I was appeased. Around this ruin [Jupiter

Olympus] was the profoundest silence, and it stood utterly alone . . . the only living creature a Turk, whose barbaric garb harmonized, to my mind at least, with the scene in which I found him. It was *his* ruthless race which had made Athens desolate . . .' Now you can't step out of modern Athens.

Or so I thought, as I left the summit, and the Propylaea, and was walking down by the road. I saw the entrance to the Theatre of Dionysus and walked in. I found I had come upon the very scene I was searching for – I mean 'searching' in the sense that when travelling you are looking for what you couldn't exactly define until you see it. You are pursuing something as yet unseen. Here was an arrangement of nature and art which satisfied my imagination. Here was tumbled marble, and dusty earth, and ruin and peace. Here were walks under the shade of cypresses, or amongst oleanders, or across clearings where half-buried columns lay in the sun beside abandoned hoisting-tackle, and here was space and silence to stroll about amongst these suggestive remains and crop nourishment from them as a sheep crops the wild hillside. It was entirely deserted, except for a man sitting sketching under a wide shady hat on a fallen column. He might have been Warburton's Turk, in the way he harmonized to my mind with the scene in which I found him. For the first time since I had watched him cross the Sava from Semlin to Belgrade I was able to observe – to see, not just to think about – the figure of the nineteenth-century Traveller I have come to spy upon. There he was, with three or four other tall, spare men in linen coats and wide-awake hats, strolling about in the company of Mr Wyse, our Minister at King Otho's court, whilst the director of antiquities at Athens, M. Pittakys, pointed out the lions of the place, and a discussion went forward amongst them as to the oratory of Demosthenes from the rocks overhead, or whether the Frankish tower should be demolished, or why the Ilissus no longer flows as it did two and a half thousand years ago, in the days with which they were all more familiar than with any epoch since. In Greece they found themselves at home, in the way that a Campbell from whatever country might feel himself at home in Argyllshire.

They thought and chatted about the ghosts who, for them,

inhabited these ruins, and I thought about them. Later that same day, in the Agora, I found another scene which exactly suited what I wanted from Athens. With your back to the reconstructed Stoa, in the vista across dust and maquis and marble to the lovely abandoned symmetry of the Theseion, you see that arrangement of art and nature which appealed so powerfully to imaginations formed on Gibbon and Pannini in the firelit libraries of English country houses. They took this romantic view of classical times. Now archaeology, as an exact science, has pared away the fingers and noses they added for picturesque effect to antique statues, and a distinction has opened up between appreciating the pared-down purity of classical art, and indulging a taste for ruined temples at sunset. The first is the rather severe, but clear-eyed and intellectual, pleasure of visiting museums; the second pleasure is an altogether murkier mélange of emotion and the melancholy Northern temperament, shot through by vague perceptions of the rise and fall of empires.

It is this second pleasure which is now harder to come by, with so many sites overcrowded and tidied up into parks, but in the carelessly gardened Agora I found it. There are views upward to the Parthenon, clear and uncluttered on its rocky brow. Amongst palm or cypress on the slopes below show the ochre-coloured villas where travellers lodged so pleasantly with consuls or other residents of the little town. The summit crowned with marvels – slopes, villas, palms, cypresses – all are struck golden in the evening light. Behind the whole grand scene hangs the hazy blue of mountains. You need nothing more, as a reason for being here and nowhere else on earth. I walked and thought. Hoses watering shrubs hissed and pattered, darkening dust paths, making cats scamper. In the fading light I entered the little Orthodox church to think of my children 'in their small corner' so far away. A degree of loneliness sharpens the perceptions wonderfully whilst travelling. Alone you note everything, and note, too, the effect of everything upon you. You are free to look hard and reflect in peace. The relationship of two people insulates each in their relations with the world. A comfort at most times, such insulation blunts the point of travel.

5

The Agora was what I liked most in Athens. I walked there at odd times, coming to like even the rattle of the little train trundling round its perimeter, as a relief from screaming car-horns deluging the rest of the city, and from the fumes and frantic ugliness of Constitution Square. Eating breakfast out of doors is the pleasantest single advantage of a warm climate, to a Northerner, and after breakfast under the trees in the Adrianou Square I more than once started the day by walking through the Agora on my way elsewhere. I did so on my last morning, before loading myself with my bags again and carrying them out of the dirty little room I had grown used to, and down the shabby stairs of Silver House, and past the bath-ridden ancient whose hands were like the withered leaves falling faster now than she could sweep them up. I was quite fond of the place by the time I left it. It is the arrival at an expensive hotel which is all the pleasure of the thing; thereafter enjoyment deteriorates, and leaving such places, when you have to pay the bill for your extravagance, is pain and mortification. Exactly the opposite is true of cheap lodgings. There the arrival is the nadir; custom inures you day by day to the drawbacks, and you leave (having paid each night in advance) in a mood of smug thrift.

The Piraeus bus was packed full, so that I had to stand all the way. At the quayside my spirits sank. There was a large signboard by the customs house showing which islands were FULL and which still had VACANCIES. Full islands! After Belgrade and Athens a new and even more uncomfortable concept of fullness seemed to impend. Pilgrims under backpacks tramped about by the dirty sea in their mild, damp way, or waited in lines at doors into sheds, or sprawled over the cafés. Such numbers reduce vision like a snowstorm.

You should never ask people who live in a place, as I had asked the friend on Rhodes whom I was going to stay with, what conditions are like. Possession of his own house insulates him, and prejudice in favour of what he has chosen gives selective vision, blotting out what's undesirable. My friend had said

Athens wouldn't have many tourists now, in late September, that there was no need to book hotels ahead, and that the islands would be nearly empty. What would she say if I pointed out the noticeboard showing islands FULL? 'Incredible!' she would say, 'I never saw it before.' And she wouldn't see it again, either, because her eyes would go straight through it. Residents see through tourists to the permanent features of the place; tourists are condemned to see each other.

My bags were heavy, the sun hot. At last, at the furthest end of the port, the fine white superstructure of the *Homerus* rose above the clutter of the quay. I went aboard, and was delighted with the ship, and with the second-class cabin I was to share with a small nervous Austrian whom I found nibbling grapes in the bottom bunk. I had lunch on the quayside, the white ship before me like the very idea of Travel, her engines audible, the bustle around her increasing, a fume of smoke from her funnel. No departure – no plane or even train – so extracts all that is significant from the word 'departure' as does a ship slowly shaking herself free of port, and turning towards the sea.

If that sea is the Aegean, and the sky under which she sails grows heavy with storm and undischarged lightning, the meanest feeling in the passenger's bosom is dignified into an Emotion. Impossible not to think of the upsets in *The Odyssey*. Anyway, I can't help looking at the people I share a boat with as prospective companions on a *Raft of the Medusa*: on a boat thunderclouds of gloomy expectation brood continually over my head. I look down from the deck with dread at the seething water laving the ship's sides. No need of storm for the sea to invade my mind with fear. The sea has only to lie in reptilian quiet at the foot of the rocks; its wash and draw, its chuckle – *ce rire amer* – are suggestive enough on the calmest day of depths, and darkness, and malignance. A torturer need only snap a matchstick between his fingers to empty his prisoner's mind of all but fear. No epitaph so touches me with sympathy as the one attributed to Archias in the *Greek Anthology*: 'Beneath the spray-beaten reef, near the disastrous main, I found a grave at the hand of strangers, and forever do I wretchedly hear roaring, even among the dead, the hated thunder of the sea.'

So here I was, prisoner of the most ancient and haunted of all seas, in rapidly deteriorating weather, watching from the deck the coast of Greece slip by under a wreath of mist cast by thunderclouds. I don't feel agitated on boats; on the contrary, a kind of sombre fatalism weighs me down in bench or chair, and I watch sea or land indifferently hour by hour, and allow my thoughts many a melancholy turn down Memory Lane. It is not a bad mood to travel in. 'The slow and rocking movement of the dromedary,' says Charles Monk of desert travel in the 1840s, 'tends to produce that state of reverie, when the memory recalls events long past by, and conjures up to the imagination faces and things that once were familiar, and now, in the midst of silence and solitude, present themselves as food for deep and sober meditation.' Monk doesn't tell you what he thought about; it was conventional amongst travellers that they revealed nothing of their lives before they set out on their journey, and that when they returned home they closed the door in your face. Exceptions – Captain Abbott in his *Journey from Heraut to Khiva* speaks with bitter pain of his disappointments and ambitions – strike you as ill-bred. By buying the man's book of travels you haven't bought access to his confessions, and he doesn't show you his weaknesses any more than he would show them to the enemies he encounters on his road. That isn't to say that weaknesses may not be deduced: a pretty accurate account of a man's character may be made out from the most tight-lipped book of travels, for the narrator is continually before you, whilst a succession of incidents illumines different facets of his personality. Even the title page may give something away; Mr Monk, for instance, though not sharing with us the subject of those 'deep and sober meditations', thought it worthwhile to add, after his name on the title page of *The Golden Horn*, 'MA, Trin. Coll. Cam.'.

All afternoon the *Homerus* ploughed her furrow through the oily sea, the white of her paint flashing in the livid light which spilled out under towers of cloud. When evening darkened the scene, we sailed at last under the far high image of Sounion on its headland against the sky, and the ship steered into the dusk eastward between the rocky claws of islands. Still I sat on deck and watched. Out of the physical nature of the Aegean – so full of the incidents of rocks and islands – *The Odyssey* suggests itself: you couldn't sail through the Archipelago without a thousand incidents befalling you. Twenty years ago I last sailed under Cape Sounion from rather a stormy yachting excursion around these seas and islands. 'Few friendships can survive ordeal by water,' wrote Trelawny; 'when a yacht from England with a pair of these thus tried friends, touches – say at Malta or Gibraltar – you may be sure that she will depart with one only.' I thought about the incidents of that voyage, and about the lives and deaths since those days of the people aboard the yacht. One of the pleasures of being young is that an episode can seem so permanent. I believed at that time that those people, those occupations, my life in Rome, were my settled course. Really it was just an excursion through a patch of sea crowded with islands, before the true course for the long haul was set. Few of the lights by which I now steer had then risen. I meditated, soberly if not deeply (myself only BA, Trin. Coll. Cam.), on such subjects whilst the *Homerus* surged into Eastern darkness. I went in at last and read in a corner till it was time to take a shower in a rusty washroom which heaved and creaked with the ship's movement, yet seemed to me magnificently sybaritic after the shower in my Athens lodging. I know of nothing cosier than a bunk in a boat crossing a calm sea. With a pleasant sense of adventure at the back of your mind you can read in your little lair as snug as a wren in its nest amid winter snow.

When I woke up in the morning the Austrian from the bunk below had slipped away, very kindly leaving a bunch of grapes on my clothes for me. I carried them up companionways, and along those dim throbbing corridors smelling of oil which are like a ship's intestinal tubes, towards the sunlight and sea air above. I stepped out on to the deck into brilliant light to find the ship sailing close to the wildest sea-coast imaginable.

Disquiet which the idea of Turkey had put into my mind whenever I had thought of it – as I'd done off and on all summer, reading about Turkish towns in the garden at home – disquiet at once took the shape of that dangerous sea-coast I now saw for the first time. Here it was, close at hand. Here were the ramparts of

Asia crumbling into a sapphire sea. We were surging through bright water off the promontory of Knidos, to which Praxiteles' Venus once drew all travellers, and I could see the waves dashing against many a lonely rock, and breaking on many an empty shore. I looked at that stony coast as if into the basilisk's eye. What was it that frightened me? Desolate cliffs rose out of the sea like outworks of a hostile stronghold into whose grasp I dreaded falling. I did not want to land. Far worse than landing, I was committed to crossing the entire country from this Aegean coast to the remote mountains of Armenia which overlook Russia, Iran and Iraq. Six weeks ago in Turkey there had been a military coup; there hadn't been much news since then through the heavily censored press, and it was hard to know if martial law and curfew had really ended the terrorist killings which had taken two thousand lives so far that year, or if the murders went on unreported. Since I had left England, war had broken out between Iraq and Iran, both of which countries share borders with Turkey, and that fact, too, added uncertainty, even danger, to the harsh sea-coast I stared at. But it wasn't calculable dangers of that kind which glittered in the stony eye that stared back at me. It was something else, more like the dismay, or dread, you feel in face of a test of the very abilities that you can feel draining out of you just when they are to be called upon.

For the moment, though, I was safe. The *Homerus* sheered away from Asia's desolate coast. The rocks, the breaking sea, lost their immediate sharp power; distance began to give a haze of beauty to the wrinkled mountains of Caria sinking behind us. High up amongst those sea-cliffs of that promontory of Knidos, which he was exploring whilst Acting Consul on Rhodes in the 1850s (with the duty of 'watching over the British Museum's interests in the Levant'), Charles Newton discovered an enormous marble lion. It was ten feet long, by six high, and weighed eleven tons. But he could not persuade any of his Turkish or Greek labourers to see a lion in what, to them, was a familiar white boulder amongst the purplish crags above the sea. With much difficulty, and several accidents, Newton crated the lion and lowered it off the cliff into a warship for removal to England together with the Mausoleum from Halicarnassus which he also excavated. On this promontory Newton discovered too a creature much more unusual than a Hellenic lion: a Turkish squire. The life of this Aga of Datscha Newton describes with much satisfaction – his fishing and partridge-shooting, the shoe-making and gun-making and carpentry going on around his house, as well as his lively interest in history and foreign countries – as though the existence of a country gentleman after the pattern of Squire Hastings, on this wild promontory, proved that all the world tended if it could towards the English way of doing things.* To see a squire in a Turkish bey – to make out the English pattern behind foreign ways – required equally trained perceptions as it took to see a marble lion in a white rock. The combination of hardihood with scholarship, a particularly English mixture which Newton possessed in a high degree, made him value the least trace of such a combination in this desolate land where he found himself. 'A well furnished and tempered spirit, qualified to appreciate both the past and the present' was how he was described by Lord Carlisle, who stayed on his Eastern tour at Newton's house on Rhodes in 1853 (together with 'young Mr Colnaghi, who is engaged in taking views with the Calotype').

The island of Rhodes now arose slowly on the starboard bow. In stately style, dwarfing the harbour, the *Homerus* docked under the dark stone battlements of the castle, described by Lord Carlisle as suggesting 'bits of Kenilworth seen under cloudless skies and topped with occasional palm trees'. Whilst staying with Newton here, he was attacked by the smallpox, and his rather unctuous diary describes how a Dr M'Craith came at once from Smyrna to attend him, while 'the good Admiral' of the Fleet sent Dr Rees from his flagship, and 'my good Dr Sandwith' came pell-mell by steamer from Constantinople. We may see in this incident, and in all Lord Carlisle's account of his being wafted in battleships through Greek and Turkish waters from one embassy to another, how smooth an excursion round the Levant might be made for a grandee, always provided he didn't catch smallpox.

* When put ashore at Calymnos by HMS *Firebrand*, Newton says, 'I remained like a waif thrown on the sandy beach, seated on my carpet bag, and plunged in a reverie about home.' He had been brought up in Shropshire, a parson's son.

6

On Rhodes I stayed several days at Lindos in the house of a friend. I stayed on from day to day because the ferry service between Rhodes and the Turkish coast had been suspended due to worse than usual ill-will between Greek and Turk, so it was necessary to wait for word of a private passage to Marmaris. I had given up my passport to a gold-toothed ruffian in a mean house behind the port of Rhodes, who had closed the door upon me with instructions to ring him up now and then for news of a boat. This I did, and was told one evening to be on the quay next morning. I packed a leaner supply of clothes into my two bags. Early in the morning I walked up through silent white streets to catch the first bus to Rhodes. After breakfast by the harbour there was time to look about the town and castle before the hour of departure. The dreads and doubts of anticipation had turned to the buoyant excitement of being on my way towards that challenging outwork of Turkish mountains watched at all hours, and in many lights, from viewpoints at Lindos. From the acropolis one evening I had watched the onset of dark across the wind-shadowed sea from the east, whilst a column of swifts over my head wavered out like thoughts towards that wild and furrowed sea-coast, and the Eastern darkness, with the same half-hesitant tendency which I felt drawing myself towards it.

At this early hour the emptiness of the Street of Knights, the stone-flagged lane leading up to the castle gate, seemed somehow sanitized. You don't need tourists, but you need the piles of filth, the rotting carrion, the wild dogs, to give the place its true character, as the palaces of Venice require Venice's stinking canals to rise above. If you know a great deal, the atmospherics of the place don't much matter to you because you study the minutiae, not general effects, and if you know absolutely nothing, the wrong effect is as enjoyable as the right one; but if you know just a bit, like me, that bit, that spark, needs atmosphere as a flame needs oxygen, if it is to burn up bright and clear to throw light upon the figures I want to see. In Rhodes the period that interests me is pretty well submerged by Fascism and tourism.

I could see no figures from the past in the castle, except possibly Mussolini's. Most of the large stone rooms containing a writing table and a florid chair give the impression of having been set aside for signing treaties in. It now seems freakish that such a creature of burlesque can have conceived of himself as ruling a Roman Empire from this royal seat of Rhodes. In other corners of the island crumble into ruin other props of his *opéra bouffe*, concrete conduits split by brambles, a lonely Italianate friary decayed into a haybarn, town halls, rusting bandstands. How can the Italians ever have believed in him as a conqueror?

Maybe the answer is in the courtyard of the castle. Statues, a row of disagreeable-looking Romans, stand there. Their presence provides a provenance for the Italianization of the island – indeed of the known world – by a modern dictator. He has only to rescue these neglected stone Romans from the walls of Turkish or Greek houses, where they are doing humble duty propping up usurpers' homes – he has only to set free these true spiritual rulers of the Mediterranean world – and things fall into proper order once more. Those petrified Romans in the courtyard provide a continuity of lineage which makes Mussolini's claim legitimate in Italian eyes. Such lineage, such continuity linking antiquity with modern time, cannot be understood in England. Norman castles arise from the bare soil. No statues from ancient times stand in their courtyards. For this reason Lord Carlisle was quite wrong to compare Rhodes with Kenilworth, but maybe he betrayed in doing so the Englishman's desire, at the zenith of British power, to connect himself and his empire by direct descent with those that had gone before in ancient times. And long before Britain was a mighty power there was felt a need to provide brave deeds with an ancestry linking them to antiquity: the opening lines of *Sir Gawain and the Green Knight* refer to the fall of Troy, and give as Britain's founder and ancestor of her brave knights Brutus, the grandson of Aeneas. His statue was dug up from England's bare soil to stand in Arthur's courtyard at Camelot, but it is less convincing, like the quarterings of a parvenu.

I didn't want to miss the boat, and was at the dockyard before time. My passport was returned to me. Soon the three or four people waiting in the customs shed were called out into the strong white light. I saw no ship at the dockside. I saw the sea, and the far-off mountains of Turkey, but no boat to take me there. I followed the man who had called us out. At the edge of the dock I looked down into the water.

Below, lower far than the dockside she bumped against, lay a little caique with her engine beating and a pair of villainous Turkish sailors looking up at me. I threw down my bags and jumped on to the foredeck after them. No tickets were sold, no money asked for. Others jumped down, ropes were cast off, we put to sea. I settled with my back against the little deckhouse ready for a rough crossing of the thirty-mile strait to Marmaris.

But the sun shone and the sea was blue. Steadily, climbing and descending the swell, we motored towards the pale mountains of Asia Minor. The grizzled skipper leaned on the rail and gazed outwards, his feet scratching the deck like a lobster's claws, whilst the mate smoked and steered. The spray's white needles hissed mesmerically into the dark blue sea. The India-paper pages of my book flickered in the breeze.

Close at hand a suggestive family scene unfolded. On the foredeck, as well as the skipper and myself, was an Australian couple with a six-month-old baby. Between them they handled the baby with wonderful adroitness. The father was a large man in slacks, his feet in shoes with tremendously wide welts, whose honest face gave the impression of trusting all four corners of the earth, as well as the seven seas, to treat him square. He smiled a trusting smile when our eyes met. Perhaps on account of me and the skipper, he was a little coy about handling the baby-food, which he helped to make up into a feed; and he very decidedly stared out to sea whilst nappies were being changed behind his back. His size, and cumbrousness, and air of innocence, made him more appealing than his wife, a neat, sharp woman who was amazingly practical. She got along with the jobs in hand, pinning, mixing, feeding, cleaning, with a dexterity which took not the least notice of being aboard a rolling caique halfway on its passage from Rhodes to Turkey across the wine-dark sea.

With a moment to spare, baby asleep, she sprawled along the gunwale on her front, poking a jersey-trousered behind into our meditative skipper's face. He contemplated it without much response save a scratch or two of huge fingers under his cap, before returning his gaze to the sea-coast arising out of the Homeric deep.

It is impossible to guess what responses to a given set of circumstances or surroundings may be going through the head of someone from the other side of the world. Here, to me, were the storied capes and headlands of Asia Minor towering out of the haunted Aegean over our little craft; was the scene to her just a barren coast rising out of an empty sea somewhere in far-off Europe? Is it only out of all those chimerical and half-remembered complexities laid on my mind in childhood by the names of 'Caria' and 'Aegean', 'Greek' and 'Turk', that shadows and dreads are formed? I couldn't change the baby's nappies out here for fear of storms, monsters, waterspouts, rocks hurled by blinded giants. Fabulous obstacles would utterly prevent me from taking a baby to Turkey in a caique. The Australians bounded over the obstacles as simply as you hear untaught voices, in a village church, bound through the complexities of the Creed. I think I probably prefer to travel with my chimeras, and leave the baby behind. Someone said once that travelling with your family was like waltzing with your aunt.

We made our landfall and ran close inshore along the steeps of the peninsula which shelters the bay of Marmaris, where Sir Sidney Smith's Fleet lay in the French Wars. Visits of the Fleet were the precursors of mass tours, or perhaps of football supporters' trips abroad; sailors swarming over a town, fighting, drinking, mocking, insulting, a nuisance to everyone and barely under control by their officers. Newton speaks of trouble on this coast from the crew of a warship sent to carry away marbles, but it wasn't the convention in those days for middle-class travellers to acknowledge the presence of their lower-class countrymen abroad. Officers appear in books of travel – at the time of the Crimean War the Levant swarmed with British forces, and in every Eastern port a British man-of-war was liable to be found at all times – but of the seamen and soldiers we hear nothing.

Nor do English merchants travelling with Birmingham and Manchester goods figure much either, though the adulteration of Eastern bazaars by their wares is often deplored. In short, travellers mentioned only those like themselves, who would hold to the convention that to reach the spot where they had met was a bold and hazardous enterprise, not to be undertaken by mere merchants out for profit. They suppressed the merchants because they got in the way of the sense of adventure they wanted to convey. I would have done better to have suppressed the Australian baby if I was to convey the sense of adventure I really felt as we ran along that wild shore. If it had even been a Turkish baby! You may share an adventure with a Turkish baby.

I know of nothing I look at so eagerly as a shore, and a port, I am about to land upon for the first time. A long gleaming swell washed beaches we motored past. Promontories, wooded down to the water, divided the bay into creeks and coves revealed as we crossed their mouths. All were deserted. Above forested foothills at the head of the bay rose the harsh and stony line of the mountains; against the dark of these forests, low on the water where the bay ended, white buildings clustered above their reflection in unrippled calm.

It was now that the mate left the tiller to the skipper and climbed about the boat with a fierce grin to collect our passage-money, 1,000 drachmae a head, just about what I had paid for a cabin from Piraeus to Rhodes. Impossible to dispute the sum, so we paid up and looked pleasant. We had been three and a half hours in the boat when we pulled ourselves up on to the quay at Marmaris, and the Australian baby had behaved like an angel.

Nervous high spirits was my reaction to landing. As soon as I was clear of the customs chief, who held court under the vine-trellis of a tea-house, I ran about cashing a cheque, looking into hotels, finding out the times of buses to Selçuk. Momentous to step ashore, but you don't see much of the character of a country in a seaside town. A lane or two led off the bright new square into suggestive shadows, an old house or two amongst the concrete blocks showed its rickety wooden front; undoubtedly this was Turkey, but I decided to take a bus that evening directly to Selçuk, and so begin my journey.

I bought some food, bread and fish, from a kiosk on the waterfront and sat down to eat it, and to drink black tea and sugar out of the little urn-shaped glass so familiar on return to Turkey. Running about the town I had noticed a couple of interesting things to think about as I sat there. First I had seen a young woman I had met before, whom I knew to drug heavily, talking earnestly to a sallow Turk in a café. If she saw me she made no sign, but continued to lean forward in the urgent manner of a creature bargaining for her soul. The hunt for drugs, let alone the taking of them, steals away half a person's life, and impoverishes, as obsessions do, the half it doesn't steal. I saw that woman, and then I saw, in the bus office, the Australian couple from the caique with their baby. I asked them their plans (on the boat I hadn't spoken for fear of starting a three-and-a-half-hour conversation). They were going to Gallipoli. The penny dropped. I understood. Those are the straits, that is the seashore – not nearby Troy but Gallipoli – which is the setting for Australia's *Iliad*, and the burial place of her Homeric heroes, and the landscape of her legends. Until they reached those straits, and saw that coast, the Australian couple wouldn't see the ghosts, or feel the awe, which Europeans see and feel all over the Aegean. 'Gallipoli,' wrote Edmund Spencer in 1837, 'now only interesting as being the fatal spot on which the Turk first planted the Crescent in Europe.' In fact now, to a modern European, the Gallipoli disaster stands as a catastrophe heralding the end to the epic which *The Iliad* began. A monument to men killed at Gallipoli in an Australian church, on the other hand, has the same function as those Roman statues in Rhodes castle, or mention of Troy at the beginning of *Sir Gawain*, in linking the present generation to heroes of old. Europe's end is Australia's beginning, as the end of Troy, Aeneas' escape from the burning town, made possible the founding of England 'far over the French flood, where Felix Brutus set Britain on bluffs abundant and broad'.

I sat with my glass of tea on the breezy quay, in dancing, sparkling light from sun and wave, and gazed at a fine long prospect of the deep bays, and wooded headlands, and sail-studded water, of the gulf. Soon it was six o'clock, time to start.

People had told me it was possible, easy, even pleasant to travel about Turkey by bus. But such different people: what did they mean, what was their yardstick? One was a woman who had travelled over Afghanistan and Persia, and wouldn't know discomfort if she saw it; another was a redoubtable Dorset doctor who wouldn't admit discomfort if he'd suffered it; and so on. What would I think? That was all that mattered now. I walked along the waterfront, bowing gravely to the customs chief who had laid aside braided cap and official jacket to play backgammon under the trellis, until I reached the bus company's office. I felt the buoyancy of being afloat on currents of uncertainty and adventure, not unusual when you are young, a famous corrective of middle age.

II

❖❖❖❖❖❖❖❖❖❖❖❖❖❖❖❖❖❖❖❖❖❖❖❖❖❖❖❖❖❖❖❖❖❖❖❖

I

      I wrote the draft of this chapter in as remote and romantic a scene as I had ever hoped to find when I set out from home for Turkey. An oil lamp threw its light over the interior of a long low hut whose walls were hung with Eastern rugs. On the floor of tamped earth more were scattered, and others covered the raised platform where I sat crosslegged behind a brass tray of little dishes which had contained my supper. Beyond reach of the lamp's rays the open doorway at the further end of the hut led out into the darkness where lay an extensive plain amongst the mountains. In this plain was a ruined Greek city.

My host, a handsome if melancholy Turk, had just made up a dummy bed across the doorway, with a bolster for the body and the water jug wrapped in a scarf for the head, in hopes of keeping out the nocturnal prowlers whose visits he feared. Twice in the last months he had been wakened by a terrorist's pistol at his head. 'C'est pas possible, une vie comme ça,' he said sadly in his grating but fluent French.

There had been another man with us earlier that evening, cloaked, leaning on a staff, who had kept out of the lamplight whilst the hut's owner, M. Mestan, had shown me coins and curios dug up from the ancient city. I had seen figures similar to his, as evening approached, sentinels watching from the mounds surrounding the ruins of temples and theatres through which I had been wandering. For romantic reasons I hoped that they were Turkomans, these gloomy shepherds picketing the landscape amongst their flocks, savage dogs of great size in packs at their heels. As the sun declined they had seemed to become taller, and darker, and to ring the ruins closer. One of them, as I say, had been in the hut with us but had now gone, as too had M. Mestan. I was alone. Through the darkness at the door, in another hut a short distance off, I was to sleep in a nest of rugs I had put together earlier on the earth floor. The silence seemed very profound.

Of course it wasn't really a wild spot. No doubt it is easy to reach the site in a coach from a cruise ship, and walk round it, and motor away before night falls. But a place is as remote as it feels to you, and it is the means by which you reach it which gives you a sense of remoteness. The way I had come made this lamplit hut in the darkness of Anatolia seem wonderfully remote.

The first bus I had taken, that evening in Marmaris, had swept off the waterfront in a blare of horns and dust with the dash of a mail coach leaving Mount Pleasant, and had climbed immediately into the hills above the lonely sea-coast. Away to the west, into the sunset, stretched long stony peninsulas of mountain enclosing the silver sea-lochs; ahead of us lay the darkening interior. I remember clearings in the pine woods studded with beehives, pale bee-cities glowing in the dusk as we thundered by, and my neighbour at the window of the bus preparing some miles in advance, face at the glass, to wave at a woman and child waving back from a glade amongst the hives. Then he settled back in his seat to smoke and doze. All the forty or so Turks in the bus dozed and smoked. The men mostly wore shabby tight suits and cloth caps, and nearly all were handsome in that harsh piratical style which runs to a swarthy skin and a flourishing moustache.

The interior world of the bus as it dashed through the dark was ruled by an agile conductor moving about the vehicle like a sailor through his ship's rigging, now sprinkling our hands with eau-de-Cologne, now taking bottled water from his ice-chest for those who signalled him, now consulting with the driver, or tuning the radio to rock music. Very far from the country bus I had half expected, this was a modern, large-windowed, well-sprung Mercedes; and evidently Turkish coaches rule the road by weight and power.

45

After an hour or two the bus stopped for a meal at a roadside *kebabci*. People awoke and poured into the place, stirring it from darkness and somnolence into frantic life like an ants' nest you kick, shouting orders, snatching bread, spitting grape-pips. On the principle that the traveller's best friend, a strong stomach, must be allowed to signal when hungry, and have no food pressed upon it, I ate nothing but a *simis*, strolling about in the warm darkness whilst the Turks wolfed down their kebabs. To fall ill is amongst the worst things that can happen to you travelling alone through a country where you haven't an acquaintance and can't speak the language, and it is what you eat and drink, in the first days especially, which puts you at risk. If you wait and watch, you find that the kind of food you like exists in a slightly different form in most cuisines, and at last you hit upon a tolerable diet anywhere where there is food at all. Until that time comes, far better to be hungry than sick.

Before long a horn-blast collected the passengers, and we were carried on through the darkness for two or three hours more. I could not tell where we were, or how near to Selçuk, for the villages we dashed through never gave a glimpse of a name. I trusted our conductor, and at about ten-thirty he signalled me. The bus stopped. I climbed down. The bus departed into the night, leaving me alone in the ill-lit roadway.

Because of Belgrade and Athens I was still anxious about finding hotels full. Down a lamplit side street I saw a sign OTELI. I hurried towards it, entered a smoky tea-house through a glass door, and took a room upstairs at once. This rather surprised the owner, who did not know of my sufferings in Athens. A huge bumpy bed with a pillow like concrete filled the room completely, and the window looked not outside but into the public washroom. Still, I had embarked on my Turkish travels. Happy with that, I drew the curtain on the washroom, turned out the light – the switch was in the passage outside my door – and fell asleep to the cheery clatter of backgammon, and the buzz of talk, coming up from the café below.

I had the café to myself in the morning and, after breakfasting off bread and tea, I set out to look round the town and make a plan. A plan I must have. For peace of mind, I need to have taken steps to settle all questions in view. This usually means finding the best way to leave the place I am in; once I know how to leave, I am free. So I found the stop where I could catch a bus eastward next day and, with that settled in my mind, walked into the town. Despite the tourists in the museum, and at Ephesus, few stay the night in Selçuk. It isn't much of a place, but to me, thoroughly Turkish. The tea-house at the station, beside empty tracks and deserted platforms, made the railway seem an adjunct of the café, attached to it to amuse the customers, and its inaction confirmed what I had been told, that trains are not the way to travel about Turkey.

I walked the mile or so to Ephesus along the tree-lined road. Through gaps in the acacias you can see across cotton fields the walls of the castle of Selçuk girdling the summit above the town, dark walls with deep battlements. This is the architecture which dominates the Turkish landscape, stone keeps in stone walls, the same harsh architecture which loured over medieval Europe. In the late seventeenth century came the country house with its park to bathe our English landscape in smiles of peace. No such era had come to Asia in 1850, or even in 1914. It occurred to me that it was partly this threatened scenery – the feeling that the Middle Ages had not ended – which attracted adventurous young Englishmen, their minds influenced by the Gothick revival and the rage for Chivalry, to travel in the East. Here were cruel pashas, wild horsemen armed with lance and sword,* inhuman tortures, stone castles guarding river-crossings – all the trappings of Romance through which the knights-errant of Scott and Southey and Tennyson rode so bravely. The dark tower is essential to the landscape of Romance. The idea it suggests, of a tyrant or enchanter into whose hands the traveller might fall, added to the view a frisson lacking from European travel. Listen to Robert Shaw describing his feelings

* In the Caucasus existed a tribe, the Khervisours, who wore a red cross on the breast, and the armour of Crusaders, and whose swords bore French inscriptions. But in the London Library copy of Spencer's *Circassia*, where this tribe is described, is a manuscript note asserting that Spencer never visited Circassia at all.

whilst detained at Kashgar by the king of that city and of Yarkand:

Darkness is the rule of the land . . . one is reminded of those tales in which some great enchanter guards his castle from intrusion. Those who seek not to fathom its mysteries pass by unmolested; while those who, however innocently, have acquired a knowledge of the secrets on which depends its owner's power are sacrificed to his safety. I feel myself now in the grasp of some such magician. Uncalled, I have entered his castle; should he believe that I have obtained any knowledge that could be dangerous to him, I am not likely to cross its threshold again.

If we had the diary of one of the Grail knights, it would perhaps read like that – in Tennyson's translation.

The road was sufficiently empty for it to seem as though I walked through fields and quiet hills towards the site of Ephesus. It isn't easy for a tourist to scuff his feet in country dust, but when he does, he learns what's meant by 'keeping your feet on the ground'. I sat in the shade of an archway where my path entered the site, the sun burning down on a waste of dry grass, the marble of the city gleaming in the distance, the blue sky above, and I thought what a perfect piece of ground my feet were on.

The Via Sacra, the deep lane by which I walked on towards the ancient city, wound under the roots of old cypresses like a marble stream-bed. I kept away from the centre of the site for a bit. In the country round, where marble shows from sheep-cropped mounds, you are aware of the stone the Greeks worked sinking back into the earth it was quarried from by men who made from it the pillars supporting our world. The shaping of the stone is just distinguishable before marble sinks back again into formless rock, as Newton's lion had vanished from his labourers' sight though not from his. I was summoned from these thoughts by an extremely ragged workman who had been following me, and who now beckoned me with many gestures of secrecy into the depths of bushes and even caves to show me some bronze coins done up in his handkerchief. Instead, from the dusty ground, I was later able to pick up what I much prefer, a fragment of marble just shadowed with fluting – my own little Newton's lion – which I could put in my pocket and carry off.

The distant hubbub of visitors pushed occasional pulses of people out of the car park into the ruins, especially into the theatre. There people sat in groups on the tiered marble benches and applied sun-cream, or fiddled with cameras, or looked vacant under sun-hats. Through megaphones lecturers described St Paul speaking in this very theatre to the rioting Ephesians. Those who attended looked around appreciatively at the flights of seats, the stage, the perfection of it all. Murray's guide to Turkey for 1854 says, 'Of the site of the theatre, the scene of the tumult, there can be no doubt. Every seat is now removed, and the proscenium is a hill of ruins. The memory of the past,' the writer continues, intending to soften the blow he has delivered, 'perhaps led travellers to indulge their imaginations too freely, while contemplating the stones that remain. Thus a visit to Ephesus will often be productive of disappointment.'

Since those days it is the authorities who have indulged their imaginations, so that the mass tourist will not find his visit 'productive of disappointment'. How much of the library of Celsus, and all those fine buildings lining the streets, has been dug up, and how much has been simply put up? Archaeological excavation has evidently struck a bargain with speculative building, to produce as much of a town as the Turks judge the tourists want to see.

The appeal of the place is pretty crude. Where ruins mouldering into the earth pluck faintly at your sleeve, these marble buildings shout in your ear. They result from the impact of tourism on the half-tones of archaeology, which has become a much duller field of activity, to ordinary people, since its adventurous days a hundred or more years ago. You could have run bus tours to watch Layard excavating Nineveh, where there was action, and crowds, and excitement, with Layard himself driving on teams of Bedouin to drag sledges loaded with carvings to rafts on the Tigris, or swinging colossal stone images about the sky with block-and-tackle, or quarrelling with the pasha, or pig-sticking with Dr Sandwith in the reeds along the river. Now archaeology seems to be slow and careful work you couldn't run a bus tour to watch. But people come in huge numbers to sites easily reached. Lured by the overstatements of brochure-writers, which give the impression that the excitement of visiting an ancient site is scarcely bearable, most would be disappointed, as Murray warned, to find a mere 'hill of ruins' where the famous theatre stood. So a theatre is built. In this way sites convenient for tours are annexed by the entertainment industry. It doesn't offend Asiatics, who possess no instinctive reverence for old stones, having always sold them to foreigners, or burned them for lime, or thrown them down in the search for treasure. The Disneyland approach to antiquity suits more people than it upsets. Though upset rather than suited by what I conceive has been done to Ephesus, I always learn a lot from the information given out by noticeboards and loudspeakers; in the library of Celsus, for instance, there were charts showing how the Austrians had rebuilt the place, in comparison with Roman methods, which were very instructive.

By midday the buses had returned to Kuşadasi, and Ephesus was deserted. I had a quiet walk back to Selçuk by way of the temple of Artemis. This they have not yet rebuilt. Its grassy knolls were grazed by ponies, and ducks dabbled on a pond where the altar once was. On fragments of marble I saw traced the lovely designs we know from the decoration of eighteenth-century houses, Greek key and egg-and-dart, which always seems to make the private lives of these people more accessible to me than their books and statues and temples do. To know that the library moulding is of Greek design establishes more intimate contact with the Greeks than does the presence, on the shelves below the cornice, of their literary works locked up in a dead language. I don't mean that you learn anything of use by contemplating the cornice; I mean that the presence of the Greek key design above the bookshelves persuades me that understanding the Greek books isn't beyond me.

I had been walking about on my own amongst ruins most of the day. When you are alone, trains of thought have a continuity they can't have when a companion is there to break in on them, or add to them, or alter their direction. Often the continuity is not valid, depends on a false connection the solitary mind doesn't sufficiently test; and I don't know if I can convey the continuity of ideas which seemed to me to connect my morning with the Greeks to my evening with the Christians.

In the morning, on the fringes of Ephesus, I'd been thinking about the foundations of our civilization chipped out of the earth's rock by the Greeks; in the evening I turned the page, and found myself amid Christian scenes and ideas which seemed to continue the story. I had walked up to the grave of St John, open to the sky amongst the ruins of his church. 'In the beginning was the Word, and the Word was with God, and the Word was God.' It is a very Greek metaphor: indeed the Tractarians recited St John's version of the Incarnation every Sunday for its Platonic content. Maurice Bowra says of Greek syntax that it was 'a triumph of the organizing mind over the obstinate material of consciousness'. The Word is an edged tool equivalent to the sculptor's chisel, for chipping form out of the inchoate mass. That is the Greek contribution. But in the Old Testament the organizing power is attributed not to the Word but to the Spirit, which moved on the face of the waters. There, with that Hebraic idea, enters the strain of mysticism. Like the two Testaments of our Bible, the two strains – logic versus mystic, Greek Word versus Judaic Spirit, classic versus romantic – have pulled different ways inside Europeans ever since. I spend my life trying to squash Spirit into Word, life into sentences, unruly feelings into orderly syntax, trying to get the naked kicking baby into its clothes. I know I value articulation too highly, and so risk attending more to the clothes than to the baby – risk exalting words above the Word. This tendency leads in the end to denying the validity of all language save your own, like the woman spoken of in Richard Jenkyns' *The Victorians and Ancient Greece*, who said, 'It's a funny thing, the French call it a couteau, the Germans call it a messer, but we call it a knife, which is after all what it really is.' This is the danger of overvaluing words, but all the same I am dismayed by the 'alternative culture' which believes that words are mere assemblages of letters, and that 'communicating' is 'something else' not dependent on the magic spells of language.

Light, the glory of evening, poured down on the roofless aisles and dust and whitened stone of the ruins where once lived and wrote 'the disciple whom Jesus loved'. It was a picture to be remembered whenever I hear the opening words of St John's Gospel read on Christmas Day. 'In the beginning was the Word.' Hard to believe that Rite A is the Word that was with God, but that, too, is the result of my susceptibility to the magic of language perfectly used, perfectly flexible, of great subtlety, as it is found in the Prayer Book of 1662. Rite A seems to me to stem from the same contemporary impulse, to diminish and even falsify what is beyond common understanding, which has rebuilt the theatre at Ephesus; with this difference, that what Rite A replaces was by no means a 'hill of ruins'.

In unimproved churches you can still find the old forms used not as curiosities but as workaday services; and in unimproved corners of Greece and Turkey, even here, by turning in at a narrow gateway, or by following a crooked street, or by looking over a wall, you can still find the country's true past surviving into everyday life in the present. There is the Turkish village of Selçuk, for instance, on the slopes under the citadel, which is as different from the Selçuk I had slept in, built on the road and railway, as Asia ought to be from Europe. For there to be any point in travelling, you have always to be looking for things as they were, and dodging things as they are. As much as anything, what I had come to Turkey for was to learn what it was like to walk through a Turkish village as it might have been in the last century. Here, under the castle walls, I found lanes as rough as stream-beds running amongst the stone cabins, and heaps of rubbish, and doors into black interiors shared on easy terms by babies and fowls. There were sleeping dogs, and children playing in the dirt, and women in bulky headdresses ascending the street slowly under burdens, or resting on stones at the wayside. I followed a lane downhill to where the mosque of Emir Isa lay outlined against the blues of evening misting the plain below. Its rickety towers were full of jackdaws and golden light. I entered a spacious courtyard, where there was a gardener carefully watering his vegetables in the square framed by high walls. There was enough room for him to garden, and for weeds, and hens, and rubbish-heaps, and there was room too in a neglected corner,

I noticed, for the graves of old Turkey to moulder under turban-carved stones. Here was continuity with a remote age. Perpetual use of the ground gave it a vitality which, makeshift as it was, burned brighter than any mowed lawns and neatened ruins could have done.

I walked away from the place with a happier idea of Islam than the mosques in cities give me. It was familiar. The basilica of St Francis, which was being built in Assisi at about the time this mosque was rising from its hillside, encloses courtyards of weeds and flowers and rusty wells which used to give me the same idea of tranquil continuity as I felt here. The finding of such a point of similarity – a spot I recognized – was like finding a safe beach on a stormy coast, where I could land from the sea and so begin exploration of the interior of this strange land.

2

Early next morning, from the bus-stop on the highway, I began the journey eastward into Anatolia. By eleven I had reached Nazilli, where I knew I must get out of the bus I was so comfortable in if I was to make the excursion to an ancient city in the mountains which I had been advised to see, if I saw nothing else in Caria. Just finding my feet with main road buses, I didn't want to branch out all at once into local bus or worse. I jumped out to go through the form of inquiring a way to the ancient city forty or fifty miles off. I hoped it would be impossible. Heads were shaken, a taxi in the shade pointed to. Its driver asked a sum I had no trouble turning down, and I walked back to the bus which would carry me on to Laodicea. I had qualms that my behaviour lacked the adventurousness of the traveller, but it all seemed so difficult, and so hot, and so hard to accomplish compared to sitting where I was. Anyway I had tried.

I felt a tap on my arm. It was the taxi driver. Wouldn't I take a seat in a *dolmus*, the shared taxi or minibus of Turkey, going in the direction I wanted? He led me to another part of the *otogar* (bus station), where two or three little vehicles waited in the sun amongst clusters of Turks. In half an hour, he assured me, one of them would start for a town in the hills ten or twelve miles from my destination. And how would I reach it from there? He shrugged, spread his hands. I changed my mind. The minute I saw the Turks gathered round the minibuses, with their bundles and country possessions, I knew I'd enjoy it. I ran back and pulled my two bags out of the bus I had come in, which then departed.

The driver of the *dolmus* which was said to be bound for the town in the hills was an active, cross-grained little fellow in a fawn suit. He stepped rapidly about the yard drumming up business whilst his vehicle dozed in the heat with its doors open, and one or two Turks, the prospective fares, sat on the ground in its shade eating fruit. I put my bags beside theirs, and walked about, and bought tea from the stall, and walked about some more. When half an hour or so had passed it became clear that the driver wasn't waiting for the hour of departure to strike, rather a Western idea of travel, but for sufficient passengers to make the trip a profitable one. More and more people collected round his *dolmus*, on whose four bench seats there was room for eleven passengers besides himself. Still he waited. At last, when seventeen of us were assembled, he packed us in with great quantities of baggage, leaped in himself, threw the car into gear, and dashed away with us out of the yard on to the cobbled road.*

I was fortunate in being next to a window, unfortunate in having the tool-box to sit on rather than a seat. Though squeezed tightly against neighbours, there was no sense of infringing on a neighbour's privacy. It is a thing I have noticed before, that Asiatics preserve a kind of unchippable wholeness in a crowd, so that we rattled along like a box of billiard balls, no one denting his neighbour, each managing elbows and feet with neat self-sufficiency. The chat between those who knew each other was friendly, if desultory, but those without any acquaintance, and the heavily swathed women clutching bundles, kept silent. All, save the women, smoked as though their lives depended on it. The owner drove furiously, brows knitted, so cramped for room – there was even a man standing between the steering wheel and the door – that he had to fight out sufficient space to change gear, or hurl the *dolmus* round corners.

* I did not then know that *dolmus* is the past participle of *dolmak*, to be filled.

We soon left the valley of citrus groves watered by the Maeander and climbed the slopes on its southern flank, the country round us warm, autumnal, full of apple orchards and shady trees. Now and then we stopped to set down a passenger at the mouth of a lane, or by a solitary house, and now and then we stopped to pick up another, who stood waiting, apparently for just the very miracle we presented, a speedy *dolmus* with room for one more to be crushed in.

We were climbing a hill steep enough to slow us to walking-pace when I saw ahead a sight which made my heart sink. Under leather hats bought in tourist shops stood two shabby pilgrims with their backpacks by the roadside. They held out their thumbs. There was a chuckle or two, contemptuous, in the *dolmus*. Two sun-scorched young faces prickled with gingery stubble peered in when we stopped. Somehow they crammed their packs and themselves on top of us, driving me from my window into the dark interior. The others, the billiard balls, gave ground; but I, the Western egg, was smashed into mixing with them. One was American, the other German, both twenty-two or -three. They were hot and smelly, and seemed to be sitting on top of me, sticking bits of themselves into me in a way Asiatics don't.

'You going to whatsit?' the American asked.

'Yes I am,' I said.

'I hear it's something else.'

The *dolmus* rattled on, crossing a gorge by a stone bridge, plunging through chestnut woods, climbing on to bare hillsides. I couldn't see out so well now, and my enjoyment was much diminished. 'Something else'! It's like Rite A, where anything subtle isn't attempted. I was aware of the Turks watching us derisively through smoke-wreaths. There was no doubt of the contempt for these Westerners. As the wandering race despised by the natives of every land, 'students' have replaced gypsies and Jews.

At the town, or large village, which was our destination the *dolmus* dashed into the square and stopped for good. We all spilled out. The village immediately absorbed the Turkish passengers: only the Enid Blyton pilgrims and myself were left high and dry to peer about for means of leaving. Mountains and pine forests rose above the rooftops: the noon sun beat down on the square. Nearby, as yet empty, I found another *dolmus* whose driver said that in two hours he would start on a trip which would pass the nearest crossroad to the ancient city. I reported this to the two youths slumped in the shade. The American sprang to his feet. 'Two hours!' He sounded shocked, a tycoon told his plane is late. 'Why, we'll hike it, I guess!' They shouldered their packs and trudged out of the square to walk the ten or twelve miles to the site in the heat of the day. My opinion of them rose. I might quarrel with the words they slopped out to describe the place, but they were surely as keen as mustard to get there. Aimless and indifferent was how crowds of them had struck me on the train from Belgrade and in the streets of Athens, and I was interested now to see two of that crowd separate from the rest, and so close to their destination. 'You going to whatsit?' 'Yes I am.' 'I hear it's the Land of Far Beyond.'

I wasn't sure I could be much more precise than that myself, in my reasons for travelling to this ancient city. I could tell you a bit about its history, and its place in Greek and Roman colonization of Caria, but I hadn't come to find out more facts, or verify the few I know. I wanted to see it, to know whether or not it was what I was looking for. When I saw it, the question would be asked and answered; until then I didn't know what question to ask of the place. It has always seemed to me an illuminating piece of psychology, in the history of the Grail, that Sir Gawain (whose character much resembled that of a nineteenth-century traveller – Layard, for instance) was so fascinated by merely watching the procession in the Grail castle that he forgot to ask what it meant. It was adventure and sensations he wanted from the Quest, not answers. Of one of his Himalayan journeys Francis Younghusband confessed, 'In my heart of hearts I did not care a rap for the military part of the enterprise; but I did care mightily for the adventure.' Those travellers might set out in their preface a scientific or commercial object for their journey, as Robert Shaw professed an eagerness to extend the market for Indian tea through Yarkand, or Arminius Vambéry claimed to be searching through the wastes of Turkistan, disguised as a dervish on one of the most reckless journeys ever made, for the source of the Turkish tongue. And they prosecuted their inquiries. Shaw was forever asking his wild gaolers the price of tea, and noting down that 'it never used to sell lower than four to six tangas a "jing" in the Chinese times'. When Bukhara Burnes encountered a river he recorded smartly that it was 275 yards wide, ran at 2¼ miles per hour, was 12 feet deep and had a temperature of 57°: then he crossed it at the risk of his life.

To the measurements and surveys and maps and copied inscriptions with which these men came home there is no end. I believe they were subscribing in this, superficially, to the contemporary view that proper scientific inquiry elicits facts which, if accumulated in large enough piles, will amount to total truth. These were the methods of the 'German school' of historical writing, which affected all fields as the century went on. On the surface travellers subscribed to it, because that was what was asked of them. But such a mentality never made a traveller of a man. What it did was give him the respectable flag of 'utility' to seek adventures under. No amount of dedication to increased sales of tea would drive a grocer over 20,000-foot passes in the Karakoram into blood-soaked kingdoms which reminded Shaw of twelfth-century Europe; nor is this a grocer's description of an undeveloped sales area: 'The first sight, on cresting the col, was a chaos of lower mountains, while far away to the North the eye at last rested upon what it sought, a level horizon . . . it was the plain of Eastern Toorkistan, and that blue haze concealed cities and provinces which, first of all my countrymen, I was about to visit.' Or would a philologist pure and simple so revel in the romance of this description of Vambéry's? 'The moving caravan and its fantastic shadows, upon which the pale moon shed its mysterious silvery light, flanked on the right by the Oxus rolling its darkling waters with a hoarse murmur, on the left the awful desert of Tartary stretching its endless vista.' No, Vambéry admits, it wasn't only philology, for 'I doubt not but that my innate fondness for travel, and my insatiable curiosity, and eager pursuit of adventure, had as much to do with my resolve' to make the journey. Sir Henry Layard wasn't an archaeologist until he found himself amongst the mounds of Nineveh with an urgent desire to continue his wandering life, rather than to arrive at journey's end in a Civil Service job in Ceylon; his matchless *Early Adventures* were written, as he says in the preface, to answer the question of how he came to interest himself in Assyriology. It is a vague answer, a book of adventures; but a truer answer, as far as the traveller's motivation is concerned, than all the meticulously drawn plates of Assyrian carvings he published in two weighty folios, or all the Assyrian monuments he dispatched to the British Museum with that comment which seems to mock museums: 'And who can venture to foretell how their strange career will end?'

In the square of the little town, where I had settled down on a wooden chair at a tea-house door for a wait of two hours till the *dolmus* should start, there was a change of plan. The crosspatch in the fawn suit from Nazilli had found enough passengers to see a profit in a trip onward himself, passing the crossroads I wanted, and he signified in surly fashion that I might climb aboard again. We crowded in and were immediately off at his best pace on a road of pot-holed cobbles traversing the hillside. Before we had gone a mile we again saw ahead of us the two leather hats, the two backpacks, standing by the road with thumbs at work. In they piled once more on top of us. The German boy had with him scraps of food in a plastic bag, *pide*, and dried apricots, which he munched, having offered the bag round first. The Turks declined with significant smiles at one another, half-raised hands indeed warding off the food. I took a fragment of bread from the boy as a gesture of solidarity with Christendom. One of the harmless self-deceptions of travelling alone is that you grow to believe yourself like the people you travel amongst, as a dog believes itself human if it lives entirely with humans; but the moment someone of your own race appears, it is as though you saw yourself in a mirror amongst this unlike crowd, and then of course it is absurd, even treacherous, to align yourself against your race. Back to your basket! I chewed their leathery bread as we rattled along. Again they had pushed me away from a window, and I could hardly see out.

After twenty minutes or so the *dolmus* stopped, and signs were made to the three of us to get out. When I did, and felt the heat of the sun on my back, I found that we stood at a crossing of two dust roads in open country. High hills, and mountain peaks, stood sufficiently far back for this level tract to be called a plain. A severe elderly figure in dark clothes who had got out with us trudged off immediately down one of the cross-tracks towards a stand of poplars shaking their silvery leaves above the roofs of some humble buildings in a hollow. I paid the sum asked for my fare and picked up my bags. The driver asked the two pilgrims for the same fare. They were aggrieved. 'We were hitching!' the American cried out, brandishing his thumb. The sum was trivial, their pockets full of money. They paid, with a bad grace, and shouldered their packs and followed the old man's diminishing black figure downhill towards the poplars. Doors slammed and the *dolmus* dashed away.

I was left alone. Dust from the departing wheels powdered down on whitened thorn bushes beside the road. Silence and heat reclaimed the landscape as sleep reclaims a sleeper momentarily disturbed. Here I was: here was isolation, and dusty roads under a blue Asian sky, and here I was in the midst of it, just as I had intended to be when I set out from home. There came that vivid and rare stroke of light, as a shaft of the sun spills between clouds and whitens one winter tree in a dark landscape, which assures you of the lustre of life. Here I was, with all I needed. I slung a bag on each shoulder and took the track opposite that taken by the others, to read a sign nailed to a thorn tree a short way down it.

MESTAN'S RESTAURANT said the sign in Turkish, German and French. I followed the track. In the midst of a devastated area of dried mud I soon came upon a tin-roofed shack built of poles, with a second smaller, if possible humbler, hut at a short distance from it. Building of this rural slum seemed to have been suspended before completion, since poles and tin and other rubbish lay strewn everywhere. The track ran in front of the huts, scrubby fields sloped up behind them; the site had no advantages. Over the mud scampered thin cats and thinner chickens, while in its midst, leaking on to a dark stain, stood a rusty iron tanker such as is used for taking water to cows. From the smaller hut, through glassless windows fringed with rags, came the dismal wails of children. My hopes were not high as I approached the larger hut and looked in.

I looked into another world. From the dusty brilliance at the door the scene extended deep into dimness and coolness like a cave. Rugs were scattered on the floor and clothed the walls. At the further end rose a Turkish platform on which sat two men crosslegged. The shadowy light, the colours of the rugs, the sense of an encampment in the wilderness – it was an Eastern scene, all that was intriguing. Both men rose, the taller of the two coming towards me, the other gliding out by some door in the hangings which I could not see. M. Mestan introduced himself, a dignified and handsome man of thirty or so, and offered me a place on the carpeted dais without inquiring what I wanted. He spoke good French, saying (when I asked) that I could of course stay, eat, make my home here if I wished. The room he showed me, which was in the other hut, had a collection of worn-out rugs and old clothes heaped against its bare walls, an earthen floor, and a door with so large a gap under it that cats and even chickens merely ducked their heads to follow us in. This room was offered to me without either the servility or the disdain usual in people who let rooms, but as a friend might offer to share what he had with you. M. Mestan's manner was grave to the point of sadness, and very reserved. I took the room, and left my bags in it. He promised that his wife would make a meal ready for me in half an hour's time, at three o'clock, and I set off at once for the ruined city beyond the crossroads.

I didn't get as far as the ruins. I was following the track taken earlier by the Far Beyonders when I came upon a scene whose significance made me stop. The track had dipped into a little valley sheltered from the austere landscape of the plain. Huts of stone, their roofs turfed, clung to the stony slope of the valley. Each had its garden wall thrown round the fruit trees treasured in Asia, and I could see that these walls too, like those of the cabins, were freely packed with dressed marble. Hence their destruction. For the village was silent, deserted, ruinous; indeed, half the cottages were already levelled with the ground, a scatter of stones showing where they had stood, and in the part of the village still standing you could see through gaps in walls into abandoned rooms, or into wasted gardens. Many a pomegranate tree lay uprooted, its leaves withered, its trunk gashed. No scene could have been more Turkish. It was a picture such as might have been found in a village laid waste by a pasha's order for non-payment of taxes, or a village in which had been quartered a squadron of bashi-bazouks, the irregular cavalry who left nothing undestroyed.

What had been extracted from the ruination of this community was heaped together around the engine of destruction. Not taxes, but stones; fragments of marble, of columns and entablatures and pavements, such as have been taken from ancient cities to build modern villages ever since the legions withdrew. These blocks of marble were stacked round the yellow bulldozer used in pushing down the village to reclaim them. I wondered what was their destination. There was nothing of 'museum' quality; they were the sort of fragments powerful men might like beside their swimming pools. It is a fact that successive governments, following on no matter how many 'revolutions', find different reasons for performing identical actions. So the government of Turkey continues to knock down villages whenever those in power want what the villagers conceal. 'Bashi-bazouk' even sounds as if it might be the Turkish for 'bulldozer'; and the yellow machine squatting in the ruin it had caused gave off rather the same baleful air you see in Horace Vernet's paintings of subjects such as 'Irregular Horsemen resting after a Foray'.

The centre of the village, where somewhat larger houses of two storeys surrounded a dust square on the floor of the little valley, remained a fine Eastern scene, only in decay through time and carelessness. These houses were deserted, their window-glass gone, doors boarded, balconies rickety, but the little dusty *meidan* they looked on to was made magnificent by a large old *chenar*, the Asiatic plane tree, which shaded a wide extent of ground under its rustling leaves. From somewhere in the valley came the trickling of a fountain, but its source I could not see from where I stood in the heat of the sun, though its sound seemed to lay the dust in my mind. What I could see in the shade of the *chenar* was a marble seat against the trunk, and I crossed the square to sit down on it. I found that it was a theatre bench, its armrest carved in the form of a dolphin, much worn by use, dragged here, I suppose, heaven knows how long ago, from the Greek city. There I sat, watching the brilliant light fall hot and still outside the ring of shade cast by the tree, and listening to the fountain which I now could see. Water spouted from a pipe into a marble sarcophagus, which it overflowed, sparkling down over the mossy marble lip to run off in rivulets darkening the dust. There was no other sound, and the village was entirely deserted.

It was now time to go back for the meal M. Mestan had promised me, so I did not take the track which followed the valley towards the stand of poplars and, as I supposed, the ancient city. In recrossing the square I noticed a faintly painted sign on one of the housefronts, CHAI EVI MESTAN. I guessed at once that he had been evicted, driven to new ground to set up his unpromising business in those huts. Though this house in the village was dilapidated, I was sorry not to be sleeping there. Its wooden front tottered; one end of its balcony had collapsed into a heap of rotten sticks, and the other had only been saved from ruin by its strut being propped on the drum of a marble column. I looked at that fluted drum supporting the old house, so harmonious a component in the scene of picturesque decay – as was the theatre seat under the *chenar*, and the sarcophagus serving as a cattle trough. Is it shocking to see antiquities obliged to earn so humble a living? I don't think it is, in fact it seems to me in the largest sense their proper end, dust to dust so to speak, and I hate to see a picturesque scene such as this dismantled in order to rescue the elements composing it. All the same, half the world's most famous antiquities had to be rescued from lime-kilns, or pulled out of house walls, or taken in some way out of common use to be preserved in museums. No doubt the marble Aphrodite we have at home was trimmed off at neck and knee to fit better into someone's wall in a village like this one. By now there would be little left of the ancient world if nineteenth-century travellers had not 'liberated' what they found, or located important pieces which the museums of Paris, Berlin and London would then compete for through their ambassadors at the Porte. I shouldn't complain at the destruction of the romantic scene by hands rescuing its classical components, but the pull inside me between their two appeals means that I want both. If the time comes when no village exists where you can rest under a *chenar* on a Greek seat, and listen to water falling into a Roman sarcophagus, then the world will have lost something wonderful. You can look at classical sculpture in any major city in the world, but for the romantic setting you still have to travel, and travel without taking along with you the other tourists whose presence immediately destroys what you have come to see. 'Our party was a large one,' says Warburton of an expedition to Delos, 'and consisted moreover entirely of English, a circumstance which, I know not why, is always fatal to research or even to reflexion; a scoffing spirit inevitably prevails, and whether on Parnassus or in Jehosophat, our countrymen seem to think that everything is unreal except themselves and their sandwiches: this is the very triumph of objectivity.'

I had reached the crossroads, on my way back to Mestan's, when I saw two figures receding on the road towards the hills by which I had come. Although made hazy in the heat and distance, by outline of hats and backpacks I knew them for the two pilgrims. So they had already left. What they wanted wasn't here. How did they know so quickly? I felt a twinge of uncertainty at being left behind. They were looking through their own young eyes, navigating by maps they carried in their own heads, and what they had hoped to find wasn't here at all, but somewhere further on. I travelled in a country mapped for me by many hands since ancient times, scrawled over with names in languages not my own. Poussin and Pannini frame what I see, Strabo and Gibbon and a hundred other voices tell me what to think. When I thought I had found what I wanted, was I looking not at the stones themselves but for sermons which an outdated education had hidden under them? I was satisfied with the answer the place gave me, but was I asking the right question on my travels, a question of my own worth asking? I stood at the crossroads and stared after them. It is said that πoθoς, the overruling yearning for something absent or lost, was the spur which drove Alexander across the world to India.

A car horn sounded on the road behind me. Bucketing along in a cloud of dust came the *dolmus* which had brought me here. The driver thought I was waiting to be taken back, and slowed down. I waved him past. Away dashed the busy little vehicle, receding towards the two distant pilgrims on the road whom I saw stop, and stand with bent backs and heavy burdens, and no doubt hold out their thumbs for another lift towards the Land of Far Beyond.

3

I heard the story of the destruction of the village from M. Mestan after I had eaten my meal, seated on the carpeted platform in a cloud of flies, and watched by five extremely dirty children with runny noses who came to stare and smile shyly, hand in hand, until chased away by their father. He brought me a bunch of grapes which I was dismayed to see him douse in filthy water before handing to me; but the time had come to eat and drink what was offered, and hope for the best. M. Mestan had brought tea, too, and sat down himself on the dais, having kicked off his shoes, and he smoked and drank tea and ate grapes beside me.

The director of antiquities of this area had given orders for the demolition of the village in which (as I had seen) Mestan's Tea-house had stood, in accordance with a general order forbidding habitations within so many hundred metres of any ancient site. Of course, whether such an order was applied in a particular case or not depended on many things. In this case, M. Mestan believed, interests in Ankara had made it worth the local authorities' while to clear the site, and evict the competition, before building a tourist hotel. There was a sad dignity about him which his dry voice, and correct French, gave fine expression to. The only ground which had not been withheld from him by the authorities' influence was this patch of mud where he was building, as money allowed, a replacement for his requisitioned home and business.

'From this place,' he said, his black eyes burning and his index finger wagged from side to side in a stubborn gesture, 'from this place, I do not budge.'

*

When I set out for the ancient city, which I did after reading and drowsing for a while till the sunlight at the hut door looked less heavy, I crossed the fields to avoid the official gate, feeling that by following M. Mestan's advice in this matter I was supporting him against the authorities. From these fields pieces of marble had been gathered and thrust together into dry stone walls like those which divide the little fields of Connemara. Between them a path white with dust, and well worn by hoof and boot, wound amongst dust-whitened bushes towards brick walls which rose above scrub trees and tangles of ivy. These were the Byzantine walls. The far blue heights of the mountainside looked down on their ruin as they had looked down on their building. Beyond the walls, on every hand lay a scene of colossal destruction. Vast works have been thrown down. Fragments as large as these, scattered so wide, convey an awful sense of the power of the destroyer. You picture the hand of giants, Titans, the Lapiths whom the Greeks feared, and the mountains seem to stand closer, the ground to shake.

There still stood, above the chaos of levelled stone, clusters of columns, walls, doorways, fragments of the marvellous fabric of ancient buildings. But thorn pushes up the paving: marble was splashed purple with the juice of pomegranates dropping from the tree: blackberries scrambled over metopes: the scene 'mingles Grecian grandeur with the rude wasting of old Time'. The sunlight from the deep blue sky drew full value from fluted column or carved frieze, and a deep silence gave weight to every thought. Far off on the flank of a mountain above the plain a forest fire burned amid dark woods: distance purged the fury and rage of fire, and turned it for me into a stately column of white smoke hanging majestically in the view. I thought of the destruction of this city many times in blood and fire more terrible than a blazing forest; and of how the ruins now hang in the landscape purged of terror by time, whitened by the sun of centuries into a smoke of elegiac suggestions.

General themes are pushed into the dullest minds by the spectacle of ruined splendour on this scale. I did not fail to preach to myself many sermons hidden under the stones by others who have passed this way. I could see them plainly here, my predecessors: a couple of raw-boned ponies switching their tails under that tree, the Greek servant squatting by them smoking his chibouk, a fire for the bivouac throwing up a thin column of blue vapour, and, at a little distance, the Traveller seated on a fallen column in contemplation of the ruins of ancient grandeur. I walked in his company over the ground, pushing through sun-scorched grass, crossing a marshy stream by way of a plank, jumping down on to the floor of an ancient house, uncovering different views and further ruins at every turn, until we climbed to the topmost tier of a small white theatre commanding a wide view of the landscape, and there sat down on a dolphin-armed bench identical to the one in the village square. He quoted Tennyson's description of Virgil:

> Thou majestic in thy sadness
> At the doubtful doom of Human kind . . .

That was the elegiac note I heard struck by the scene from his mind.

It seems to me that there was very often something in these travellers' circumstances which enabled them to draw consider-able comfort from the contemplation of fallen empires. The qualities which such a traveller prided himself on possessing, though they might have been made use of fifty years before in building an empire, weren't rewarded in Victorian England as he thought they should be, when it came to governing the British Empire. It was the cautious and the well-connected who got along quickest nowadays. Throughout Victoria's reign the popu-larity of Sir Gawain, in character most English and most robust of Arthur's knights, lost ground before the duplicitous courtliness of Lancelot, and the simperings of Sir Galahad. Well, the empire wouldn't last for ever. It gave a man of Sir Gawain's character singular satisfaction, surely, to sit at the tent door of the sheikh of a wild tribe, dependent for his life on the force of his own personality, a solitary Englishman practising the qualities he had been schooled to prize, and to watch the rising of the moon over the ruins of some Imperial city where the Bedouin now grazed his flocks. So I imagine anyway. Layard, in his *Early Adventures*, often reflects on the transience of human power; and it was

Layard who suffered a snub from the governing class which angered him exceedingly, when he emerged from a dangerous journey in Constantinople, with information he had been told the Ambassador was anxious to hear, and found himself prevented by some frilled and scented Secretary of Embassy from making his way into Sir Stratford de Redcliffe's presence. Layard in his early twenties had already had audiences with Sultan and Shah, as well as living intimately with the rulers and chieftains of innumerable tribes which nowadays form entire nations, so we can picture the fury and frustration he would have suffered, had he known that Queen Victoria wrote to Palmerston of him, in objecting to his employment by the War Office (when he had become a Member of Parliament and a celebrated man): 'In contact with foreign countries we should be represented only by gentlemen.' Eastern society, where the English middle-class traveller ranked himself with rulers, and the Eastern landscape, which was full of ruins presaging the downfall of an 'establishment' he resented, were balm for such wounds. Moreover, ruins on this scale, such mighty works destroyed, go far towards reconciling a man to the destruction of his own designs. This magnificent devastation shows private ruin – the decay of hope – old age and death – as a microcosm of the great original. In place of petty discontent arises elegiac melancholy such as Tennyson described in Virgil, the mood most proper to man or mankind faced with his own history.

It was certainly my mood as I sat in the theatre above that tract of country, and those ruins, which had begun to grow a little misty with the decline of day, in the onset of the autumn evening. I had been watching a young flycatcher trying its wings at the moths which now fluttered whitely out of grass and nettles, when my attention was caught by a thin sound. Over low rough fields, as the sun sank, there came to my ears a faint quavering song accompanied by the tinkling of the flocks' bells. I looked out into the plain, but couldn't believe that the sombre figures of the shepherds would produce so plaintive a melody. Children mounted on donkeys, or leading goats, came in from the country through the sad misty light, and passed below the hill of theatre seats where I sat, while still the far-off singing rose and fell.

Never was a landscape better accompanied by music. I had begun to think it supernatural – 'That old song Apollo sang' – when I saw its source. Into a pomegranate tree in the midst of the fading plain a boy had climbed, and was throwing down its fruit to a friend, and singing as he worked.

By now the flycatcher had gone, and a brown-backed hawk hunted low over the ruins, swerving between white columns, gliding through doorways, whilst I descended the tiers of seats and walked amongst the children and goats towards the village square. There I left them watering their animals at the sarcophagus and walked away up the lane towards M. Mestan's independent venture in the darkness ahead.

I was perfectly satisfied with all I had seen. To be here answered the purpose of the journey. As I walked through the blackness of night I was aware of the landscape behind me enriched by ruins; knowledge of their presence loaded the darkness like music. It seemed that I would never forget that they were there.

4

The colours of Eastern rugs by lantern-light, and wavering shadows, made the interior of the hut look more than ever like an encampment in the wilderness when I walked in. From the platform, as he had done before, M. Mestan arose and pushed his feet into his shoes to come forward. Again there was a man with him, who moved into the shadows. When I had kicked off my shoes, and was seated on the rugs with a glass of soda water in my hand, I looked into the shadow to see him. He was a wild figure. A long cloak reached to his ankles, his hair was dark and tangled, his hands gripped a staff as tall as himself. I recognized at close quarters the figures I had seen picketing the low hills amongst their sheep, and who I hoped for romantic reasons were Turkoman shepherds.

M. Mestan had not sat down, but had removed a stone from the hut wall. From this hiding place he drew an old boot, from which he shook a knotted cloth on to the dais at my side. He unpicked the knot, looking in conspiratorial fashion to left and right into the shadows, and then spilled out a hoard of bronze coins chinking and gleaming in the lamplight. I know nothing about coins. These lumpish tokens bearing clumsy heads looked gross to me. But I was intrigued by another twist of rag which had fallen from the boot. I asked for it to be unwrapped. A movement forward, though still in shadow, showed the shepherd's interest. The rag was unwound, I saw the flash of crystal, and out twinkled something brilliant on to the dull heap of money. I restrained myself from reaching out until this little glitter of light was put into my hand. It was an intaglio enclosed in a bronze clasp, the work delicate beneath dirt and oxidization. Held against the lamp it showed faintly the profile of a goddess incised in the crystal, the light striking a bewitching gleam of green fire out of the gem, and the touch of the thing in my fingers arousing hot cupidity. I dropped it back, and cooled off my fingers by stirring them in the coins I didn't want. The shepherd watched me. When M. Mestan found that I wasn't going to buy any of his coins, he turned his attention rather reluctantly to the intaglio.

It was the shepherd's. I was told how the intrepid fellow had descended to three metres – *non, jusqu'à quatre metres!* – to steal the gem from an ancient grave, digging secretly by the light of the moon. Neither the age nor the beauty of the object was spoken of, only the depth and hazard of procuring it. By his interest, the shepherd had been drawn into the lamplight. In his eyes I saw that uncertain watchfulness you see in the eyes of untamed creatures tempted by hunger into the presence of man. A price was named. I said I could only spare a certain amount from the money I needed for my travels, and that this amount, though payable in pound notes, wasn't even a third of what was asked. The price fell by half.

A general discussion began. Sometimes M. Mestan argued with the shepherd, translating the guttural Turkish into French for me; sometimes he told me of the life and character of such a man as this shepherd, whom he described as a peasant so rusticated that he had never in his life seen the sea, or Smyrna, with the result that he had no idea of values, and couldn't grasp the concept of foreign money. The difficulty was that we weren't really bargaining over the gemstone itself, which none of us knew the value of: they were selling the work and danger of digging it up, and I was trying to buy a keepsake of this scene and its participants, and of the day I had spent amongst the ruins. When only a few pounds separated us, the shepherd suggested through M. Mestan that I should throw in my watch – and my radio, too, if I had one – which put all calculations into disarray.

It convinced me, though, that I wasn't dealing with swindlers. If the thing was a fake, it had been planted on them. I wanted it badly, the scintilla of light on the carpet beside me which contained all the lustre of the day. Adjusting the exchange rate in my favour I added a few dollars to my offer. In that sad, resigned way of Asiatic traders, spread hands portending self-ruin, they accepted.

I had the money on me – all my money, as well as traveller's cheques and passport, I carried in a belt round my waist – but I didn't want to reveal my secret to the two of them, so in order to extract the cash I had to retire to my room across the yard, pretending to them that my money was in my baggage. I lit a candle in a tin dish on the windowsill, and had undone my trousers and pulled out my shirt-tail, and was fumbling notes out of my money-belt, when I saw the rays of a lantern and two pairs of feet appear at the gap under the door. The door opened. M. Mestan and the shepherd peered round it, advancing their lantern into the room. Its beams exposed my position. I smiled as brightly as I could, caught out in a lie with my hands full of money. The shepherd, a wild enough figure to encounter anywhere, would have pushed on into the room, had not M. Mestan restrained him with a gesture which delayed rather than forbade his approach to my money. I counted out the pounds and dollars I had agreed with them, hoping to conceal the thickness of the wad remaining as I crammed it back into my money-belt and hauled up my trousers. M. Mestan picked up the banknotes from the bed on the floor between us and pushed one into the bear's paw of the shepherd, who examined the writing on it with the extreme care of the illiterate, rubbing his thumb over it as he did so. With the notes counted, M. Mestan held out his hand for the intaglio. Given it reluctantly, he handed it to me in the twist of rag it had been rewrapped in, and I dropped it into my shirt pocket next my heart. Bonhomie then returned. We went back to the larger hut in the quavering beams of the lantern, though before we reached it the shepherd had vanished into the night.

An hour or so later I sat alone in the lamplight, amid the shadows of the hut, writing the draft of this account of my first days in Turkey. On the floor slept the dummy which M. Mestan hoped would frighten intruders away. We had talked as he made it up – we talked since he brought me a glass of wonderfully dark strong-flavoured tea to finish the supper I had eaten alone – about the state of his country.

He had the brooding temperament of the chronic malcontent. No régime would suit him. Calling himself a Communist, what he resented about government was that it interfered with his capitalistic ambitions. He believed that he resented 'inequality', but really he resented inequalities that didn't favour him. All his rancour focused on the authorities in charge of the ancient site, whom he accused of exploiting the place to benefit themselves and other strangers from Ankara – whether politicians, or hoteliers, or holders of 'research grants' from American foundations. Exploited instead by M. Mestan and his friends, in their makeshift way, the site would provide the community with a living, just as its stones had furnished the community with building materials for their homes ever since the Roman invaders went away.

So he clung on here in his two half-built shacks with an obstinacy which would not give further ground, except to a bullet in the head. The authorities denied him piped water – hence the water-cart in the yard – and so, because he had no tap, no lavatory, the authorities denied him a licence to sell food or lodging even at the humblest level of Turkish categories. He had no illusions about their wish to be rid of him. I felt strong liking and respect for this difficult, independent man.

Towards me he was ambivalent. His instinct for hospitality inclined him to make me as comfortable as possible as his guest; but now and then he remembered that I was exactly the fly, the none-too-common passer-by, which he had built his web with such labour to catch. He couldn't allow me to slip through his fingers. He returned to the old coins I had rejected, would have sold me anything he possessed just to assure himself that his enterprise was in working order. I asked once or twice how I could find my way back to the world beyond the mountains next morning, and each time he said impatiently, with a gesture pushing aside such questions, that a bus would pass. I had seen no bus all day, and I knew the road led nowhere. 'It will come,' he said, 'you will see.'

He had finished the dummy in the bed by this time, and sat down by it for a moment, his hand resting on its water-jug head like a man saying goodnight to a child. Twice in the summer, he said, terrorists had awakened him demanding money. Such a life wasn't possible. The military junta would be tolerated, if they stopped such things, for six months or a year. Then what? He shrugged, rose from the bed. I guessed that when the junta had had its period of grace, and some sort of order had been restored, then M. Mestan, like several million other Turks, would require a government which not only repaired all the injuries done him, but favoured him at the expense of everyone else. He was condemned to an embattled life. Away he went to bed, and I was left alone.

I got up to stretch my legs, cramped from sitting on the dais. The hut was a cave of lantern-light hollowed out of darkness and silence which began at the door; I had the impression that my lamp was the only light burning in this whole tract of mountain and plain, whose blackness seemed intensified by curfew and martial law. It was not hard to picture the gleam of the pistol which had awoken M. Mestan. Nor did the dummy bed seem much of a defence against intruders, a mere dying fire in a forest inhabited by wolves. I wondered if it had been the Grey Wolves, the right-wing death squad, who had visited M. Mestan, or some other group of killers now lying low. What, too, was the meaning of the relics of earlier 'guests' which were the only furnishing of my room beside the rugs I was to sleep in? A safety razor, one walking boot, a bundle of denim clothes – not possessions a tourist leaves behind willingly. I saw again in my mind M. Mestan and the shepherd advancing their lamp and their heads round the corner of my door, exactly in the style of First and Second Murderers, and I remembered M. Mestan's hand restraining, or delaying, his companion's approach to me and my money.

I went back to the dais, and to my writing, trying to set down if I could the interest and amusement of Turkey so far. Hardest, because most important, was to find words for the certainty of happiness which had filled me as I had walked away from the ruined city in the dusk. I could not – cannot – crush that kicking baby into its clothes. But I had in my shirt pocket the gem which expressed it all. No need to look at it: I possessed it, a talisman which gleamed in at the corner of my mind like the moon on a child's bed after a happy day. No need to struggle on with words – I had something else.

III

✦✦✦✦✦✦✦✦✦✦✦✦✦✦✦✦✦✦✦✦✦✦✦✦✦✦✦✦✦✦✦✦✦✦✦✦✦

I

The next chapter of this book I wrote in draft in the town of Ürgüp, in Cappadocia, in the course of a day of suspended animation I was obliged to pass there. A hush had fallen on Turkey as unnatural as utter stillness on the sea. I looked down from my window on to white, empty streets. No one stirred through them, not a child, not a cart, not a car. Only in the shadows of windows, standing well back, could faces be seen. The sunlight fell hot and heavy on the ash-white town in the middle of its fantastic landscape.

The sounds which disturbed the silence increased its uneasiness. Occasionally a troop-carrying truck crawled up the steep street in low gear, the sun gleaming on weapons and helmets. Static spat from the loudspeakers rigged to iron posts above the streets: the electric crackles heralding military announcements as the shuddering, slave-beaten gong in Hollywood's Old Testament movies used to preface the pharaoh's commands. *Dikkat! Dikkat!* The staccato order crackled out. I got that part of the message, but I couldn't catch a word of what followed. If my life had hung on understanding, as it might do in a revolution or civil war, I couldn't have grasped the meaning of those volleys of Turkish echoing against the housefronts in the silent town.

Luckily it was neither a revolution nor a civil war, but Census Day. The decree had gone out that all Turkey was to be counted. To effect this, no one was to leave their home until the counters had tramped the streets in pairs and reckoned up the numbers house by house. From one corner of Turkey to the other – from Aegean to Persian border, from the mountains of the Black Sea to the plains of Syria – not a soul might stir out of doors. There was something pastoral in the idea, like a shepherd counting his flock: at the same time, despotic power is required to cause silence and stillness to fall upon the whole land.

It had taken this decree of daytime curfew to show me what the Turks knew already, that the underpinnings of military power – the armed troops, the public address system rigged to lampposts, the jeeps parked at street corners – were omnipresent. Usually masked by the rush and noise of everyday life, the harsh bedrock of dictatorship was revealed today like the stones in a river-bed when the flow of water is dammed off above. You saw people's apprehension in their absolute obedience: in streets emptied of all but soldiers.

I found out that foreigners could get a pass allowing them out of doors, so I went to the police station to ask for one, as much for the interest of seeing the mechanism of army rule at close quarters, as for the pleasure of walking about the empty town. The military were courteous if chilly, rather touchingly showing their humanity by the way they had made themselves as comfortable as possible for the day's work, stretching awnings between fruit trees for shade, and having at hand a good supply of tea and melons and suchlike homely solaces. Though as a race the Turks don't care a jot for preserving what is beautiful, or even what is useful, they have the instinct (the nomad's instinct?) for making the best of what chance puts in their way to achieve a little comfort in a stony place. They were comfortably bivouacked. I caught a feeling, too, of their camaraderie; but self-sufficiency in this respect is, I suppose, forced upon them by their isolation from the rest of the community, whom they rule over, rather than resulting from *esprit de corps*. It is a conscript army, and how do you isolate a conscript from the population you have drawn him from? Yet you do; and I saw the process take place before my eyes, later, in eastern Turkey.

I walked about the town for a while with my pass, now and then meeting the solemnly marching pairs of officials poking in and out of doors and gardens with clipboards under their arms, or seeing a mother anxiously rush to grab a child that had run into the road, or watching more phlegmatic householders prepare for winter by splitting wood in their yards, under yellow apple trees. But I didn't care for the silence and emptiness of the place, or for the troops in the streets. The little town was shown up in all its dustiness and dilapidation by the ceasing of its life to flow. I soon walked back to my hotel, an ugly block of concrete standing on end in a builder's yard, beneath which I noted with pleasure two or three of my shirts hanging limp on a line, a signal, like the struck flag of an enemy admiral, that the management had undertaken my washing. A pretentious hotel exists in Ürgüp because it is, or was in less uncertain times, a tourist centre for the rock churches of Cappadocia, and I had chosen to stay there in order to get my washing done, and to ring up England. I had already had several rows with the management on both subjects, and planned more. It isn't the badness of bad hotels which is distressing, it's the badness of 'good' hotels.

2

As in the yards of houses in Ürgüp, so across the high country of Anatolia I had watched people preparing for winter. Gathering and storing fuel as well as food is an obsession with the inhabitants of those high, cold, unforested plains. I sympathized with a man I saw stand tapping his moustache before his hoard of wood, heedless of the heat of the sun on his back as he reckoned up the long bitter weeks of January against the stock of logs in his yard. Was it enough? I knew how he felt – it is never enough, there isn't enough firewood in the world to quench the craving for plenty which gnaws at the wintry heart of the lover of fires. All this storing away of summer and autumn gave me an idea of the ferocity of winter in those highlands. In the shelter of fast-yellowing poplars I saw peaches and nectarines and apples ripening in orchards, but the leaves were reddening and falling, the days grew short, and everyone was intent on tasks of gathering and storing. In the village I first came to after leaving M. Mestan's establishment I saw the roof of the bakehouse heaped with sheaves of wheat and firing, whilst the flat roofs of many of the houses round about held a store of melons as yellow as moons.

A bus did indeed come for me that morning, just as M. Mestan had predicted. I was drinking a glass of tea he had brought me, and eating a piece of bread, at perhaps half-past seven in the morning, when we heard the horn-blast of a bus bellowing towards us over the plain. We dashed up the track to the crossroads and there, whilst the old bus trembled and snorted, we wrung one another's hands with the strength of feeling which had for some reason arisen between us. Then the bus rolled forward, full of men on their way to work and women going to market, and carried me out of an episode I had very much enjoyed. I had slept beautifully, rolled up in the rugs on the floor of my bare room, stars shining in on me through the black window, and I looked forward eagerly to whatever might happen next.

Constant diversion, the turning to something new, is a chief attraction of travel. Especially this is its siren song if your nature lays on you the obligation – as a writer's nature does – to make something out of yesterday before you go on to today. When you're travelling you can't stop for such spoilsport ideas as that. Let it go! Let the water flow over the lip of the fall into oblivion. Fresh scenes will divert us today.

I was aware of this improvident waste of experience as the bus carried me away from the ruined city and the day I had spent there. Couldn't I turn it to some account? It had happened, I had been there, let that be enough. Let the experience, like the ruined city, sink into the landscape I left behind, to enrich if it will the darkness of what is past. In my pocket I had the intaglio, which contained what I needed to keep. The bus rattled along, and I gazed out of the window, where the interest of what was passing soon stifled the regret of letting go what was past.

We collected workmen from one village after another, winding about the valley, crossing the slow green river, steering by dust roads for the slim sun-whitened minaret, or peaceful dome, of a village mosque amongst orchards and trees. Dogs and children and hens stopped for a moment in the dirt square whilst the bus throbbed and men shouted to one another and swung aboard.

Blue smoke rose into the sunlight from cottage roofs. Everywhere, as I say, was the impression of autumn, harvest, winter to come.

I took another bus eastward from Nazilli. Soon the vale of the Maeander becomes a little threadbare; sandy hills show above vineyards, and rocks above fig trees and lemons; outcrops of stone begin to wear through the soil. Through bare hills the road climbs on to the vast bare plain which is the central tableland of Turkey. Still there was an impression of harvest, enormous grain fields cleared and burnt, ripe orchards, melons, maize. In cotton fields, above the bent backs of hundreds of women picking the crop, rose the solitary upright figure of a male overseer smoking his pipe in cap and braces. The road keeps on and on.

The landscape hardly changed all day. Here and there, besides stopping in towns, the bus made halts at wayside eating-places, where passengers strolled about in the hard bright light eating grapes, whilst an active boy or two washed dust off the bus with hose and broom, the work rarely finished before the driver swaggered out in his bell-bottomed trousers and high-heeled shoes, dark glasses and cigarettes in a pouch on his belt, to swing up into his cab, start the engine and blow flourishes on his horn, the conductor meantime hissing automatic doors open and shut to harry latecomers.

The buses were full: I never had an empty seat beside me. On and on the driver battered across the interminable plain. People ate heartily, nectarines or pomegranates drawn from their bags, rubbed on shiny sleeves, offered to neighbours, devoured in a fountain of juice. They dozed, a lighted cigarette between lips or fingers, or they slept with their foreheads resting against the seat in front. They looked out of the window, but without much interest. I don't believe that answers to the questions which puzzled me about the landscape would have emerged from conversations, if I had spoken Turkish. Why, for instance, on two strips of land side by side should one man plough with a new tractor, his neighbour with oxen? The dust from both ploughs rose above the question, and we were past them.

Towns were few, and dilapidated, their decaying old centres almost swallowed by concrete suburbs rising from dust and rubbish encircling them. I saw nowhere I wished I was stopping, though I peered out at Akşehir with interest, thinking of Layard's description of riding into it in 1839:

> We arrived towards evening at Ak Sehir, the principal place of the district – a considerable town, but filthy beyond description. The narrow streets were up to our horses' knees in mud, and the putrefying carcasses of animals lying in them tainted the air with the most offensive odours. This barbarous and unclean habit of leaving the bodies of horses, camels and other beasts to rot in the streets prevails in most parts of Turkey.

The marshy lake of Akşehir I saw, too, far-off shimmering water under pale mountains. An example of Layard's character can be seen from a telling discrepancy between his description, and that of his companion (Edward Mitford), of an incident which befell them between lake and town of Akşehir. An old woman hailed them, both agree on that, and Layard's version goes: 'Seeing my fez, and taking me for a Turkish official, she thus addressed me: "May the blessing of Allah be with you. Whilst father and mother weep for you at home, you are away from them, toiling through the rain, on our Lord the Sultan's business." ' Now listen to Mitford: 'An old woman on the road, as we rode along in the rain, mistook us for Turkish *recruits* and cried out', etc., etc. Now Layard's fiery and arrogant spirit never would have let his ear hear, or his heart believe, that any old woman, or any human being whatsoever, could mistake him for a mere recruit. But Mitford, destined for a life in the Ceylon Civil Service, did not insist on being mistaken for someone important. Both wrote their accounts of the incident nearly fifty years after the old woman had accosted them on this road – Layard by then an ex-Minister, ex-Ambassador, father of Assyriology, connoisseur of Italian primitives, a famous old lion; Mitford only a retired Civil Servant with quiet mild eyes which look softly out of his photograph – and you could say they were right to hear the old woman's words in differing versions, as though she had been a soothsayer prophesying their different futures.

After three or four hundred miles of this steppe, travelling east from the Maeander as I did, you come to Konya. I arrived pretty late one evening, and fell for the draw of a cool-looking hotel entrance within the precincts of the bus station, rather than finding my way into the town's centre, and looking there for a hotel. Of course the glass doors and marble foyer were a trick, the one I always fall for, imagining the room I get will be in keeping with the luxury I've seen looking in from the street. Upstairs I was soon in regions of echoing concrete and rusty iron. In my room both light bulbs and the lavatory were broken; there was no water and the window wouldn't open. When told, the desk clerk uttered the most unpatriotic sentiment I have ever heard, even from a hotelier: 'This is Turkey, sir,' he said with a shrug. Still, I had a meal in the *locanda* nearby, reading Trollope's *The Three Clerks* amid a wilderness of empty tables, and enjoyed walking about the dark and rather hostile-seeming quarter around the bus station before going to bed. I passed a new mosque rising from a litter of raw wood and stone: above it in the darkness, red lights flashing and rotor-blade slashing, hung a military heli-copter. I knew that Konya had been the centre of religious fanaticism before the military coup, and this combination struck a significant note.

3

Did Konya seem hostile because of the amount of armour visible in the streets, and the incessant chatter of helicopters overhead? When Layard and Mitford were there, they, too, found the town an armed camp. 'The streets swarmed with idle, disorderly soldiers shabbily dressed in European clothing, and discordant sounds of drum and fife came from every side. The conscription was being rigorously enforced . . . every khan and coffee house was filled with this wild and as yet undisciplined soldiery.' I was aware, as Layard probably was, of tension, even apprehension, caused by the presence of so many armed men, and steel-helmeted troops in the back of khaki trucks, and rotor-blades cutting the air like sabres overhead.

Perhaps it seemed hostile because of Konya's eminence as a stronghold of the fundamentalist Islamic party. Here fanatics and army confront one another, a touchy mix in a town. I wondered if there might have been some move, or countermove, amongst the forces of the country whilst I had been gallivanting about in buses far from any newspaper I could understand. So, taking a *dolmus* early my first morning, I was dropped at the Alaeddin Tepesi, a charming round green hill in the middle of the town, and walked from there to the chief square, Hükûmet Meydani, where I found a tourist office. Through plate-glass windows I spotted the regulation easy chairs and potted greenery, the regulation leaflets fanned out on shiny tables. I went in. There were no customers. Dust lay deeply on tables, on greenery and on leaflets. From some recess hidden from me there entered a courtly, much-decayed citizen in a double-breasted suit of great age and a spotted bow tie. I had the impression of a wig, even of rouge – of a creaky old suitor rigged out for the tea table of a rich widow. I asked him if he would be kind enough to translate for me the headlines of the Turkish newspapers I had also seen through the window, explaining that I knew nothing of Turkish developments, or of the Iran–Iraq War which was a week or two old, since leaving Rhodes, and that I was hoping to travel to the east of his country.

He rubbed together his hands with a papery sound, a ring or two twinkling, and offered me tea, a seat, whilst he reflected. I took the seat. The tea soon came, as it seems to come of its own accord into Turkish affairs, two piping hot glasses and plenty of sugar on a tray like a pair of scales swinging from the hand of a speeding child. Once it was coffee; now the price of coffee, all imported, means that everyone but the rich drinks tea. The old gentleman meanwhile appeared to have sunk into reading the paper for his own amusement. I cleared my throat. He looked up, recollected my request, made a gesture exhorting patience whilst he turned the paper back to page one. Smoothing it out on the table between us he began to translate one headline after another with quiet confidence into a fluent but absolutely unrecognizable language. At first we had spoken French, but when he learned that I was English he had switched into this other language, which he spoke much more rapidly and confidently than he spoke French. No word of it was intelligible to me. I questioned him in French, in Italian. No, I was an Englishman, and I should have the news read to me in this tongue which, by some mistake never to be rectified in a tourist office in Konya, he had long ago filed under English in the recesses of his head. At last his moving finger reached the bottom of the page, the smallest headline, and his voice ceased to jabber. As I rose and thanked him, I wasn't sure that a smile didn't lurk amongst the rouged wrinkles. As I stepped out into the dust of the street again, I wondered if he and the rich widow, both furious Anglophobes, weren't perhaps shaking with laughter at this prank, over the tea table in their recess amongst the greenery from which he had emerged.

No wiser about Turkish affairs I walked along the bare bright boulevard, between the shabby buildings, still wondering at the hostility I felt in the place. It wasn't directed at me particularly; it was a general uneasiness, a lack of amity, which put distrust into every eye. In the bazaar quarter of the town, where I enjoyed walking greatly, the prickle of unease was intensified. It is a fine warren of life, and light and shadow in narrow streets, every nook animated by people and colour and trade. Here I saw the faces of men of many Asiatic races converged together in the intimate dealings of stalls and shops. Heavily decorated baroque minarets hang above the lanes, impending Islamic banners, with something of the menace of old Turkey towards the *giaour*. I thought I caught here a whiff of the atmosphere of the East which used so to strike the Western traveller when first he crossed the Golden Horn amid the confusion of Asiatic races swarming across the Galata Bridge from Pera to Stambul. What Istanbul still promises, or threatens, in this way, was first fulfilled in Konya: the faint unease of the European at finding so very Eastern a city encamped on his own Mediterranean (which I think is at the bottom of many people's dislike of Istanbul) became in Konya, for me, a realization that I was now in a remote Asiatic town inhabited by men from many Eastern lands and races and traditions. The young men, of course, are squeezed into tight, bright, cheap Western clothes, and give you just the arrogant stare of the young provincial anywhere for a foreigner walking through his town; but the old men are the vessels in which the race is preserved. Bearded and shawled, skullcaps above walnut faces, the old men watch you pass from behind their deep eyes, incurious and contemptuous. I saw the dignity of old Turkey in them. Brought up before the Westernization of the country by Atatürk, they knew in their youth an ancient world. If one of the old men you sometimes still see sunning himself on the bench outside an English country pub were able to tell you tales, not of England before 1914, as he certainly will, but of England before the Civil War – Cromwell being the English Atatürk – then we would have old men with a span of memory to match these ancients squatting against the walls of Turkish towns. They were like old volumes outside a bookshop, whose pages might contain a lot you would like to know, if only you could make out the script.

So, when a carpet dealer drew me by the arm off the bazaar into his den lined with *kilims*, I was persuaded to stay by seeing one of these interesting old men – 'volumes of forgotten lore' – crosslegged on the floor. The merchant talked sufficient French, tea was sent for, rugs were flung down before me in that careless profusion which is designed to impose on your conscience an idea of the trouble you are causing, and I was told how much cheaper and simpler it would be for me to furnish my own house from Konya than from Bridport. I kept my eye on the old man, hoping that he would be brought into action. But he never stirred from the wall against which he leaned, his back full of repose, a cigarette smouldering in his gnarled knuckle, his glass of tea set down carefully before him by one of the boys who pulled out the carpets and flung them down before me. The moment came in the transaction when the dealer switches from asking you if you want to buy a carpet, to asking you which carpet you want to buy. I saw I could never read the old man, only look at his binding. Which carpets would I buy? But no one who had survived shopping in India with an Indian grandee could be embarrassed into buying what he doesn't want by the techniques of a provincial Turk. I drank my tea, kicked the carpets, thanked everyone in the place, and walked away into the bazaar. It isn't possible to behave quite as you would to an English shopkeeper; because of the necessity of altering natural behaviour, it is an easy descent into becoming arrogant and rude, mistaking the Asiatic's bargaining posture for actual humility.

It is a difficulty which shows up in a nineteenth-century traveller's accounts of the East. What view should he take of the native population, the more or less opaque inhabitants of the lands he travelled through? In general, when he came to compose a book of travels, the writer employed Asiatics as the crowd of extras and bit-players forming a background of atmosphere and Eastern colour whose function was to show off himself as the central figure in successive exploits. The natives were, so to speak, the raw material to be used as required in constructing an episodic novel of which the narrator was to be the hero. To this end, the same Turk or Persian might appear in different character in two books of travel – as the Matamet, ruler of Isphan, appears in Layard's adventures as a monster of depraved cruelty, and in the book of a contemporary Russian traveller as a civilized host – depending on the writer's need for a black or a white character at that stage in his tale.

The natives the traveller knew best were his servants. Often Levantines or Greeks, their function was to smooth their master's path in every respect, and to act too as insulation; mitigating the Eastness of the East by their knowledge of Frankish customs and habits and languages. For this reason their presence is played down by the intrepid traveller pitting himself against a strange land, except where the servant's reaction to a situation, particularly one of danger, might be used in dramatic contrast to the Englishman's reaction. Thus Captain Fred Burnaby, an unpleasant hero of the bullying heavy-dragoon type, makes his Turkish servant the butt of his John Bull soldier-servant Radford: laziness, cowardice, dishonesty, false piety, dirtiness – all these are discovered in the Turk by Radford, the stolid, stupid Briton, who plugs along through the mud at his master's heels. Burnaby praises Turks in the abstract (obliged by his Russophobia to be pro-Turkish) but mocks and disparages the only Turk he knows, this poor servant obtained cheap in Pera. Even the kindly, delightful young Arthur Conolly admitted his patience was tried by a servant in Persia: 'To add to our perplexity, Meshedee

Noroz all of a sudden took a wild freak, got acquainted with some jolly Topchees, married a temporary wife, and got into debt 30 tomauns.'

Of the many hundreds of native servants underpinning these books of travels, very few surface as individuals. There was Misseri, dragoman to the author of *Eothen*, who later kept the Hôtel d'Angleterre at Pera, and is often mentioned; but a more usual tone towards these men is that implied by the Murray's Handbook advice, to inquire at Smyrna for a dragoman answering to the name 'Faraway Moses'. Like servants in nineteenth-century novels, they rarely get their faces into the picture.

The date of that Murray Guide was 1874 (the year of Burnaby's ride across Turkey), and by then I think Englishmen's attitudes towards Asiatics had deteriorated. Joint-commands with the Turks in the Crimean War (as at Kars) had made Englishmen contemptuous of the incompetence, corruption and cowardice of Turkish officials. 'Turkey is all fine words and misrule,' wrote the Arabian traveller Palgrave. 'Who chats with the elegant Osmanli in his carpeted kiosk beside the Bosphorus, may not believe these tales of massacre and violation.' Experience of India, too, especially after the Mutiny, was likely to make an Englishman dislike and despise Asiatics, as well as giving him an exalted view of his own superiority not found in earlier travellers. Robert Shaw, who lived in India, says of one of his gaolers at Kashgar, 'I really look upon him quite as a friend, a feeling one can never have towards a native of India'; and Captain Abbott, an Indian officer, agonizing as usual about everything, says, on obeying the King of Khiva's summons to his palace: 'None but a resident in India can realize what this sacrifice cost me.' These are what Byron called in Stanhope 'his Nabob airs from Hindoostan'.

Such an attitude towards the natives might have been safe enough in British India, but it was a dangerous one to take up in the deserts of Tartary. Colonel Stoddart's offence in Bukhara, which caused him to be imprisoned, was to refuse to walk through the streets, although an ancient edict (obeyed by Burnes a few years earlier) forbade any but Mussulmans to ride through Bukhara the Holy. He was an Indian officer, and so was Arthur

Conolly, who came with such bravery to rescue him: both were murdered.

Knowing the dangers they ran amongst fanatics and lawless tribes, most Englishmen behaved with more discretion towards Asiatic custom, though they might throw their weight about a bit in their memoirs, where danger was a principal selling-point. Claudius James Rich, Resident at Baghdad of the East India Company, a most curious and knowledgeable traveller, as well as a collector of 800 volumes of Syriac and Arabic manuscripts, says, 'I have always made a rule of conforming to the native customs as far as my conscience and the honour of my country would admit.' Englishmen on the whole took the line of perplexed acceptance of Asiatics and their ways. 'Flatter them or beat them,' wrote Arthur Conolly, 'they still look down on you.'

A traveller didn't come to the East in order to study contemporary Eastern life or character; the contemporary East was just the condition prevailing, like the weather, in the lands he chose to travel through. What interested him was research into the classical or biblical past of these countries, not their present; and research into his own character and capabilities seen in relief against a background which had passed away in Europe. Just as he delighted in dressing up in costume – there was in Pera a painter named Preciosa who would paint your portrait in full Eastern rig of turban and pointed shoes and long-barrelled musket, any number of knives thrust through shawls twisted around your waist – so the traveller made of Asia and its people a stage-setting and crowd-scene behind the drama of his journey.

It was Turkey's past that I was interested in – the 'past' which was the contemporary scene to nineteenth-century travellers – but there was precious little of it to catch hold of in Konya, in any material way. Very occasionally amongst the concrete boxes I saw an old Turkish housefront of starved wood cut into fantastic patterns, but very little of this singular Osmanli character remained. What is being built now – like the cheap Western clothes the young wear – doesn't differ from quick building elsewhere.

Maybe it's a bit uglier. A Turkish town, seen extensively from a height, as you can see Konya from the Alaeddin Hill, is a grim

86

sight. Every horizon is dominated by high-rise blocks of concrete, and what is not in process of being built appears to be falling into ruins. There is a universal shabbiness not found elsewhere. There is no chic, however temporary, about what's new. I walked about the shady green hill, followed by two little boys anxious to clean my shoes, and wondered from different viewpoints why the town was so dreadfully ugly.

In part it's due to a lack of continuous development from past into present: the want of a soundly built eighteenth- and nineteenth-century base for the modern buildings' ancestry and foundation. You see nothing remaining except a few old wooden houses in odd corners. Here is how Konya looked to a traveller in 1840: 'We passed through a fine gateway, with numerous guards lounging in the portico, and found ourselves amid a heap of ruins, crumbling houses, wretched hovels, deserted mosques, and falling minarets. The modern houses were mostly built of mud, and had a miserable appearance.' Nothing there to serve either for a basis or for a model when the rush of development building began; no strong framework of streets and squares to hold the place together and set the style; no continuity of development: mud huts and ruins, then suddenly the leap to high-rise concrete. Take as an example the street lighting: because they didn't arrive at sodium by way of gaslamps, whose design still influences European street lighting, the Turks are content to stick up an iron tripod with a cluster of bulbs on it. Multiply this instance by a thousand others, and you have a Turkish town.

Modern materials don't suit the Turkish genius either. Concrete makes impossible the embellishments – fantastic balconies and carved façades – which the Turkish taste wrought upon their houses in wood or stone. The Asiatics' love of bright colours, too, is betrayed by the plastic paint they slap on everywhere, which flakes and peels as the colours of their native fabrics and tiles never did. All this makes for shabbiness. Nor is there any tradition of civic responsibility or civic pride. The pashas regarded their appointments – bought with huge bribes – as a chance to make their fortunes rapidly, before a rival schemed their downfall, out of the towns they ruled, in order to retire rich to a *yali* on the Bosphorus. With such a tradition I doubt if local authorities feel that they owe much to the citizens in return for their taxes. Certainly they don't spend anything on beautifying the towns, apart from providing what I now enjoyed on the Alaeddin Tepesi, those two necessities of Asiatic life, shade and water. I sat in the shade, by the green water of a pond, and both little boys cleaned my shoes with peals of laughter (my shoes were the sort that has little holes all over the uppers, through which their polish dribbled on to my socks) whilst I drank a bottle of water from the spring at Afyonkarahisar, which is delicious stuff.

Water and shade, not fine buildings, satisfy a nomad's needs, and I believe that much of what has always distressed and surprised the European in Turkey may be understood by accepting that the Turks are a nomadic race. They are at heart nomads, and their country is subject to devastation by earthquake; you have to take these two fundamental facts into account when you look at a Turkish town and wonder why they don't seem to care that it is so dreadfully ugly.

Ugly or not, I loved my stay in Konya. The mosque I wanted to see, the Alaeddin Camii, was closed, its walls cracked and tottering; and the Mevlana mosque-museum of the Whirling Dervishes appeared to me so like a great-aunt's drawing-room – all carpets and chandeliers and glass cabinets and hushed gloom – that I couldn't achieve a proper frame of mind to get up my interest in the sect. But I hadn't come for the famous buildings. As usual it was what I came upon by chance, walking casually here and there, that I loved about the town. I didn't move to another hotel, and I was walking back to it from paying visits to various mosques and medresses, one hot afternoon, when I found myself in a backwater of the town, an old suburb lying unruffled between two concrete arteries carrying traffic in and out of the centre. Here it was quiet. Dusty lanes led between old walls, and within these walls were orchards, and comfortable-looking little villas washed the colour of an apricot, and trees shading red roofs. The roofs were low; trees, and the domes and minarets of Konya beyond, were what you saw under the vast shining sky of the steppe when you looked back. From that view modern Turkey was eclipsed, and there existed instead the idea of a fruitful and well-watered oasis, shady houses, children playing by street fountains and, in corners of ground here and there, the humble mud huts of the very poor under roofs of stick and turf.

You are soon out of that quarter, and back in the glare and glass and dust of concrete canyons between half-built high-rise blocks, the strip of sky prodded by cranes, and shedding on your head the ominous metallic chatter of military helicopters.

4

From Konya north-east to Aksaray the road shows the traveller the extent and the harsh nature of the Anatolian plateau. As soon as you are out of Konya you are in the midst of emptiness. Long, low, dreary levels of steppe extend to a rim of hills webbed in mist. By nature a barren soil clothed with tussocks of weed, this wilderness has been forced to support a grain crop, so that against its obdurate distances you see figures toiling with mattock and hoe, whose purpose might be to represent the ineffectiveness of Hope. These wretches inhabit low oblongs of mud in the dismal wastes. How such a landscape exhausts the soul of man! Even the rim of hills, little hopes you might cling to in a failed enterprise, let you down; you reach them, the road climbs through them, and you find you have gained only a higher and more desolate level of the steppe. A curious eclipsed dimness darkened the scene, as though I saw it through tinted glass.

Of course the buses dash through this sullen waste as they dash through everything, spilling out muzak, insulated by speed and glass windows from the reality of what they drive through. People read, eat, doze, smoke; these tracts of their own country are no more to them than the ether outside an airliner's window. Few look out, and if they do there isn't interest in their eyes, there is disdain.

I looked out, missed nothing, because I am a foreigner who had come specially to see such vast un-European landscapes. To get the measure I wanted of these wastes I had to imagine crossing them slowly, at a horse's pace. At a horse's pace there would have been time for every dent and hillock, or patch of shadow, or crescent of marsh water, to be speculated upon and wondered about. The solitary shepherd leaning on that ridge, made singularly tall by his cloak, would have become as familiar and permanent a part of the scene to an approaching horseman, by the time he drew level with the flock of fat-tailed sheep, as a watchtower of stone. And that pack of huge mongrels, their collars spiked against attacking wolves, would undoubtedly have set upon him. The half-wild dogs of Asia were described by Charles Monk as 'the great unmentioned hardship of Eastern travel'. Said to know a *giaour* by his scent, they raged and roamed in town and country, and had certainly eaten sufficient human flesh in graveyards to be very dangerous indeed. 'A Frenchman,' says Spencer in his *Circassia*, 'the master of a brig, having spent the evening with a friend, set out after nightfall [in Constantinople] to return to his ship; whether he lost his way, or indulged too freely in the use of the grape, is not known. Certain it is, that the next morning, all that remained of the miserable man were his bones and attire.' Unable to shoot the brutes – though Edmond O'Donovan, *Daily News* war correspondent in Russian Tartary, shot one who climbed aboard his horse by way of its tail – because he depended on the dogs' owners for hospitality, the traveller had to wait on the fringes of a village, or of an encampment of these Turkoman shepherds, until some ragged fellow laughing in his sleeve should choose to call them off.

To a horseman crossing these plains I could imagine many disappointments of his longing for relief from their monotony. Into any chance arrangement of rock or ruin seen far off, in this tricky light, he could build hopes of a caravanserai. Are those not trees, walls, shadows of stone? Is it a mirage? Nearer and nearer, hour by hour. Will it dissolve? At last he could dare to trust in the shape of trees, the shiver of leaves, the thought of water. There stands the conical stone lantern above the khan! Yes, there are the strong, square, windowless walls, and the shadow of the deep gate-arch, and the promise of rest. In the bus dashing past the walls of these caravanserais it's hard to reconstruct the scale of time and distance they were built to, or to appreciate the weariness of an English traveller who sank down on a mat infested with fleas in one of the stone niches in its courtyard, whilst his servant bartered a little English gunpowder for some eggs with the merchants crowding at the gate. The old measure of distance used across the Turkish dominions, and in Persia too, was the *farsakh*, which confused time with distance in a thoroughly Eastern manner, a *farsakh* being the distance (about three and a half miles) covered by pack animals in an hour. It was also said to be the distance at which you could tell whether a camel was black or white. Such scales of time, or distance, or eyesight, mean as little now as do the ruins of the caravanserais to modern Turks speeding past at 80 k.p.h. in their bus. But it isn't very long ago; the grandfathers of people in the bus inhabited that prehistoric world; whereas the English traveller of 1850, looking out now from his stone niche on to a courtyard full of camels and turbaned merchants, could have spent his last night in London amid the splendours of the St Pancras Station Hotel.

One of the changes of bus I had to make, the day I went from Konya to Ürgüp, was at Aksaray. It is a dusty little town packed with people. There is no bus station, only bus-stops and wooden kiosks in a square selling tickets for the various private bus companies. Passengers descending from my bus at once dissolved into the crowd thronging the street. I was uncertain how to find my way on, not sure where I should try to go next, unable to make myself understood in any of the little kiosks.

I walked about the rutted street and dusty square rather anxiously till an old man, quite toothless, his head wrapped in rags and his naked feet folded under him on a rickety chair outside a tea-house, called out to me in German. Cursing myself for idle hours up to Mr Hogg, when I never learned a useful word of the language – I used then to quote Sir William Temple, an ambassador, who said of German, 'It is a language I never would learn, unless it were to affright a baby when it cries' – I outlined my plans to this old ruffian in any scraps of German remaining. He grinned and scratched. But he said nothing, pointed nowhere. I waited for a bit whilst sun and baggage grew heavier. As I walked off, he grabbed by the arm a boy running past, muttered a few words in the lad's ear, and propelled him after me. Beckoning to me, the boy set off at a rapid pace through people and traffic with me hurrying behind. We came by many a twist and turn, and through many an alley jammed with sheep and hooting trucks, to a narrow cobbled lane in which he led me to a doorway in the rotting wall under one of the houses. Here was the waiting-room for the *dolmus* to Nevşehir. The boy would take no money, and trotted away before I could even push a few lira into the pocket of his ragged shirt.

It was just the place to wait. An interesting scene was presented, and all the time in the world to consider it. So decayed were these housefronts on the lane that they looked more like mud cliffs than buildings, their windows such holes as martins might nest in, and the waiting-room like a cave quarried out of crumbling stone.

The air was cool and dark. The cave contained, on three or four benches, a cross-section of the travelling public. A young soldier and his wife had their baby of two with them, whom they fed and played with, and then turned loose to amuse himself with other passengers whilst they talked together hurriedly as people do on the brink of uncertain partings, their eyes anxiously on each other's face. The youth in charge of the office, who sat at a large desk he unlocked and locked up again every few minutes, and who possessed an office-boy whose head he could cuff, took charge too of the tottering child as if it was part of the bus company's service, a crèche, and amused the baby with scissors, and bits of broken glass, and paperclips and all sorts of other rubbish taken from his desk. An old peasant woman wrapped in twenty layers of cloth, so that only a glimpse of her nut-brown face could be seen, also had a baby with her, but this she kept close to her, amongst her other bundles, like a secret as well wrapped up as herself. Another young couple, with a brand-new suitcase, I put down as honeymooners. They were silent, no joint relationship for public display having as yet been arrived at by custom. Three single men between twenty and thirty-five completed the sample.

An efficient, widespread, and cheap system of travel is, I'm sure, as necessary to a nomadic people as water and shade.

Nomads aren't 'travellers', but people who regard journeys as part of ordinary life. Hence the Turks' ceaseless movement to and fro by a system which reaches efficiently into the smallest villages and the largest towns; and hence, too, their lack of interest in anything so ordinary as the journey they are making. There is a perceptive comment on this, relevant to understanding English travellers' motives and attitudes, in a book by Sir John Malcolm, who led an embassy to Persia in the early nineteenth century.

The love of travel, visiting the remains of former grandeur, and of tracing the history of ancient nations, which is so common in Europe, causes wonder in the Asiatics, amongst whom there is little or no spirit of curiosity or speculation. Men who live in ill-governed or unquiet communities can spare no time for such objects from the active occupations incident to their place in society. In better regulated or more settled governments, the state, by divesting men of all immediate care respecting life and property, almost compels those of its subjects whose minds are active, and whose time is at their own disposal, to provide for themselves such a portion of vicissitudes and trouble as shall overcome that apathy and inertia into which they might otherwise fall. From these motives they court toil and care, and sometimes danger, to make them relish the feast of existence.

Had I been able to explain to these Turks why I was sharing with them a waiting-room in Akşehir, my reasons would have seemed to them quite insufficient for leaving home. Yet they have the perfect temperament, as Europeans have not, for the vicissitudes and trouble of travelling. Watches were not looked at. Instead, tea was sent for, cigarettes exchanged, a bunch of grapes shared, the soldier's baby played with as a responsibility and diversion common to all. Opposite our waiting-room, on the sunny side of the alley, three or four greybeards reposed on wooden chairs outside a tea-house, their days of making journeys done. The tractors, pick-ups, carts, which all came nosing between the houses, compelled the old timers to draw in their toes, or even pick up their chairs altogether and press themselves against the wall. For a flock of sheep, however, they sat tight whilst scurrying hooves and curly backs pattered by.

Finally our *dolmus* came. We crowded in, and rattled away, at a pace contradicting the long placid waits at either end. I remember it used to amuse me in Italy the way Italians would dawdle away half the morning in a tipped-back café chair, putting off the moment when they must set out; then, once their hand had touched their car's doorhandle, a perfect frenzy of speed and impatience possessed them till they reached another café, another tipped-back chair, in which the afternoon could be idled away. After this rapid dash of thirty or forty miles to Nevşehir I seemed once again to be in for a long wait, in a dusty sunny square amidst crumbling walls tangled with ivy. Hurrying down through the sloping town to find the departure place of the Ürgüp *dolmus*, I had asked an old man eating a melon on a mound of rubbish which way to take. He extended his melon, a fleshy beauty dripping juice, and encouraged me to gouge out a handful with my fingers, as he was doing, whilst he considered my question. I commended my health to Providence, and plunged in my hand. The Ürgüp *dolmus* I found by his directions sitting in the sun half full of passengers, and to pass what I expected to be a long wait for all the places to be taken, I put my bags into the vehicle and went over to a little wooden hut under a ruined wall in a shady corner of the square, where tea was being sold. In Nevşehir the sense of decay and collapse was even more striking than elsewhere; so lately, and so constant, was the fall of buildings about the ears of the inhabitants, that the dust of their collapse seemed to hang in the air. I was watching the scene contentedly from an iron chair in the shade of the ivy, tea in hand, when I saw the *dolmus* suddenly clap shut its doors and begin to move off, hooting as it went. I dashed after it and hammered on the roof. A door opened and I jumped in.

The passenger who had opened the door for me was a likeable young American, very thin and wry, in owl spectacles, who was examining Cappadocia for his thesis, and lodging in Nevşehir while he did so. It was he who told me that the day following was Census Day, when all Turkey was to be counted, and that no transport would run anywhere in the land. He said he was sharing his room in the town with an elderly Turk, and 'Tomorrow,' he said, 'I guess we'll just stay home and get drunk together.' Today he was on his way to the Goreme valley, and at a certain crossroads he left us. I thought when he'd gone that I must strike someone like him, an earnest and efficient American of twenty-five, as strangely ill-informed and purposeless to be blundering about the interior of Turkey, the White Knight at large. But had I told him that I was a novelist turning over in my mind the possibility of writing a novel about a nineteenth-century traveller, I would have been excused further questions, for my reasons would have seemed to him – in contrast to the Turks in the Akşehir waiting-room – perfectly sufficient. It illustrated Malcolm's point in the passage I quoted. Both he and I, and the Enid Blyton pilgrims, too, fulfil Malcolm's conditions for Western travellers.

A Turk touting for business for his brother's hotel met the *dolmus* at Ürgüp. Obligingly, when he heard I needed 'laundry service' and 'telephone', he led me down the steep white street to another grander hotel like a concrete shoe-box in a builder's yard, where I soon fell out with the management. However, I had some lunch in the town, and met my obliging Turk at his cousin's carpet shop, where a bargain was struck for them to drive me about Cappadocia for the afternoon, an extravagance forced on me by movement being impossible on Census Day.

They were a diverting pair. Handsome, with big black moustaches and pale suits, they were evidently making a fat living out of tourists – or had been, until the Emergency shut off the supply. They remained sanguine, however. At first I sat in front, and they pointed out views and features to me, like guides eager to please, speaking only English; after a stop or two, though, they sat together in front, and very soon we were speeding from place to place whilst they talked together in Turkish, laughing a good deal; and our itinerary, it soon became clear, was a shopping and business trip for the two of them at Muggins' expense. They bought meat in a butcher's shop in Ortahissar whilst I toiled up the castle's spiral stair to the neon sign on the topmost tower; in Avanos they tried to buy a dog, collected parcels, waved to friends, bargained for pots in a store beside the wide pebbly flow of the Kizil Irmak river (which was the Halys of the Greeks), and tore home through the weird landscape in the evening light. I enjoyed it. They were light-hearted, and good friends, and altogether it reminded me of the way I'd watched Italians make the money of tourists finance their fun when the development of Monte Argentario first began twenty years ago.

Another aspect of the afternoon made me think of an incident on that Italian coast one early morning long ago. Driving along the sea road at dawn I had looked down into a bay and seen there, resting in the translucent water, a whale. Of course I jumped out of the car to gaze at this great wonder. The whale rested, I stared. The sunlight strengthened. The whale revealed no plans to entertain me with action of any kind. In the end all I could do was climb back into my car and drive home to bed, reflecting, as I went, that interest in a freak of nature is quickly satiated, for a freak raises expectations of further amusement which it doesn't fulfil. If you want to look with interest and contentment into a bay for any length of time, it is better that it doesn't have a whale in it. Now, it occurred to me that the freakish landscape of Cappadocia illustrated the same truth. What you need of such a weird spectacle is one good view of it, and this I had from the top of the castle rock at Ortahissar. The uneasy moonscape stretched away on every hand, and, below me, clinging to the roots of the fortified pinnacle of rock I stood upon, were the ruinous mud huts of the old village, their terraces heaped with melons yellow and green. Fantastical that landscape is, the tufa towers riddled with painted churches, like the sandcastles of giants' children, and I was amazed by it; but amazement is pretty soon exhausted.

I walked about the Goreme valley for an hour or two, where my Turks left me on my own, and I climbed in and out of the churches on view; but I would rather have walked in the valley below these curiosities, which my eyes kept straying to for rest, a sweet natural valley of orchards and shady gardens, where the birds sang ardently. That was the bay without the whale, which I preferred.

However, I mustn't run down whales on all points, because the rock churches produced a one-liner as expressive of a marriage as any I ever read. I was about to climb one of the iron ladders which lead to the church door cut in these rock pinnacles, when out of the church above me emerged an English couple in their middle fifties. The man had an expression I have often seen among clergymen and men who boss boys about: jocose if humoured; temper rapidly deteriorating when crossed. His wife was a thin-faced, dry woman who set foot on the ladder above me first. 'They oughtn't to be allowed to put up these contraptions if you ask me,' she said in the tone of one focusing general disapproval on whatever was to hand. 'I think they're lethal.' By way of comment her husband emitted an exasperated cough, quite justified in my view. She turned on him, hand on the iron railing:

'I hope to goodness *you're* not starting this cold now,' she said bitterly.

And she click-clacked down the ladder past me with her head in the air. He followed, attempting insouciance. Between each of them and the view stood the other, more fatal to research even than Warburton's sandwiches. Of a tour made with someone else, I believe your chief memories of each place are the details of your relationship there with your companion. And love is insulation, quite as much as quarrelling.

There is in *Eothen* an instance of this insulated travelling which produces the very opposite effect of, say, Vambéry's caravan beside the Oxus, or Captain Abbott's loneliness in the deserts of Khiva. 'As for me and my comrade,' says Kinglake,

we often forgot Stamboul, forgot all the Ottoman Empire, and only remembered old times. We went back, loitering on the banks of the Thames – not grim old Thames of 'after life', that washes the Parliament houses and drowns despairing girls, but Thames 'the old Eton fellow' that wrestled with us in our boyhood till he taught us to be stronger than he. We bullied Keate, and scoffed at Larry Miller and Okes; we rode along loudly laughing, and talked to the grave Servian forest as though it were 'the Brocas clump'.

Eton seems to have been used as a means of telegraphing social credentials to the reader. Such meagre tokens of worth – like Monk adding his 'MA Trin. Coll. Cam.' on his title page, or Spencer putting 'Esq.' after his name – look from this remove more like uncertainty than self-confidence, and, as I've said, I think that impatience with their position in English society made the East an attractive field to these middle-class 'gentlemen', for in the East, as well as placing themselves in the highest rank of society, they found opportunities (like the chances in Campaign or Quest) to prove a knightly character through Ordeal by Travel, and to put themselves before the public in this character as the hero of a book of travels.

As I ate my dinner that night in Ürgüp, outdoors in the wan garden of a once-handsome villa, sitting alone by a stagnant stone pool whilst the yellow leaves drifted down around me, I was glad I had no comrade from Eton with me, indeed knew of no comrade at all closer than Rhodes to the west or Delhi to the east. Under an elegant kiosk in this garden, half in ruins, a wooden shack had been erected, where a kitchen was installed. I was the solitary customer. A huge German waiter in a leather cap tramped to and fro between this shack and my table by the pool, carrying meat and wine and melon over the gravel by the light of neon strips tacked to the trees. I wanted no one interposed between myself and the scene I was in the midst of.

IV
※※※

I

I had thought that its position in the very middle of Turkey, and the inaction of Census Day, would make Ürgüp a neat spot to decide whether or not to travel on into the east of the country. In the eastern mountains Kurds and refugee terrorists might still be giving the army a run for its money. I didn't want to do anything dangerous or foolhardy. I had said to myself on starting that I would go eastward as far as the country seemed safe, reaching, if possible, Kars, on the Russian border – apart from a stretch in Norway, NATO's only first-hand border with Russia – before turning for home. Now I should decide.

But I didn't have any data. I knew as little about the state of the country now, in the middle of Anatolia, as I'd known in the middle of Dorset a couple of months ago when news of the military coup first broke. In fact I knew less, unable now to understand either radio or newspapers, or even to grasp whatever imperatives the military grated out over loudspeakers in the streets. Travelling seemed safe enough. Indeed a repressive régime suits the traveller better than the anarchy which preceded it, so long as his documents are in order, and he isn't unlucky. If there was to be a counter-revolution tomorrow, or if the eastern highlands were a nest of guerrillas, I would not learn of it from the Turkish newspapers under military censorship. All I missed hearing, by my ignorance of Turkish, were rumours on one side and propaganda on the other. They wouldn't have made it any easier to settle the question rationally. But I wished all the same that I could muster a persuasive case either for or against going on.

The line to England was extremely bad, voices faint as if from another life. There was no one on whom I could lay the responsibility of deciding. Earlier travellers were given advice in dramatic terms, usually against proceeding, by consuls and pashas and shocked merchants met by chance in khans after alarming experiences. Or did he only record the advice of those who begged him to turn back from so dangerous a course – to make a detour to avoid a nest of robbers – to wait for a guard of *serbaz*, as he valued life and liberty – so that the traveller's calm pursuance of the road, and of his plans, should seem all the bolder by light of the perils he has leaked into the reader's mind by this device? For one of the difficulties about presenting his travels as an exciting narrative, likely to appeal to the armchair adventurer at home, is how to instil in his reader a proper appreciation of the dangers which he, the bold narrator-hero, must make light of. Here is an incident during a night ride made alone, by Eliot Warburton, along the sea-coast towards Beirut. Escaping a madman whom he has surprised fighting with dogs for human bones in a cemetery, our hero rides into a party of silk smugglers running their cargo on to a moonlit shore. A Syrian, anxious to save his life, implores him to turn back from a road on which a young Frenchman was murdered by smugglers last week. The scene is set. 'I must proceed,' says Warburton. 'The Frenchman was perhaps unarmed. I shall not die alone, you may depend upon it!' His way is barred by the Arab smugglers. He draws a pistol and calls out, 'The first man who puts out his hand to my bridle, dies as sure as I live!', sets spurs to his horse, and charges them. Warburton's tone is defiant, independent, aggressive – all that Sir Gawain's should be when challenged at the Beach Perilous by the Knight of the Literary Device.

There was no one at Ürgüp whom I could consult as to the dangers of the road, not even a literary device. You get the impression from old books of travel, as you do from the letters and diaries of people in Victorian society, that, whilst there were very few people about, most of them were known to the writer. As in a sequence of novels, the same characters occur and recur time and again in books of Eastern travel, turning up now in Tehran, now in Baghdad, criss-crossing the deserts and mountains of Turkey and Persia, their characteristics illuminated a little more fully at each meeting. Dr Wolff, as he darted about the East to 'circulate the Word', makes an appearance in every book; indeed he says himself, 'As was always the case, without one single exception, whenever Dr Wolff was in trouble, a British officer was sent to him by God.' Darker figures too, as in a sequence of novels, run through the works and never fully show their hand: there was a renegade Pole abroad in Persia at the time, named sometimes as 'B—', sometimes as 'Borowsky', now glimpsed as an adventurer in the Persian army, now as 'an amusing fellow with a fund of stories', poor but arrogant, who challenged Baron Hyter to a duel at Tabriz; denounced by Dr Wolff ('Be on your guard, Boroski is not a Polish nobleman but a Jew'); finally killed, it was believed, at the siege of Herat. Travellers knew each other, and ran across each other, yet each moved as a solitary figure against a background all his own of adventure and loneliness amid a hostile scene, for these were the necessary conditions of a book of travels. Emerging from the wilderness, it was allowable to meet up with an acquaintance at once. My namesake Philip Kirkland Glazebrook, catching a boat between Berbera and Djibouti during a shooting trip in Abyssinia before the Great War in which he was to be killed, finds on board that 'Our table is a cheery one – Venables of Burma whom George knew before, Tillard, who had rough experiences in the Somali War, Dunn, with whom I travelled from Khartoum to Cairo last year, and Murray who was at Eton with me.' No risk of an evening without bridge amongst friends, once town or boat were reached, despite 'observing in my cabin, or entomological museum, a large brown rat and two cockroaches as big as mice'.

The only chance meeting I have had on this trip was in Rhodes. I had gone for a longish walk on my own one day, in the southern part of the island, and was returning across a wide vale between mountain and sea, upon a dusty track, when I made out two figures approaching from a distance at a cracking pace. Both were tall, one a deep crimson, the other a lighter, more glowing, scarlet, and both (I saw as they drew nearer) wore only gym shoes, bathing trunks and dark glasses. They, and I, were the only figures in an extensive landscape. As the distance between us closed, I saw that both were known to me, one having been in my house at school, the other a famous actor. We met. Introductions were made, news exchanged. The actor said, rather angrily, 'I don't know you, but I know your cousin,' as if some excuse ought to be made for not knowing everyone in the view at that time. As in my interview with the whale, no development promised. They went their way, and I mine.

However, if I'd seen either of them, or anyone I'd ever met, walking down the street at Ürgüp on the day of the census, I would certainly have asked their advice in the question of whether or not to travel eastward into the mountains of Armenia; just as I had plagued the only person I knew in Pondicherry about how to get out of the place, whether by bus or train or car; to which he had answered, 'Why not just walk out and let India take care of you?'

I thought of his answer now (made, I don't doubt, in exasperation at my fussing). Oddly enough, I trusted Turkey in a way I hadn't trusted India. Maybe it was the greater efficiency of Turkish buses I trusted. Anyway, by the time evening came I thought I might as well carry on now I was halfway to Kars; and I was immediately aware of relief that I was going on, which is as good an endorsement as I ever hope for of a decision I have taken. To have turned back, or to have turned north to Samsun for a boat to Istanbul – to have turned any way but east – would have been failure.

So I went east on the morning following the census. The return of noise to the town silenced by curfew restored an essential prop of the Turkish scene. Noise! – how they love it. Turks deluge themselves in uproar as they deluge their palates in sweetness. Louder is better, whether it is the mullah's cracked chant to be amplified by loudspeakers necklacing the minaret, or the muzak in buses, or the radio at an open window, or a motor-bike gunned at the lights. Never was an invention so abused as is the electric amplification of sound abused by Asiatics, an example of the fact that a culture like Islam, which has never invented anything, is sure to misapply the inventions of other races. Like the garish colours they dote upon, this pining for loud noises and sweetmeats makes the Turks seem to have the tastes of children. Out of a town seeming to shake with noise I started for Kayseri, fifty miles or so to the east, in a *dolmus* which picked me up at my hotel.

It wouldn't have picked me up there if I hadn't by then been standing on every guest's right I could find in the small print, with that sense of injury and peevishness which ever succeeds confrontation with a long bill in a bad hotel. I had shown the clerk a notice promising that a *dolmus* would collect guests from the hotel. 'Impossible!' 'Why?' 'Because our guests don't take *dolmus*.' 'How do they escape then?' 'By coach they come and go.' 'Have the first *dolmus* for Kayseri stop here for me.' 'Impossible.' I kept my eye upon him until with many despairing sighs he sent a boy off to take a place for me in the *dolmus* in the square and keep it until the vehicle stopped at the hotel.

The consequence was that I wasn't very popular in the *dolmus* when I climbed in, my bags obliging the packed interior to pack itself tighter yet. I was stared at in an unfriendly way by flat, cold eyes. Fortunately an accident soon happened which made us all comrades: the *dolmus* was speeding along over the usual rutted road which climbed through yellow and russet orchards towards bare hills, when the young man next to me was violently sick. We slewed off the road, doors flew open, out bundled all affected to clean themselves up with grass and leaves; on getting back in again, I was able to offer my window seat to the boy who had been sick, taking instead his place on a box between rows, so putting myself in the company's good books for the rest of the ride.

It was a wonderful drive to Kayseri. The road at first climbed, as I say, to a long bare crest, cold in the morning light; then down it swooped upon a magnificent landscape of plain and shimmering lake, and the lines of hills fading into mist. At first I didn't look sufficiently high up into the eastern sky to make out what it was – what mighty presence – that dominated the scene below. Then I looked above the hills, above the leaden mists, into the sky itself, and saw the snowy grandeur of Mount Argaeus, Erciyas Daği, its peaks clear above all else with the lonely detachment of a solitary mountain, its shining snowfields isolated as far above the earth as high, pure ideas above the reach of man. A hundred and twenty years ago it was agreed all round here that no human ever had, or ever could, affront Mount Argaeus by climbing to its summit; and if you lived under the eye of the old volcano, whose peaks are about 13,000 feet above the sea, there might seem sense in keeping to the human side of the bargain, if the chthonian god kept to his by not erupting over the works of man. Though it has smoked, it has not erupted in historical time.

Still, that presence at the town's gate, above the town's roofs, adds a tremor to the air not easily forgotten. Kayseri impressed itself on me as altogether a remote and uneasy place. My day in it was full of interest, but added to the interest was a sense of strain I hadn't felt before.

A day was all I spent there because I had become enmeshed in the imperatives of the timetable in a way which always seems so trivial and irritating when you read about such pressures in other people's travels – 'I had to press on, and so unfortunately missed Angkor Wat/the Zambezi/Symond's Yat, which I had come so far to see' – but which, none the less, contain your movements, however free you may desire to be. In this case I had to take into account the winter timetable of the boats on the Black Sea, with which I needed to link up at Trabzon for the passage to Istanbul, after I had reached the coast from Kars. Consequently I took a ticket at the *otogar* in Kayseri for the only bus service plying to Erzurum, the old capital of Turkish Armenia, which left on its twelve-hour journey into the eastern highlands at half-past five that evening.

Then I caught a *dolmus* into the centre of Kayseri. Modern buildings here are fewer, and lower, than in towns to the west, and I was looking out at these, and at the empty spaces and collapsing walls along the roadside, when a muffled cry leaked out of the bundle of wrappings on the knee of the woman next me. She herself, well bolstered out with cloaks and shawls, looked like the Duchess in *Alice*; and when she had unbandaged the source of the cry, a black and wizened baby, she handed out treatment very much in line with the Duchess's views on pepper and childcare, before binding it up tightly as before. We all got out together in the *meidan* between dark old walls of the citadel, and humped roofs of the *hammam*.

A crowd bustled through the square in every direction. It was bright, rather windy. Dust blew about, and pigeons fluttered up at people's feet. Through the noise of the crowd came the jangle of a bell, and there approached a water-carrier, an old man with a round cap on his shaven head, and brass cups strung on a crossbelt on his chest, and his waterskin under his arm like a set of bagpipes, who stationed himself between mosque and *hammam* to dispense water like a human fountain to the people hurrying by. He was there all day, tinkling his bell when business was slack, or making the circuit of the mosque and Turkish bath, but present whenever I passed through the *meidan* – which I did many times that day.

Half-past ten to half-past five is a long time on your feet without a base, and I thought I would take a room in a hotel where I could rest for an hour or so before my night journey to Erzurum. But I did not. Something prevented me. I found a dirty eating-shop with rooms above it to let, but sudden inhibition prevented me taking one, or even entering the door.

In my experience of travelling alone there is no telling when your confidence will evaporate, in face of the most ordinary little everyday dealing, and let you see only the vulnerability of your situation, and your awkwardness in it. This happened to me now.

There wasn't in Kayseri exactly the hostility of Konya, but the town's remoteness, and the busyness of everyone about their own affairs, and the old volcano clothed in snow, gave me a feeling of being very far from home. I saw myself as a curious and outlandish figure wandering about amongst the proper inhabitants of the town. People stared without smiling. I was not welcome in the mosque, where I had gone as any stranger might enter a church in Christendom, to sit quietly at the base of a pillar. The tea-houses were not like cafés, with tables on the street, they were like dens under the ruinous houses, and I didn't care to enter them. My confidence had gone. Instead of looking out at the world, forgetful of self, I saw my own reflection with all its oddities thrown back at me by the eyes of passers-by. I walked into various *medresse*, and *türbe*, and mosques; and soon walked out again.

I walked, for something to do, far out along a pot-holed street, into regions of crumbling masonry and dust and weeds where the town petered out, in search of the archaeological museum I had been told of. Here at least the road was almost empty, and in places shaded by trees, so I walked slowly and thought about my situation. The more isolated and solitary my position became, particularly in the somewhat threatening atmosphere of this town, the closer I felt I might come to understanding the feelings and ideas it would be interesting to explore in such a character as I proposed to invent for the Traveller in my book, so I did not try to quench, but rather to exaggerate, my twinges of uneasiness.

'No small part of the pleasure of Eastern travel,' says Murray briskly, quoting David Urquhart, 'arises from sheer hardship and privation.' That is quite true, but further to that, as Malcolm hinted in the passage I quoted, an element of 'danger', too, was a draw. Murray's zestful attitude to the risks of desert travel, in the 1854 Handbook to Turkey, show that they would be an attraction to the traveller: 'The sons of the desert, mounted on wild-looking but high-bred mares, come down upon him like a whirlwind, with a loud unearthly yell, shaking their lances over their heads; and the interview is soon over, the tourist finding himself again alone upon the plain, with or without his shirt, as the case may be.' All right; the traveller is prepared for that much danger; would he go on to agree with George Hayward, who said in a note smuggled to Shaw whilst both were imprisoned in Tartary, that he was 'possessed of an insane desire to try the effect of cold steel across my throat'? Newbolt, in his poem about Hayward's murder in a high pass of the Himalaya, makes of the killing just such a picturesque and romantic incident as most appealed to the reading public. Travellers had a duty to Mudie's patrons occasionally to be murdered.

Hayward was reckless, as no doubt were many who never returned; what is of interest is the attitude of less extreme cases, of the many travellers who survived great dangers, towards fear of death deliberately encountered. 'In the long struggle between us,' wrote Arminius Vambéry, 'fear was finally subdued; but it is this struggle which I blush to remember, for it is marvellous what efforts are required, to grow familiar with the constant and visible prospect of Death.' And dear, good Dr Wolff, who bearded the Emir of Bukhara to ask him what he'd done with Stoddart and Conolly, and feared no man, said of a boating trip he was once obliged to make, 'Wolff was so much afraid that he is ashamed to this day to think of it.'

Englishmen, of course, don't speak so frankly, but I am sure it was with the intention of calling out and subduing fear that they chose such unsettled regions for their researches. Privation, long days, lean meals, toughened their bodies; danger hardened their nerves. The ordeal proved to the traveller that he possessed the qualities he had been taught to admire. His life might depend on the force of his character to impose its will on superior numbers and strength and arms, just as authority in 'old times' – and at beloved Eton, too – had depended on these strengths, rather than on the gradations of society. 'In the East,' says Robert Shaw, noting the sudden familiarity and rudeness of his captors in Yarkand, 'want of respect is the precursor of danger.' He responded by giving out orders like a drill-sergeant; but how closely he must have watched and waited for the executioner! As Captain Abbott did, night after night, in the tents of the Kuzzauks, amongst whom he had in his mind identified his executioner, a half-mad giant of whom he conceived a horror.

There were plenty of gloomy examples, not only of blackening heads over gateways, but of Europeans who had paid with their lives for an ill-chosen word, or a blow, or just for the misfortune of finding the country disturbed. A chair, or a silver watch, or an English gun, might be spied in the possession of a sheikh in whose territory an Englishman had vanished. The penalties were severe. All had watched the bastinado, many had seen natives executed, or blinded; Vambéry, in the courtyard of a castle in Tartary, watched the executioner kneeling on prisoners' chests to blind them with a knife, knowing that his own fate would be theirs if his disguise was discovered.

Sang-froid was cultivated by these conditions. 'G. Fowler, Esquire', faced with a deteriorating situation in Kurdistan, tells us, 'Our position now became critical; but, I do not know how it is, I can never bring myself to the anticipation of danger, so I lay down on my mat and slept most soundly.' Did he really? From the point of view of constructing the character of a traveller, as I mean to do, it is interesting that Fowler should claim for himself such excessive sang-froid as is found only in romances, or poems by Newbolt. The narrator, for all his assertions that 'pressure of friends' had obliged him against his will to place 'these few notes of a rough traveller' before the public – the narrator was very conscious of his reader. There was conscious art. James Fraser (who wrote a number of novels 'of Eastern life' or, more accurately, of Victorian life in Eastern costume) says in a book of travels, 'In a well-told tale now, as one sits in his snug parlour before the bright fire, a foot on either hob, and a decanter of old port or madeira at his elbow – in such a tale, an incident like this [he was lost at dusk amid the Persian mountains] would bring delight to all the hearers.'

The behaviour and conduct of the traveller – at any rate the ridiculous degree of 'stout heart and cool head' sometimes claimed – were dictated by the expectations of the readership. When Alexander Burnes made his journey to Bukhara it is evident that he was cautious and canny as well as brave – in obeying the Emir's edict forbidding infidels to ride in the streets, for instance – but I wonder if his fame as a hero to his readers, which the runaway success of his *Travels* brought him, didn't encourage him in an arrogance and foolhardiness which in the end made him hated by the natives of Kabul? Faced with capture by tribesmen whom he suspected of murdering an earlier traveller, Burnes says, 'I will not conceal my feelings at this moment, which were those of vexation and irritability.' If those really were his feelings, they were inadequate. The fragments of his body, after he had been torn to pieces by the Kabul mob in 1841, remained hanging in the trees of his garden until the bones dropped out of them.

The archaeological museum at Kayseri, when I eventually came upon it among compounds of a military sort, behind wire defences, wasn't a sanctuary at all. The officials were very surprised indeed to receive a visit. Staff scattered to their posts, settling caps on their heads, and holding cigarettes behind their backs, until it was discovered that I wasn't a superior come to vex them, but only a foreign tourist. I bought a ticket from one, had it ripped by another, was directed into the proper traffic-flow by a third; and found myself, at the end of all this administration, in the two small rooms comprising the whole museum. Battered fragments of marble from the West, a few Assyrian cylinder seals from the East: meagre remains from the empires it lay between testify to the fact that a city so strategically important as Kayseri is sure of total destruction by each invader. Towns built in the wrong place, like Palmyra or Fatehpur Sikri, are the towns which survive whole. In these bare little rooms I was followed and watched by the whole staff until I gave way under their stare, and set out to walk the mile or so back through the glare and dust of the town's outskirts.

Self-consciousness attracts an audience. Boys seeing me pass from a window clattered downstairs and ran into the road to stare, even crossed it to walk backwards just in front of me, looking up with unsmiling black eyes into my face. With a turn of speed I caught up with a woman with a long stick in one hand, and a handbag in the other, who was driving four calves along the road. The woman I overtook, but I couldn't push past the wretched calves without them kicking up their heels and flying in all directions. So a strange race began. Past me ran the cowherd, chivvying scattered calves into order, banging them with handbag or stick; then they would stop to peer into a hole, I couldn't help catching them up, and off they would fly again. I tried crossing the road but they followed me, the nudge of their noses at my back as bad as the boys' stare on my face. In this way our party leapfrogged into the *meidan* once more, where the water-seller was tinkling his bell at the midday crowd.

I looked for somewhere to eat. In the very middle of the town is a little ruinous quarter, a lane, stone hovels with glassless windows and rotten doors, their walls supported on poles bedded in heaps of filth. Nearby I found a greasy eating-shop where men in leather caps scooped meat and juice into their mouths with wedges of bread. There was no rest from the flat, uncivil eyes. I chose food from the cooking pots and sat eating it, when it was slopped out for me, at the corner of a stained table.

I soon found myself on the street again, with four hours to fill before my bus left for Erzurum. I went to the bazaars, which I had saved up until now.

In 1856 one of those controversial figures of the Eastern scene, a British consul, rode into 'Kaiseriah' at the head of a cavalcade of horses and pack-animals bought by the British for the Crimea War and now being sold off on a peripatetic auction through Asia Minor. The consul was H. J. Ross, a fiery, touchy individual, who hedged himself in with defensive arrogance against the contempt which travelling gentlemen had for the commercial gents and half-bred Levantines lording it as consuls in seaports of the Euxine or in provincial capitals of the Turkish empire. Travellers, he wrote, knew nothing of the East or its peoples: 'It is astonishing how long it is ere an Englishman can understand the depths of falseness of the Oriental character.' Loving his garden and his spaniel and his pheasant-shooting as an Englishman should, Ross prided himself equally on his Eastern ferocity ('I am grown cruel-hearted and watch the bastinado I have ordered as quietly as any Turkish pasha'). He loved, too, the trappings of power ceded him in the wild towns of Anatolia. Here he describes his entry into Kayseri:

Our entry was very grand. Three pairs of kettledrums, the insignia of a pasha, were beaten before me . . . Tufenkjis [musketeers] escorted me through the long ranges of bazaars. I was surprised at their extent – all covered in. They reminded me of Cairo; the same Eastern half-lights, and the same heavy smell of drugs. Some twelve years ago I left Kaiseriah without a single prospect before me, and I return with the pomp and circumstance of an Eastern Pasha.

It may be surmised that the bombast in this, like the fact of the man having been born in Malta, may have made him and his like seem half-bred, not quite gentlemen, to Englishmen on their travels.

But on the bazaars at Kayseri Ross's word is sound. Very wonderful they still are. You walk down long tunnels of stone, shafted through with sunlight which falls in spots of brilliance on the heaps and gaudy piles of goods massed in front of shadowy caverns, and all the echo and bustle and glitter of life fill these stone-arched lanes. Here everyone was too busy to stare at me. I sank back into the anonymity of a pair of eyes to look through. The bazaar leads to the courtyard of an old caravanserai, that central feature in the travels of past times, where merchants put up, and sold or exchanged the goods on their pack-animals, and sat smoking *narghileh* or chibouks on a rug spread before their cell door. Here was great activity in Kayseri. Over cobbles clattered carts, boots, the rattling hooves of sheep – and amongst the bewildered living flocks were pushed iron-shod handcarts heaped with sheepskins still steaming from the knife. The stone square stank with blood and dung. In its quieter corners the sun fell on bales of wool, and on old men in skullcaps seated crosslegged at their work of sorting or scraping the skins.

In coming on this scene I had an instinctive feeling of putting my hand on what I wanted. This is what it was like. Details of clothes and all the little anachronisms in the picture – wires, motors and so on – don't signify in the sudden vivid stroke of light your imagination can receive. This is what it felt like to be there. If you catch at that, and keep it, you have a keynote. The essence is in your grasp. From a living fire you take a live coal.

I walked back through the grey stone vaults of the *bedestan*, where carpet dealers were drinking tea gravely together in front of their solemn shops, and crossed a square and busy roads to a small green park by the Kursunlu mosque, where I sat down on a small green bench, and took out my book.

But I was badgered out of all patience by inquisitive Turks. They converged by every path, crowding my bench, picking up my bag to examine it, tapping my arm to make me look up, taking the very book out of my hands to discover what language it was written in. No inhibitions restrained them; every kind of inhibition made me uncomfortable. As with their love of sweets and loud noises, this inquisitiveness makes Asiatics seem to Europeans like children. In Lindos two English children aged four or five used to come and stand in front of me whilst I ate breakfast, and shout 'Eat shit!' and 'Fuck!' in my face to see how I responded – I shook my head sadly over the bread and honey

– and these Turkish youths crowding me off the bench seemed anxious to test me in the same way. In patience they can always outlast a European. But they came closer, and the crowd grew, and my possessions were soon being passed out of the front row for others to see. So eaten up with curiosity to see the Feringhee were the villagers of Feridun that they not only filled the courtyard of Layard's house, they climbed on the roof and peered at him down the chimney. It is part of the Asiatic character; to stare is not rude, but to object to being stared at is taken as offensive behaviour. I got up, and held out my hand for my bag, which was at once given back to me. I put my book into it and walked away, and the young men drifted off in ones and twos as they had come.

I managed to hide myself away pretty well amongst the pillars and shadows in the courtyard of the nearby mosque, and so to observe the Faithful gargling and spitting, and washing hands and feet in the fountain, and laying out to bake in the sun the handkerchiefs they had dried themselves with. The domesticity is appealing. 'The Faithful' seems perfectly to describe this ceaseless traffic of people in and out of the holy precincts, fitting devotion into their lives in a matter-of-fact way which makes earth seem nearer heaven. Here is the childlike quality again, but this time in the form found in the Beatitudes: 'Except ye become as little children . . .' I didn't follow them into the shadow of the mosque.

Instead I walked away towards the bazaars again, where I had felt myself less noticeable than in other parts of the town, and I thought as I went about the ambiguous attitude towards Islam to be found in Victorian travel books. Condemnation of Muhammad and all his works, and particularly of the Mussulman's eagerness for a paradise full of 'profligacy', is expressed in strong terms. But that, you feel, is to establish the writer's orthodoxy as far as the Circulating Libraries are concerned; his real views, which leak out in asides, are more complex. For one thing, the Englishman travelling through Islam found himself, very naturally, attracted towards the powerful rather than towards the downtrodden – towards pasha and sheikh rather than servants and moneylenders – and this partiality led him to associate

himself with Mussulmans rather than with Christians. The
Syrian or Greek Christian under Ottoman rule was perhaps the
most wretched, and most despised, of all inhabitants of the
empire. True, Christ himself under the Roman Empire in these
lands was wretched and despised; but the nineteenth-century
English gentleman based the whole of his outlook on the world
upon confidence in his ascendancy, which in England did not
conflict with his support of Christian principles as they had
evolved in an English context. To find himself confronted with
a set of beggars and servants as his natural associates, by faith, in
the East, did not suit either him or his readers. Of a village in
Kurdistan Rich says sadly, 'It would be a tolerable place except
for the extreme dirtiness, which, with the smell of liquor, is, I
am sorry to say, the characteristic of a Christian village in these
parts.' Simply by recording the facts, the traveller moves away
from championing Christianity against Islam at all points.

Perhaps due to rough handling by the inquisitive, my second
bag, bought at Belgrade, required a stitch or two to secure its
strap, so when I reached the bazaars again, I looked about until
I found the cobblers' quarter. Showing the first in the row what
I needed done, I was passed from booth to booth until, down
a couple of steps into a shop like the den of some leather-
hoarding animal, I found a quick little shoemaker in a leather
apron who possessed a machine which would sew through the
material of my bag. All the family was at work. Three sons,
besides the father, were busy tapping, stitching, cutting, at their
cluttered bench in the half-light amongst a crowd of customers.
I sat in a corner waiting my turn. It is strange that there is no
strong smell, peculiar to Turkey, which pervades it as the
pungent sweetness of India reaches into everything that India
touches. In a den like this in an Indian bazaar that sweet scent
would be at its thickest; here the shoemaker's shop smelt of
leather, nothing more.

Whilst I waited – glad to rest unstared at in such light as the
shoe-cluttered window let in from the covered bazaar – a seller
of melons who was passing called down the steps. Work was
suspended. A fruit was bought, slices pared off the mighty green
sphere and handed about on the point of a cobbler's knife. With

great kindness I was provided with a share, which I ate in the usual delicious dissolution of juice and seeds. At last my bag was sewn up for me.

At last, too, the time had come to find a *dolmus* in the *meidan*, where the westering sun lit up evening crowds hurrying past the water-seller's pitch, and to return to the *otogar*. I wasn't bored, or particularly tired, but I was surfeited with the restless interest of travel, and I looked forward to a quiet seat in the bus.

2

The bus pulled out into the road at half-past five. A twelve-hour journey lay ahead. I allowed in my mind for thirteen hours sitting in my seat at the window, knowing that it is the hour after you had expected to arrive which excruciates the passenger by its slowness in passing. I looked out at sandy hillsides, and fields of dead sunflowers, for the thirty miles or so of daylight remaining before darkness shut the book in my face. With no diversion left to me I thought of what Carlyle said to Trollope, rebuking him for reading or writing whilst travelling by train: 'You should sit still,' he said, 'and label your thoughts.' So I did a little labelling of thoughts put into my head by Kayseri, and lots of daydreaming with intervals of dozing in between. At the best of times my methods of thought hardly improve on this plan.

Somewhere in the darkness we stopped at a wretched cafeteria for a meal, but the ravening passengers lapping soup and tearing up meat stifled my appetite, so I ate bread and dried fruit, and walked about in the light spilling out of the place, until the bus started again, and the speeding swaying journey through the night once more unreeled thoughts from my mind in need of labels. The crowds in the mosques at Kayseri, the quiet attachment of their devotions, had impressed me greatly. Faith is enviable, in whatever creed. It is disquieting, even to me, to know what contempt exists in those faithful minds for myself and all 'Christians'; unbelievers, pig-eaters, infidels, *giaours*, dogs. The cup you have drunk from is broken. It is a new view Islam makes you take of yourself, that you defile what you touch.

How much more startling a view for a Victorian Englishman to be obliged to take of himself! Religion was then more central to the nation's life than it is now, in the sense that all educated men were conversant with the tenets of Protestantism, and with the ideas of churchmen and the state of the Church. The educated class was convulsed by Tractarianism, and split by the row over 'Essays and Reviews', and divided by doctrinal views on the suppression of the Irish sees, or the Jerusalem bishopric, to an extent it is now hard to imagine. In writing for this class, the traveller was required to adopt the outlook of a Christian with wide knowledge of the Bible and its archaeology, and of Church history. Attacks were expected on Muhammadanism and its adverse effects on the social, political and economic condition of Islamic lands, and in almost every book of travels they were made: Rich might have been summing up the viewpoint expected of travellers when he told his English readers that 'The Moham-medan religion is a bar to all improvement. A nation could not become civilized and remain Mohammedan.'

But there is another view covertly, or tacitly, expressed. Usually an unconventional and rather lawless spirit, the traveller of those days may at first have been taken aback to find his fellow-Christians in the East such an abject and contemptible set, whilst the rich and the powerful, with whom he chose to associate, held beliefs he assumed to be wicked or ridiculous; but, with the other freedoms of a traveller's life from the restraints of home, he may well have felt, I imagine, growing independence of the received ideas of his religious education. In an English schoolroom he might not have seen the difficulty of reconciling Humility, which is a Judaic virtue not known to the Greeks, with the classical virtues instilled by all his studies; in the East, seeing Christian Humility in practice in a society whose rulers still did not think of Humility as a virtue, the travelling Englishman might have realized that he was not, and never had been, in any real sense Humble. In his narrative, by emphasizing the dirt and deceit and idolatry of Eastern Christians, and by dwelling on the enormities and absurdities of Christian sectarians in the Holy Land itself, he had the chance to mock behind his hand, so to speak, the sober church-going hierarchy of conventional society at home. It is in Jerusalem, and in the Holy Sepulchre itself, that the chance to mock lie readiest to hand. The arrangement of so much miraculous material so conveniently close is recorded with face scarcely kept straight. The erection of two walls by two factions around two Gardens of Gethsemane is noted with twitching lips. He doesn't fail to compare the shrill, seedy sectarian priests shouting down one another's services in the Holy Sepulchre, with the grave dignity of the Mussulman guard smoking on their divan above the floor of the church, posted there by the pasha to prevent Christian riots from upsetting his town. (Riot they did, especially at Easter, as Robert Curzon tells most dramatically of his visit in 1834, when many hundreds were crushed to death.) At last reverence, and cash, are demanded of the traveller for one pious relic too many: 'The cord of my credulity had been stretched to its fullest extent,' wrote James Creagh in the final sentence of *A Scamper to Sebastopol and Jerusalem*, 'but when they told me this it broke.' You feel he laid down his pen laughing out loud at last. In his beliefs, as in all other questions, the traveller was concerned to confront himself with as direct an experience as could be contrived, and to discover the line his own mind took in face of it.

Hours passed. I thought and dozed, and the bus carried me rapidly eastward over rough roads through broken country occasionally glimpsed under the moon, a dim bluish interior of sleeping Turks' heads hurtling through the dark behind the spears of headlights.

Many of the buses I had taken had been stopped at military roadblocks: in the west of the country, in sunlight, these had seemed not unfriendly checks on passengers' papers. By night, in the eastern wilds, they altered their character. They became frequent, and hostile. The first signal that we approached an army post was the violent check of the brakes on the bus's rush through darkness. All were thrown forward and awoken. The bus stopped, cut engine and lights, waited. On the road came the rattle of boots, orders, lights which flared on faces peering out of the bus. The door hissed open. Up the steps sprang a couple of soldiers under steel helmets, one running to the back of the bus, both covering the passengers with automatic weapons. A pause: then there mounted slowly into the bus an officer. He was a swell amongst scared servants. 'Identity papers!' A rustle of hands reached for pockets, and the gun-muzzles front and rear waved over us in case anywhere a weapon came out in a man's hand. Terrorists in flight were of course making their way east into Kurdistan by these buses. The officer moved slowly and carefully from seat to seat, a powerful light held for him by a third armed soldier, examining papers and looking into faces. There was a horrid coldness which shrank the heart. The shaven skulls and Germanic helmets of the guards behind their weapons made them into another race from the passengers, Mongol overlords crushing rustics under armed heels. There were young men of military age in the bus; how do you turn them from subject race into soldier? Is there in every crushed rustic a Hun tyrant longing to get out? In the seat in front of mine sat one of these young men. The officer reached him. As perhaps is inevitable under military rule, the officer had adopted the 'dashing' style of the pre-war Nazi in films, a style running to cigarette holder and loosely tied white silk scarf, and when he had looked through the youth's papers he stretched out a hand in a thin glove and tousled the boy's hair with the rough comradeship of the rugger team. The victim's head shrank into his shoulders as a tortoise's head into its shell. Then the officer came to me.

I don't know if other nationalities – indeed I don't know if other Englishmen – have the confidence I have in a British passport to shield me from harm. Certain of its effect I put this trump card, which was visa'd for many countries in many tongues, into his hand. He turned pages slowly. I saw that he disliked it for being written in languages unknown to him. Not to understand made him vulnerable. This was a vulnerable post. In the brooding care with which he turned the pages I saw the apprehension of an official who frightens his inferiors, but is himself very frightened of making a mistake. The soldier's unsteady hand shook flaring light on to his face and the white page. I wished I could have quieted his worries. When he looked from the photograph to my face, it seemed inappropriate to wreathe myself in smiles. Suddenly he stood back, my passport in his hand, and decided. An order was given. From the front, under the soldier's gun, people began to shuffle down the steps of the bus into the night. Those attempting to take hand-luggage with them had it taken from them.

It was extremely cold outside, in darkness pierced by flamelight from the soldiers' watchfire, which flickered on the flank of the bus, and on the backs of the passengers lined up against it. The firelight lit up no other feature of landscape whatsoever, no tree or hedge or wall, so that the sense of being in the middle of nowhere was complete. Baggage was being pulled out of the bus's belly by our conductor. When it was all out, passengers were nudged in the back one by one, and one by one they turned and went to the heap of belongings and identified their bags or sacks or bundles in the pallor of torches playing fitfully on faces and possessions. I had thought the customs inspection of the trainload of peasants entering Yugoslavia from Italy severe, like warder and prisoner; but here it was like occupying troops and native suspects. There was no spark of friendliness or humour. The touch in my back felt more hesitant than it looked when dealt out to others, and I went to find my bag in the luggage heap. I opened it, a complicated bag with many compartments, and the officer plunged in his hand here and there and felt about. All he examined was my battery razor, the traveller's friend. Then I took my place against the bus again, the glare of the fire not warming my back, but its light gleaming on metal hazed with the dust and mud of our journey from Kayseri. That I had not been given back my passport allowed a cold little draught of uncertainty into the picture which was otherwise one I could not fail to enjoy. Turkey must at that time have been full of scattering terrorists making for the eastern mountains, or the Russian or Iraqi border, and it was easy to imagine such a man suddenly identified amongst us, his dash for the darkness beyond the fire, the cries, the flash of gunfire. I was lucky to feel the tenseness of the scene at first hand, even if imagination was needed to inject danger into it, for such a scene was well in keeping with the alarms of travel in earlier days. All the same, I wished as I began to shiver with cold that I had my passport back. Nothing easier for an uncertain officer than to tear out a page, or smudge a number, and offer that irregularity to his superiors as a reason for detaining a man, if detaining the man turned out to be the wrong course. We waited for some time whilst nothing happened. Then at last the line of passengers was directed back into the bus. At the foot of the steps my priceless talisman, in its blue boards with the Royal Arms stamped on them, was handed back to me with a stiff nod. Soon the bus was travelling again.

We were stopped several times more that night, though not again made to get out. In the intervals, when awake, I strained my eyes into the dark to make out the shape of the country under starlight, for the moon had set long ago, and I regretted that I was not to see the landscape of this province. It seemed wild country, the roads unsurfaced, dust, and the smell of dust, filling the bus. In one deep valley we crossed and recrossed a stream which I knew to be the Kara Su – the infant Euphrates – amongst the most powerful of all rivers' names in evoking vanished might. Dark water glittering under a bridge was all I saw of it, but the first glimpse of any famous river is an event to remember.

Asleep or awake I was completely comfortable, my Belgrade bag under my seat, a sweater rolled up for a pillow, my corduroy jacket buttoned up to the chin, better rested in mind and body than I have often felt in bed. Events – stops and starts, villages, people coming and going – had the dreamy continuity of a film watched from a deep chair in a drowse.

At Erzincan, by the barracks, the bus stopped under cold glaring light shed from tripods the height of pylons on to concrete and wire fences guarding a waste land of huts. No grimmer picture of army life was ever projected. From the seat in front of me rose the youth I had noticed before, and took down his new zipper-bag from the rack. Now I knew why the officer at the roadblock had tousled his hair: from his papers he had seen the boy was travelling to Erzincan to begin his compulsory army service. I understood the recruit's head shrinking down into his shoulders under the gloved hand cuffing it, and the weak half-smile he managed for the conductor as he descended the bus steps into that desolate future under the arc-lights on the other side of the wire. Was I watching the moment of transformation I had wondered about, when the citizen of a military state changes sides from subject-race into soldier? The weak smile – the instinct that made him shrink – all feeling – would be ironed off his face by the helmet's steel rim, and his hands would be made powerful by putting a weapon into them. I saw him slouch to the gate carrying his bag, and the guard march to the gate from the other side, before the bus carried me on.

3

Day had not dawned when we reached Erzurum. The bus boomed through streets emptied by curfew, cold, lit with feeble splashes of sodium. The town by these glimpses was one of the ugliest I have ever seen. Dirty modern concrete masked any old streets it may have contained, and tower blocks of the same repellent grey overtopped any domes or minarets or fortress walls that might still remain. Before long the bus careered into a large open space at the foot of the town, dark and bitterly cold, the *otogar* where the journey from Kayseri ended. I took my bags and made for the shelter of the café, where many groups swathed in wrappings sat immovable and silent at half-lit tables amid a sea of bundles. What should I do?

Why stop at Erzurum? What was there to interest me here?

These are doubts fatal to admit into the mind in the course of a journey. Once you question why you should stop at the place you intended to reach, you begin to wonder why you stop anywhere. You let in too powerful a draught of that restlessness which, though an ingredient of the impetus to travel, must not be allowed dominance over the rest. The traveller needs restlessness as the sailing ship needs wind, to waft him from place to place; not the hurricane driving him under bare poles and battened hatches.

What had I expected of Erzurum? Was it reasonable to be disappointed already? As with most places I ever want to see, I had in my mind a misty picture, that's all, made up of old aquatints and agreeable accounts. Of Erzurum, on the road to Persia and India, so many sketches exist in books of travel that I felt I'd been there. The frontispiece of Curzon's *Armenia* shows an eastern city of minarets and deckled walls gleaming in a sunshaft against the formidable dark mountains rolling up behind. Dr Sandwith, who was attached to Layard's excavation at Nineveh (as well as running down to Rhodes when Lord Carlisle caught smallpox), gives an account of reaching Erzurum at daybreak, after a desperate journey, and of sitting next to an Englishman at breakfast who invited him out for a day's snipe-shooting, then and there, in the marshes below the town in which ibis and spoonbills and silver cranes fed in their thousands. Sandwith shot with his usual cheerfulness, up to his armpits in water all day, and ends his chapter: 'A sharp gallop brought me to the gates of Erzurum just as the sun set.'

It seemed to me probable that the marsh lay just where the bus station I was sitting in had been built. With such vague expectations as I carry about in my head, you might think I'd be disappointed everywhere. But it isn't so. From vague expectations a flavour can be distilled, and often the flavour persists, when all material or architectural hopes are utterly dashed. However, to catch the persisting flavour, it is necessary to hang about the streets of the place, and walk, and poke in alleys, and above all to be patient. The obvious and evident changes – the bus station where the spoonbills should be – have to be ignored. I was now in danger of dismissing Erzurum without giving it a chance to show whether the old flavour of Armenia's capital hung about its streets or not. This was the kind of hastiness fatal to my plan: the first blast of the hurricane which could blow me straight back to England under bare poles.

When I lived in Rome I used to drive to and from England once or twice a year, taking several days for the journey, stopping to see people in Paris or Geneva or the south of France, staying an odd night in a French or Italian village where I had never been before, and these were journeys I loved and looked forward to; yet each trip nearly always ended in impatience, and a long fast drive through the night to reach, quite unnecessarily, Rome or the Channel in the least possible time. Since then I have recognized the danger of restlessness getting out of hand, until the tour becomes a circular dash for home.

All right, I wouldn't stop at Erzurum, I would go on to Kars by the next bus. But at Kars I would stop, whether its appearance matched my misty picture or not. I went into the large dim central vault, which was surrounded with guichets and full of sacks and bags and patient people, where I soon found a bus company which would take me on to Kars in an hour or so's time. With my ticket onward in my pocket I found a seat at the window of the café looking out on the dark before dawn. Kars was the destination of my journey from England − Kars, the citadel fought over by Turk and Russian and Persian since ancient times, which commands what is to me the frontier charged with most history and romance of all the world's frontiers. Mount Ararat, on which the Ark stranded, overlooks Persia, Iraq, Russia and Turkey: an Islamic legend places the Garden of Eden on a mountain between Erzurum and Kars, out of whose springs flow the Euphrates bound for the Persian Gulf, the Araxes which flows into the Caspian, and the Coruh whose waters join the Black Sea: this knot of mountains, in short, stands at the source of the human race, and upon the frontier which might decide its future. At Kars I would stop, whatever it looked like now. The pilgrims didn't have any difficulty, as I recall, in recognizing the Land of Far Beyond when they got there.

Around me at the tables the muffled and somnolent figures waited immovably. Suitcases, in this region, had given way to bundles and sacks, with which all were well supplied. There was no tea, for reasons I couldn't fathom, but I was content with bread and warm, sweetened, goat's milk at my seat by the window. Objects against the sky now began to look blacker, and denser, than the sky itself: a glimmer crept along the roofs: the eastern gables of buildings grew pale: the sky hollowed, and expanded, and began slowly to fill with dawn and the mighty shapes of mountains. The air seemed sharpened into intenser cold by the light. The altitude is 7,000 feet above the sea, and the mountains behind the town, never without the snow which now sparkled in the dawn, reach 10,000 feet into the sky. Happy, and feeling full of health and vigour, I watched colour wash into the scene, the dry pale colour of anywhere high and cold, and the sun begin to light the summits of the mountains.

It is important to emphasize how much I was enjoying myself – and had enjoyed myself wherever I had been. The impression left by many books of travel is that the traveller disliked each place he came to more than the last, and was counting the moments until he reached home again. 'At length I reached Tehran,' says Captain Wilbraham on his travels in 1839, 'and as I rode through the Shemeroon Gate, most devoutly did I wish that my residence in Tehran might prove a short one; and that, when next my foot was in the stirrup, my horse's head might be turned in the direction of Europe.' You could find the echo of that joyless sentiment in many a modern book of travels. Partly it is the difficulty of conveying to the reader 'in his snug parlour' a proper awareness of the hardship, danger, illness, suffered by the writer, whilst preserving any overall atmosphere of enjoyment in the adventure. A stern idea of Duty is made to run through the narrative like the poker which straightens a slouching back. The authenticity of Daniel's Tomb – the exact route of Xenophon's Ten Thousand – the military strength of border towns – the tonnage of leeches exported from Trebizond – serious topics must be kept before the reader's mind as the writer's chief purpose in struggling through snowdrifts and flea-ridden post-houses on his and England's behalf. It mustn't be thought that fun was the point of the thing.

Besides lacking gusto, I believe travel writers fall into the habit of mocking scenes and people rather as inferior novelists take the easier course of creating only mockable people; a tone of lofty contempt seems to the writer to elevate himself, where enthusiasm, he fears, leaves him open to derision by people more sophisticated than himself. 'I own I am disappointed by the Euphrates,' wrote James Fraser rather grandly; but we know now which of them came worst out of the encounter. There was in the 1840s a Mme Ida Pfeiffer, an Austrian woman in a straw bonnet, a dogged traveller, who set about the Holy Land in a scolding tone which leaves us in no doubt as to its failure to reach the high standard she expects from places she inspected. With her riding whip she drove off the beggar children in Bethlehem, of all places to choose in which to beat the children; the girls of Nazareth she found 'poorly clad, many wore no covering on their heads, and, what was worse, their hair hung down in a most untidy manner'. You are reminded of a governess who takes satisfaction in being 'disappointed' so that she may deal harshly with the offence. The ugliness of olive trees – 'large leafy trees, like those in my own land, are seldom seen in this country' – the gracelessness of women carrying pitchers from the well – all our notions are upset as she looks about and pokes things with a disapproving umbrella. She even managed to quarrel with some fishermen on the Sea of Galilee. (With one sentence, however, she wins my heart: 'The finest production of Egypt and Syria, almost superior to the pineapple in taste, is the *banana*, so delicate it almost melts in the mouth.') I see how it is that the mocking, or the suffering, tone comes to be taken up, but I want there to be no doubt in the reader's mind that I was enjoying my bread and goat's milk in the bus station at Erzurum, after my night on the road from Kayseri, and that I looked forward with much keenness to the day now dawning.

At half-past seven the bus left on its four-hour journey to Kars. At first the road winds through a bare landscape of grass hills, pale and wintry with frost that morning, down towards the Araxes. In an extensive valley the river flows broad and fast over its pebbly bed. It is an Eastern scene, the level valley, the distant rough mountains, the river picking its course at will amongst stony islands, and uprooted trees with white trunks, and marsh grass, and grazing flocks; over the river at Horasan, where the road divides into a branch for Persia and a branch for Russia, stand the fine stone arches of an ancient bridge, and upon this bridge, outlined against the valley and mountains, I saw my imaginary Travellers as clear as day. Two English horsemen rode ahead, turbans and robes of the East worn stylishly, their horses stepping sharply and smartly away from a lame baggage animal ridden by a servant which crept along behind. It was a scene, like the bazaar at Kayseri, which I committed to memory as a touchstone of reality upon which to ring the coin of invention. It has to look like this. I was a bit surprised that there were two of them, besides the servant, but no doubt there was a reason for that.

The bus dashed on at reckless speed, the road narrow, rough, climbing and descending through hills. Tearing towards us, before we had reached Horasan, had appeared a convoy of twenty or more container lorries driving at a furious pace out of Persia, or at least from the direction of the Iranian frontier. Yet the Tehran mullahs' war against the Kurds, as well as their war against Iraq, is said to have closed this frontier; so where does such a convoy come from, along a road which leads only to Iran? The trucks were identical, brand new, huge, each marked 'International Transport' on the side. I had the feeling of one who lifts the corner of a window-blind and sees what he is not meant to see: 'Watch the wall, my darling, while the Gentlemen go by!' Roadblocks were frequent, the military everywhere. I shouldn't have liked to have been a spy or a fugitive terrorist making for the border in our bus.

Next to me sat an old fellow with a henna'd moustache and so very heavy a cold that he kept his nose plunged into a soggy cloth all the way. Everyone in the bus – everyone in Turkey – seemed to have caught colds, but no amount of coughing, no paroxysm of hawking or spitting, discouraged them for one instant from smoking. My old neighbour wore a kind of turban wound round his head, and when the bus was first stopped at a roadblock, and armed soldiers mounted its steps, he dragged this contrivance rapidly off his shaven skull, to slide on in its place a cap drawn from the bosom of his shirt. As he did so he muttered to me the one word 'Army!' in a derisive growl through his nose-cloth. When the soldiers left the bus he resumed his turban, determined to defy, if it could be done in safety, Atatürk's anti-clerical Hat Law (which forbids, I think, the brimless headgear so convenient for a Mussulman's prayers). He never spoke again: whether 'army' was his only English word I do not know. He was old enough to have learnt it whilst fighting us in the Dardanelles; and old enough to have learnt his distrust of the Young Turks at the same time, for 78,000 of his contemporaries were lost in these very mountains in the expedition led by Enver Pasha against Russia in 1915, a grandiloquent expedition which had as its objective, as well as the defeat of Russia, the invasion of India by way of Afghanistan.*

From the Araxes the road climbed into the pass of Sarikamis, overhung by craggy hills clothed in the first pines I had seen since leaving Caria. There succeeded regions of mountain pasture and upland valley, rough roads and stony streams, all with the pallor of intense cold about them, the sun scarcely colouring the scene.

It is in this tract of country that the Garden of Eden is said to have lain. As persistently as the idea of Eden runs through human history, the existence, and rare attainment, of an Earthly Paradise runs through the books of Eastern travellers. Their dream has certain fixed qualities: mountainous scenery, well timbered, forms the background, and flowing water runs through the foreground; a race of bold mountaineers, who accept the traveller into their midst, and show him all the spirited and freeborn virtues of the highlander, must inhabit the mountains and pitch their tents by the stream, and in their company, listening to their wild songs or joining in their mimic fights, the traveller finds rest and peace from the ordeal of his journey. This idyll is not the goal, but a happy interval along the way in which, as for knights of old in some pleasant castle, weariness may be refreshed, exile sweetened, wounds bound up by gentle hands.

The imagery used in describing this Earthly Paradise draws on two sources, one in pagan antiquity – the vale of Tempé, Dafné's grove, many-fountained Ida – the other in Miltonic Eden; together they form a Paradise Garden, somewhat Italianate, somewhat Gothick, which is sequestered within the folds of a mountain fastness.

In this touching and romantic picture many instincts and loyalties in the traveller's own mind might be traced. A likeness between these highlands and the Highlands of Scott's novels strikes the reader. By their honourable simplicity in placing trust in the word of lowland politicians, Layard's Bakhtiari chieftain, and Rich's Kurd from Sulimania, are tricked into the power of a Matamet of Isphan, and a Vali of Sinna, whose features are decidedly Hanoverian, whilst the clansmen are pursued and

* It was John Buchan's hero, Richard Hannay, who with his friends engineered this Turkish defeat in the novel *Greenmantle*.

destroyed and blinded with the ferocity of a Cumberland. With such men as these highlanders the English traveller sympathized. Jacobite by instinct, exile by force of many circumstances, he 'pines by Arno for my lovelier Tees', and the river flowing through this pass was just the sort of burn which twines itself round the heart of any exiled Highlander.

The immense grazing plain which we soon entered by way of the mountains was a wonderful sight to come upon at that altitude. Green and tender as a watercolour, grass spread out soft and far under smoke-puff clouds and the shining blue sky. This is the plain of Kars.

I was almost afraid to look into the distance and see, surely, the usual muddle of concrete suburbs in place of the dark tower which imagination had built to brood over this blood-soaked arena between the empires of Shah, of Sultan, and of Tsar. But I looked, and out of the plain a harsh and gloomy outline began to rise; square, squat, dark; stone walls ringing the stony hill; a fortress formidable enough to guard the most romantic frontier of the imagination. I was satisfied already with the eastern limit of my journey.

Through steep streets, mud and cobbles, we bumped into an open mud compound which served as bus station and commercial square, people and goods and animals all unloaded into a general mêlée. Wretched shops and other low buildings fronted this open ground, and amongst them I saw a hotel. In the entrance a number of soldiers and policemen were sitting on wooden chairs listening to a wireless without much animation. Attempts to cheer the place up with paint and plastic flowers had been abandoned uncompleted. A man came forward and showed me a room upstairs which I took, although it was so extremely dirty that I asked for it to be cleaned of the rubbish and filth accumulated on every surface. I then went out immediately to see the town and to visit, if possible, the fortress.

Despite ruinous streets and much waste ground there is a tremendously likeable spirit of liveliness about Kars. Maybe it is the number of animals you see which makes it so lively, for you are mixed up in a moment with sheep, goats, cattle, all being driven in rapid little parties along the street, whilst horse-drawn carts and traps rattle to and fro at a great rate. The imminence of winter was sharpening up people's activities, no doubt, for October is the eleventh hour before ferocious cold seizes the town. As I walked towards the citadel I thought of the October morning in 1855 when a Russian army attacked the town. On that day they were driven off, losing 8,900 dead (whom it took the Turk garrison, under General Williams and one or two other English officers, four days' work to bury), but Mouvarieff sat down before the town and invested it closely until, after two months of intense suffering from cold and cholera and famine, when every living creature in the place had been eaten, and horse soup was a delicacy reserved secretly for the dying, the garrison capitulated. Dr Sandwith (who was chief medical officer) persuades his reader that magnanimity, courtesy, chivalry – all the warrior virtues commended in Romance – persisted between the armies. A book sent to Sandwith (it was Lord Carlisle's *Diary in Turkish and Greek Waters*), which the Russians intercepted, was delayed only whilst Mouvarieff read it, then forwarded into the doomed town with apologies. And here is how Mouvarieff is made to speak during the capitulation scene:

' "General Williams, you have made yourself a name in history, and posterity will stand amazed at the endurance, the courage, and the discipline which this siege has called forth in the remains of an army. Let us arrange a capitulation which will satisfy the demands of war without outraging humanity" – I leave my readers to imagine,' Sandwith goes on, 'anything more touching than the interview between these gallant leaders, whose eyes were suffused with tears, whilst their hearts were big with the sentiments of high honour and graceful benevolence.'

The scene comes from an earlier war, such as those chivalrous affairs between Richard Lionheart and the Saladin, which the nineteenth century persuaded itself had graced the age of the troubadours and the England of Camelot. Still, official recognition agreed with Sandwith's romantic view of the 'Hero of Kars'. General Williams was made a Knight of the Bath, a Freeman of the City of London, and granted £1,000 a year for life by Parliament. Noble defeat – the Jacobite sympathy again, which touched Layard's heart in the blinded Bakhtiari chieftain's plight

– made perhaps too strong an appeal to Victorian Englishmen. To heap such extravagant honours on a defeated general might be seen to tend in the direction of those celebrations of the forlorn hope – Majuba Hill, Dr Brydon's escape from an army massacred by Afghans – which were painted into the moral syllabus by Mrs Butler, and were to have dire repercussions in the committal of men to hopeless attacks in 1916. Of the magnificent attributes wished by destiny on to the Victorians, excessive admiration for heroic defeat might be singled out in retrospect as the wicked godmother's gift which was to prove fatal to the whole.*

I had picked my way up the hillside amongst whitened cabins until I came on a track winding under the fortress walls. This track led me into an archway embayed between bastions, which was closed with a pair of timber doors fifteen or so feet in height. I knocked on these doors, but the sound was puny. I pushed at them, but they rattled without giving way. I stepped back. A high, windy solitude made the spot like a ledge on a cliff. In the shadow of its gloomy bastions the castle door rose ahead of me,

---

* The Turkish view of the loss of Kars was less self-congratulatory. 'One of the most intelligent and Europeanized of the military pashas' was asked by an attaché of the British Ambassador 'if he was of opinion that the services of General Williams had been very useful at Kars. He replied that an officer, sent as Commissioner of the Queen of England, had unwarrantably interfered with the legitimate command at Kars, where Turkey possessed a valuable army and an important town. By keeping the one in the other when everyone else was aware that it could not save it, he had lost them both, for which he said that no Turk could feel otherwise than vexed and indignant.' A reason for English enthusiasm over the siege of Kars was that interest in its progress was unalloyed by the losses of English troops, which so marred even our successes in the Crimea itself. For chivalry did not extend to Turks. The life of a Turkish ally (as may be seen from the following account written by the same attaché I have quoted above) counted for less than the life of a Russian enemy. 'The battle was at its thickest and hottest, when three Turkish soldiers pushed a wounded Russian officer back from the parapet, and followed him over it to dispatch him with their bayonets. Major Teesdale, seeing this act of barbarity, vaulted over the breastwork, cut down the foremost Turk with his sword, and called on the Russian, in French, to surrender as a prisoner of war. He did so, and was handed over to Dr Sandwith, who cured him of his wound. Major Teesdale most deservedly received the Victoria Cross for this exploit, as well as the thanks of General Muravief [sic] which were publicly offered to him, after the capitulation, for his chivalrous humanity towards a wounded enemy.'

and the rough little town straggled over the slope below. That it was a High Security Area had rather slipped my mind. Determined to get in, I picked up a stone from the track and beat with it on the weather-stained timber until echoes resounded and jackdaws dropped out of the towers. At last came the rattling of chains from within.

A young soldier looked nervously out. One hand held together his belt, the other clutched his automatic weapon. He hesitated between the two duties before putting down his gun and doing up his belt, more used, I daresay, to being scolded by sergeant-majors than overrun by enemy troops. I asked if I could look round the fortress. His face brightened, and he let me in. When he had chained up the door he led me to a grassy knoll in the sun where a pair of army boots protruded from under a blanket amongst some grazing sheep. Remembering his rifle left by the gate, he ran off to retrieve it. An edge of the blanket was lifted from within, a sleepy young face peered at me, the blanket fell again to cover all but boots. The sheep nibbled, the sun shone hot in the shelter of walls and towers. Here I stood in the fortress of Kars!

It is in ruins. At the base of roofless towers, their beams blackened by fire, are heaps of fallen stone. Crumbling stone steps climb from one grassy level to another of the castle's elaborate system of defensive architecture. All are nibbled bare, and sheep file up and down the flights in the rapid restless way of animals short of food. Round these hollow works, which appear formidable from without, the soldier led me.

Walking behind him – steel helmet and cropped neck, khaki, heavy boots, hand on weapon – I thought of him as the next stage in developing a civilian into a soldier, after the stage I had watched in the boy leaving the bus at Erzincan and approaching the barrack gates. He was not yet a soldier, except for his armour. He still leaped and ran like a boy, showing me rusty machinery, handing me his gun, or forgetting it on a parapet, whilst he wound an ingenious windlass for bringing up food from below. In his familiarity with every nook and cranny of the deserted fortress you could see the extent of his boredom. This was his playground. He ran into a tower where he showed me how the

Russians had machine-gunned some crowd or other (in which war he neither knew nor cared) by waving his weapon at the wall and shouting 'D-d-d-d-d!', which wakened, or startled, an off-white pigeon from a rafter overhead. Pitching down his rifle, the boy began flinging stones at this sorry dove, which flew wearily amongst the missiles, attempting to perch, until driven off in search of peace elsewhere. It would have appealed to a Russian in my place, if he had a taste for allegory: LACKEY OF USA STONES DOVE OF PEACE IN VIEW OF ARK'S REMAINS. Hoping that Mount Ararat might indeed be visible, I freed myself from my guide and climbed back to the tower's summit alone so as to look out upon the varying scene of plain and mountain.

The citadel commands the south and east. A grassy plain rolls away from the town to a great distance, hills pushed back to clear the ground around the fortress on its rock like sand swept away from a sandcastle and piled into heaps at a distance. Two clear pathways are driven through the distant mountains. Towards Russia opens one wide gap, and towards Persia opens another. Their width well suggests the room needed by the unnumbered thousands of an eastern invasion, the rolling dustcloud, the glitter of spear and brass, the note of the kettledrum, the profound dread struck into the watcher's heart by oncoming hordes crawling over the grassland towards him. 'Kars,' said Colonel Lake, who was in charge of its fortification under General Williams, 'is the key to Asia Minor.'

The last view of Christendom, across the waters of Danube and Sava from the dark walls of Belgrade, began a journey across the Turkish domains; and in those smoky Russian hills rimming the plain of Kars was a no less picturesque view of the road's eastern limit.

To the north the fortress is commanded by rocks as high as itself, and, between these crags and the castle, in a deep fissure, runs the Kars river. This green and scaly torrent winds its coils around the base of the rock into the town, where an arched bridge on the outskirts connects two filth-strewn banks. I watched its shallows used for watering horses driven with their carts into the stream, where they stand dreamily sipping the scum. In rapids below the bridge washerwomen were busy thumping cloth on stone, and shouting up to friends who had paused to rest heavy loads on the parapet of the bridge above them. Shabby buildings, low mean dwellings, cover the ground without plan, dust and stony spaces lying between collapsed walls, huts climbing the hillside across the river to peter out amongst caves burrowed into the slope. The clustering humps of a *hammam* by the bridge, and the Kümbet Camii, are the only old buildings you look down on from the citadel.

Kars has another quite different quarter, which intrigued me greatly when I found it in the afternoon. In 1877 a Russian army again besieged the town (returned to Turkey after the Crimea War) and this time took it by storm, a disaster to Turkish arms which they blamed (in the French manner) on 'treachery'. Kars became Russian, and was Russianized. It was this Russian quarter I found after eating rather a wretched lunch and reading on my bed for an hour.

The bequest of Russian building – I supposed it was Russian because it was so un-Turkish – stands out like British building in India: frock coat and top hat picking its way through the bazaar. I walked up a sound cobbled street with well-built town houses on either side – background for that society of exiles in remote provincial towns which Russian fiction tells you almost more about than you can bear to hear – until I reached a residential square of tall solemn-fronted houses looking down on a garden of evergreens locked in behind railings in its centre. Here, rather than in Athens, I was reminded of Edinburgh: the square achieved that most un-Asiatic of all qualities – respectability. Too large to be lived in, these, like the best houses of many a finer town than Kars, had degenerated into a warren for public officials in which I poked about because I was looking for authority to let me visit Ani, the deserted town on Russia's border. I was sent from office to office, no one seeming to have power to act, bureaucracy conspiring to extinguish, rather than to forbid, the individual's wish to do something awkward. They were suspicious. The wish was extinguished. For the non-specialist there are very few places worth arousing suspicion as the price of a visit; the hopes of the general tourist like me are just as likely to be satisfied quite adventitiously by a wayside village as they are by taking a lot of trouble to reach a ticklish spot. My wish to see Ani had at any rate brought me as far as this odd, Chekhovian quarter of Kars, and I was happy with that result.

It was cold and dusky as I walked back through the streets from this excursion. On the pavements firewood tumbled out of trucks was being weighed out on scales for customers, and the tang of split beech on frosty air caught at me from the wintry woods at home. Chestnuts roasting over braziers, too, and flaring shop-lights spilling into the dusk, reminded me of winter evenings in the North. I experienced that feeling of isolation which is one of the pleasures of solitary travel: awareness that no one in the whole world knows where you are, save you yourself, and delight in the sufficiency of that awareness. *Here am I alone in the midst of this strange scene.* I think you only feel the pleasure of this state if you've suffered at one time from homesickness, for the feeling I've described takes the same circumstances as those causing home-sickness – isolation from all that is familiar – but finds more sweetness than bitterness in its poignancy when suddenly home is thrust into your mind by a chance scene or scent. Winter dusk, frost-rimed windows, wood smoke, act most sharply on my mind: it was the winter I spent in France, between school and university, which took the child's bitterness out of these things, when they made me think of home, and put instead sweetness into the pang. It was during that winter at Nanteuil that I first learned that it was possible for me to be absolutely happy away from home. Now, as I say, the awareness of isolation amongst strange scenes is one of the pleasures of travel.

I do not speak of the terrific loneliness which sometimes visits the mind with fear in desolate places. To grapple with that, and to harden the mind by its continual presence, was a stern necessity to poor Captain Abbott in the deserts of Khiva, or Vambéry under the stars of the Kizil Kum.* On 19 February 1838, at five in the evening, Lieutenant Wood stood at 15,000 feet on the shore of the Sir-i-kol lake, in the Pamir, which he believed to be the long-sought source of the Oxus: 'Not a breath

* Suffering intensely from the bite of a scorpion, Vambéry tells how he lay watching the Pleiades 'moving slowly to the West – the beloved West, which I despaired of ever seeing again'.

moved along the surface of the lake, not a beast, not a bird . . . silence reigned around, so profound that it oppressed the heart, and, as I contemplated the hoary summits of the everlasting mountains, where human foot had never trod, and where lay piled the snow of ages, my own dear country . . . passed before my mind.' I can see that to try his character against such extremes of loneliness and isolation as Asiatic travel offered, might attract the man who had suffered the frailty of missing home and family as a child, in order to make sure that he had overcome it in manhood. The suffering is so acute in the child, that the man could never be certain that he was armed at all points until he had confronted that fear above all, and subdued it.

I'm not talking about these stern methods in my own case; I am thinking, as always, of constructing the character of the Traveller I mean to write about, from these ideas and instances. In my own case, the isolation doesn't need to be extreme, or the scene very strange; the pleasure of the thing, to me, may be partly due to lofty ideas of self-reliance, but partly, also, I recognize it for the self-congratulatory hug of the tripper on a spree, who finds himself alone on the Great Orme above Llandudno, wife and family visible, but distant, on the beach below.

Still, the pleasure is keener in a wild town like Kars which I had longed to reach. When I set out later that evening to eat at a *locanda* I had marked down as promising good cheer, I could not well have enjoyed my walk through the dark town more. It was bitter cold, and I walked rapidly by unlighted lanes full of puddles, and full, too, of enormous dogs quarrelling over rubbish heaps. Now and then came a splash of lamplight, on a wall, on a door, on a street. The houses were shuttered, shop-doors chained, the town secretive. At corners I dodged carts whipped through the dark with fierce cries, or met a swiftly pattering herd of sheep tumbling along round the heels of Kurdish shepherds. My only worry was how I was going to leave the place, for I had found out that tomorrow's bus to Trabzon was full – though that was all I had managed to find out from the bus offices. The dark vociferous men in their rabbit-hutch booths round the *meidan* seemed rather contemptuous of foreigners. Nor did the carters, or shepherds, who peered fiercely into my face, look any more friendly. I was glad to see the yellow light of the *locanda* behind its steamy window, and find myself in a wooden chair at a wooden table, with food smoking in metal vats at one end of the room, and on the wall over my head a reproduction of 'The Hay Wain'.

A curious facet of the Asiatic mind is lit up by the choice of pictures on eating-house walls. Here was 'The Hay Wain'; on another wall hung a brightly painted view of a Swiss mountain; the lush Suffolk fatness of the one, and the tidiness of the other, being at all points the antithesis of Turkey. Is it the idealized forms of shade and water, those promised essentials of a Muslim paradise, which make the appeal? Not this – not what you see, not carts driven into the green scum of the Kars river between grassless banks – not this, but something else, a heavenly cart in a limpid stream, in cloud cuckoo-clock land. These sentimental pictures, like the postcards you can buy all over Asia of girls in nighties with huge shining tears sticking to their cheeks, under-line the consciousness of exile which seems a Muslim character-istic. Exile – the powerful far from the Bosphorus, the tribesman far from his mountains, the humblest beggar far from Paradise – exile is his fate. There is always somewhere else, the thought of which brings a tear of self-pity to the eye. Maybe homesickness is a condition of the nomadic soul.

Possibly on account of being sent away at seven or eight to a boarding school, the Englishman, though haunted by homesick-ness, looked upon it as a weakness of childhood, as I've said, which must be overcome or kept secret. Their sentimentality was reserved for the plight of others – again I think of Layard and the betrayed Bakhtiari chieftain – in whose exile they might blend their own without confessing to a weakness. There is no equivalent in English writing to the theme of malcontent exiles pining for Moscow which exists in Russian fiction. No doubt Kars resounded to the sighs of Russians weighed down by the injuries of exile. But had it belonged to the British Empire, it would have had the brisk social life of an Indian or African station, where pining was not regarded as setting the proper tone, and where, at any rate, the middle-class administrator was sufficiently content with the prestige and comfort of his life, modelled as it was on that of a higher class than his own, to prefer it very often to England.

Whatever its effect upon the Turks sopping up meat juice at greasy tables, 'The Hay Wain' did not make me pine for Suffolk. I was where I wanted to be. I chose some ladlefuls of food at the counter, and a waiter followed me with my choice to the table. Odd that I should have been thinking about exiles in Kars, because here was a man, the waiter, who was an exile from the metropolis if ever I saw one. Trim and erect, perhaps sixty years old, in a grey cloth jacket, he stepped along with the quickness and neatness, and served my food with the silent courtesy, of a waiter in a great restaurant. Was the place his? Had he retired here from Paris or Rome and bought himself the business? I doubted it, because he seemed to be subordinate to the greasy cook managing the vats, and sat humbly over his paper at a table when not employed. Indeed there was no job for a waiter here, and I never saw one, save perhaps a small boy, in any similar eating-house I was in, so that it seemed probable that he was employed here, or allowed to work here, out of kindness shown to a relation fallen on hard times. The pale fat cook was perhaps married to his niece, something of that sort, and the girl had been obliged by her family to take care of her uncle when she had married, the uncle (possibly an Armenian) having blotted his copy-book politically, or fallen victim to a mania for gambling at backgammon in a far-off European capital. It was the way he laid his feet to the ground, with a kind of tender haste, as a carter drives old horses he must depend upon but fears to press too hard, that made his story a sad one.

He was just the kind of waiter you might have expected to serve you in Kars if, like me, you thought that everything about the town deserved marking with a red X in your memory. I had hoped that I'd find the eastern mountains safe, but I had hoped too that I would find them worth coming to see. As I walked back through the dark streets, amongst those inexplicable ruined walls and empty spaces of Turkish towns, where rubbish heaps stirred with rats, and when I saw the frosty stars look down on the outline of the black citadel, I never was less disappointed with reaching an objective in all my life.

V

❖❖❖❖❖❖❖❖❖❖❖❖❖❖❖❖❖❖❖❖❖❖❖❖❖❖❖❖❖❖❖❖❖

I

I always hope I'll get over those restless little worries that scamper about in my head when I haven't been able to plan my next step, which is usually, as I've said, some means of leaving the place I'm in. But I know it is a condition of my mind inseparable from travelling. I resent it for the same reason I resent all those minor themes – thinking about gardening is another – which recur and recur to fill up my head with their unworthy clutter, just when I should like to be concentrating on grander issues.

In Kars I got up very early, and breakfasted in the dark, my room very cold, off honey and tea, in my determination to catch the first bus possible to Erzurum, and so to improve my chance of finding another bus that day onward to Trabzon. I hadn't been able to find out the times of the buses, but I had a plan. Downstairs I asked the hotel keeper, who was the only man who understood a word I said in all Kars, to send a boy to buy me a ticket on the first bus to Erzurum.

It worked. At seven o'clock, in a frosty dawn, I was waiting by an old bus amid a crowd of passengers. Worries let me alone to look outward instead of inward. Dawn had by no means begun the life of the town, but growing light revealed the bustle of humans and animals in full swing around the shacks and puddly streets. Sheep nibbled any grassy spot, and boys rattled by driving pony carts with a calf or two balancing in the back on frightened legs. A man in ragged furs and a lambskin cap tied a couple of goats to a lamppost whilst he popped into a shop. Up the street came a child pulling a cow by its halter. Soon the sun was up, and the town flooded in marvellous light. In a few minutes we had left Kars.

My word how the Turks cough and spit in the morning, smoking away furiously between bouts! The bus was a lot older and shabbier, and the passengers much simpler people, than any I had travelled with before. They stared into my face unremittingly. From the seats in front, from across the aisle, black eyes gazed and gazed, not quite with curiosity, for there wasn't the lively interest that curiosity implies, but in the fish–like manner of children watching a television programme that doesn't interest them. I to them was such a programme.

Just as you have to get used to enduring silence, not smalltalk, at a formal meal in the East, so you have to put up with being stared at – though not quite in the terrific way that Edmond O'Donovan was stared at whilst a prisoner of the Tekke Turkomans at Merv:

They gazed and gazed as if they never could stop looking at the external appearance of the Feringhee. It was the gaze of the operator while endeavouring to mesmerize his subject. Utterly impatient at not being able to get within reach of the peephole, or in line with the doorway, spectators tried to lift up the edges of the tent and introduce their heads . . . All the tent pegs being removed, the thing actually subsided upon me, nearly smothering myself and the more select party inside . . . I asked the old moullah if there was no means of getting rid of the persecution. He shook his head gravely and said surely I was not harmed by being looked at.

It is a difference between Eastern and Western manners. As Dr Sandwith noticed aboard a Black Sea steamer, a pasha's servants will stand before him as long as he chooses to sit still, 'gazing anxiously into that placid face. We have nothing like this strange adoration in the West,' he concludes, 'but from time immemorial it seems to have obtained in Eastern manners.' To be stared at is interpreted by the European as hostility, and has certainly often caused a resentful outburst from the victim which might indeed provoke hostility. Asiatics staring at a Western woman, for instance, can cause the man with her to react so rashly as to put their lives in danger.

We, on the other hand, are used to smalltalk filling up silence, and to contriving to take in what interests us most in our neighbours through the corner of an eye. In this way I watched a couple further up the aisle from my seat whose relationship intrigued me. The man was a wild fellow of thirty-five or forty, a stage ruffian, and he sat like a guard beside a very young girl, who threw glances about her with the tremulous appeal of a captive. Her hair was decked up in an embroidered headdress, she was swathed in heavy garments, a cloak of sorts overall, and her hands were contained in woollen gloves; but her glance was restless, and her dark eyes, as I thought, full of terror as they rolled this way and that. Was she a bride sold into marriage? Was he a Laze carrying her off to a remote village in the Pontus from which escape was impossible? There was about him an air of squalor and licentiousness – and about her an air of timid virginity – which made their union seem brutal, like a soldier riding off with his prize from a sacked city. So I thought, anyway, as we rattled along, and everyone but these two stared at me, and I peeped cautiously at them. But when the bus stopped in a village square, out he clambered over her, to reappear in a moment or two with a bag of sweets. These they shared, hands dipping together into the paper. No narcotic could have soothed her more effectually. Soon she folded herself up on the seat at his side, and laid herself down across his knees to sleep. They made a tender picture. My ideas of a robbers' nest in Lazistan faded away.

Out of the bus windows the villages I could see on the plain looked miserable enough, low outlines of mud which offered the wind no resistance, though blue breakfast smoke arising from them, and dabs of life and colour put into them by turkeys and geese and children, gave the scene a kind of morning cheerfulness. James Fraser describes quartering himself in one of these villages when riding *tata* (post) to Tehran with government dispatches:

The entrances [of the houses] were black-looking holes into which we plunged . . . we elbowed and fought our way through the throng of men and brutes to an inner apartment full of sitters and smokers where we were welcomed by an old man, and coffee immediately served to us . . . The walls, which were very rudely constructed of stone and wood, resembled much some of the old Highland huts you have seen in the heights of Badenoch or Stratherrick, or in our own Caploch [for Fraser's home was of course close to Beauly, in Inverness-shire].

I looked at the low mud oblongs of the houses, in those days inhabited by Armenians, whom Turks and Russians have between them removed from here, and wondered if you could still walk or ride across this country and find lodging in a village. Maybe hippies wandering to India still do, or would if both Iran and Afghanistan weren't now impassable. If you found a Westerner at all in one of those huts, it wouldn't be a Queen's Messenger like Fraser, it would be one of those mild pilgrims with hepatitis and a pocketful of hash, who don't catch at my imagination as do the travellers of past times.

I was thinking of Fraser's Highland comparison when the bus was driving a little later through the pass at Sarikamis, for a fine trout river flows below the road there, and he was fond of fishing, astonishing the Turks by catching trout on the fly. I could picture him, or the Traveller I have in mind to write about, wading up this little river. Peace could be found in fishing the swift water between fall and fall, the noise of it clamorous in the mind so that no fears or worries could be heard beyond the happy ones of fishing. All flowing water is the fisherman's nirvana. To drive away loneliness or cares all he needs is the water amongst boulders and the wagtail bobbing on a stone, and the world may be forgotten in the intentness of dropping the fly just there! – where even a Mussulman trout must seize it. A tenderness for highlands goes with the love of fishing, and I think Highland sympathies, perhaps Jacobite feelings imbued by a boyhood spent in Scotland, fit in with the character whose story I plan to tell. There is also, I think, in most travellers a trace of the aggressive hardihood which is natural to the Scottish, and which shows itself at its best in indifference to cold and to minor discomfort, and at its worst in taking Calvinistic pleasure in inflicting cold and discomfort on others. The tendency to wade across rivers which might be crossed just as easily on stepping-stones is a Scottish trait often found in a book of travels.

As we cleared the pass there appeared now and again through the bus window a snowy peak far away, a summit of perfect form higher and grander than all other mountains, gleaming above the ranges to the south-east. I was anxious to believe that this was Mount Ararat. The pass was at a height of 7,000 or 8,000 feet, Ararat is about 17,000, and some eighty miles off, so to see it from that road is not an impossibility, for no mountain thereabouts anywhere near matches it in height. Anyway, I certainly consider privately that I have seen Mount Ararat.

At eleven o'clock we swung into the bus station at Erzurum, a youth in a sharp suit leaping aboard the bus before it stopped, to tout for fares to Trabzon, which made my little worries comfortable again. I had a couple of hours to wait, but I didn't go into the town, which is at a distance from the bus station, content, now that I had seen Kars, to remember Erzurum by the pictures of it painted into my head by Robert Curzon. There was in the citadel a dungeon, according to Curzon (who was here on the staff of Colonel Williams, twelve years later to become the 'Hero of Kars') – a dungeon into which the pasha, like the king in a fairy tale, cast anyone who tried, and failed, to mend his watch. At that time this fate had befallen a Frankish doctor, no doubt one of the renegade Italian or French adventurers without a scrap of medical training who imposed on Mussulman credulity to follow a dangerous and picaresque existence in the East. Arthur Conolly came across one in Asterabad drowning two vipers in a large bottle to make a brew 'selon Galen'. Ignorant they might be, but in Islamic darkness they were 'monoculus inter caecos', as Palgrave said, who himself crossed Arabia to Ryadh and the Gulf in the character of a Syrian *hakkim*, equipped with enough drugs in fifty tin cases 'to kill or cure half the sick men of Araby', and an Aesculapian treatise in Arabic. A book of travels purporting to be the memoirs of one of those renegade Frank doctors could be as entertaining, and as illustrative of Eastern manners, as Morier's *Haji Baba*. The only doctor's travels I know of are those of a respectable Englishman called Madden, whose frontispiece shows an intriguing fair hand extended to the medical man through the curtains of the harem, for in theory the pulse at the wrist was all of a lady's person that might be examined before a diagnosis was made.

In windy sunlight I lounged about the bus station, watching a huge black old steam engine shunting across the plain under a mighty column of smoke, or drinking tea, or writing postcards to anyone who might, like me, think Erzurum a far-off and romantic spot to get a postcard from.

Whilst I was writing my postcards on a bench a Turkish student speaking painfully broken English ('my special subject') sat down beside me. At once he asked me how old I was. When I said I was forty-three laughter rolled from his open mouth, and he crowed out, 'But that is very old! You are very old! Yes you look very old!' No contempt, no pity, just a droll fact he thought I should appreciate, told me, I think, without the intention of being rude, but with the frankness of the starers in the bus. I felt, not so much old, as utterly at sea in a culture where such remarks are made. Questioned about my education I told him I had been at Cambridge, at which he shouted out, 'But it is famous! Famous place! I wanted to go there.' Other students lurking about the place sidled up and were introduced, hangdog youths kicking their heels in the bus station, looking for some scrap of interest upon which to fix their flat-eyed stare. I remembered how amazingly dull are the conversations you are likely to have with strangers who don't speak your languages, and returned to writing postcards.

The bus left at one o'clock, full as ever, myself in an aisle seat, which is always a disappointment, but bound none the less for Trebizond, which of all names in the world can hardly be matched as a conjuror of past greatness, distant scenes, and ideas steeped in romance. The storm effects in the valley leading to Aşkale were marvellous. Flying cloud and cloud shadow were driven across the empty hills – twisting white spirals of snow dashed down on summits – the storm-blast blew plumes of dust off the villages like the smoke of explosions – sudden fierce onslaughts of rain hit the bus windows. It was the first rain that had fallen since I left Belgrade, that wonderful weather week after week the best possible luck I could have had in crossing a country which, in autumn, can be full of tales of mud and woe. Beyond Aşkale we left the road I had come by from Kayseri, and the valley of the Euphrates, and climbed steeply through eroded hills dotted with oak scrub. From the heights of the pass of

Kopdaği Geçidi, and a last view southward over a vast prospect of central Turkey, we went racing and bouncing down, deep down, into valleys watered by streams and lit with yellow poplars.

This is a wild region. What happened to Dr Sandwith here, and the way he tells the adventure he nearly had, shows both the dangers of travel, and the style in which the narrator depicts himself as meeting them. Whilst resting in a posthouse – whose keeper he compares significantly to 'the old innkeepers of the Black Forest, such as we read of in *The Mysteries of Udolpho*' – the Doctor observed two or three men

whispering together like the bravoes in a tragedy. Certain words of ominous import fell on my ears. 'The Giaour has been, or will be, killed' was muttered by one of these ruffians. I at once arose from my seat, and walking up to them, asked, 'What it was all about; what had been killed, or had to be killed?' The postmaster then told me, that just before my arrival, that very morning, early as it was, a man had been murdered by robbers at the very door of the stable in which I then found myself.

All they knew was that he was a *giaour*, and they had buried him not a gunshot from the stable door. An hour before, a man bleeding at the mouth and soaked in blood had galloped to the khan and staggered off his horse. Immediately there had appeared his pursuers, four or five banditti of the hills, who fell upon him and beat out his life before rifling the corpse and riding away. Soon his Turkish servant had ridden in, and had told how they had been stopped by a band of Lazi, and how his master, a French officer named Belliot, had killed a couple of them and attempted to charge through the rest, receiving a ball through the body as he did so. 'Poor fellow!' says Dr Sandwith,

I felt a strong sympathy for him, and admiration for his gallant bearing; although he had succumbed to numbers, he had yet sold his life dearly, and taught these Paynim hounds that a Giaour of the West is not the spiritless, cringing, Christian of the East, degenerate from ages of oppression . . . I ordered out fresh horses and galloped onwards, nursing my wrath against the murderous crew through whose country I was riding.

Bayburt, which we soon dashed into, was the headquarters of the subsequent hunt (by the French consul at Erzurum with an army of *zaptieh* and bashi-bazouks) for Belliot's killers – a hunt utterly frustrated by Ottoman wiliness and indifference, for if there was one thing a pasha found more tiresome than another, it was the fuss Europeans made when one of their number was murdered. As the Emir of Bukhara said to Dr Wolff, 'How wonderful! I have in my empire 200,000 slaves, and no one ever came from Persia to ask after any of them, and here I have killed two Englishmen, and Dr Wolff comes with a Bible in his hand, and demands these two!' Whilst my bus waited under some trees in the street of Bayburt I walked about in the sharp mountain air, and drank some tea from a stall. The shell of a castle surmounts the ridge, and curtain walls, much decayed, follow the contours of the hillside above the town's roofs. Curious that mountain towns in whatever country share a quality of substance, solidity – Swissness – which you don't find necessarily at lower altitudes. I suppose keeping out cold and snow governs their design, and so makes mountain towns seem to share a nationality, where towns upon plains are infinitely various. So it is that highland tribes of whatever nation have much in common. The driver drew sonorous blasts from his horn, and we were off again into the mountains.

The speed of the bus, and the corkscrew road, now began to tell on the passengers. There had been delivered to the *otogar* at Erzurum by a chauffeured car the only bourgeois people I had ever seen on a bus. A superior dry-looking man in suit and tie, very possibly a dentist, had brought with him a fifteen-year-old daughter, dressed like himself in old-fashioned rig. I had noticed that he dusted his seat with a white hand before placing himself in it, briefcase on knee, to stare severely out. During the journey he had not spoken once to the child, nor looked at her, his disdain for us all isolating him even from his daughter.

But pained disdain for bus travel turned to dismay when the girl began to be sick. She was repeatedly sick into plastic bags which he was obliged to handle. Each time she began to heave he snapped his fingers hastily at the conductor, who issued the bags and then flung them, when full, out of the speeding door. The pace really was terrific, the road narrow, steep, and a succession of hairpins. In front of me a fat Turk with a large family spread about the bus shouted furiously at them, and cuffed the heads of any who came in reach as they staggered about the bucketing vehicle, the poor little creatures moaning dismally as they were sick on the floor and on my feet. Beside me a gargantuan soldier munched food with his mouth open. The wilder the mountains, the tighter the bends, the faster flew the bus. Regardless of the scenes of misery behind him, our driver hurtled onwards like the heroes of old, his courage in overtaking trucks never daunted by the blind corner, the precipice's edge, the swirling cloud.

I've suffered from car sickness all my life. A mile through lanes in the back of a car makes me queasy. Now I refused to feel sick. I breathed deeply and looked out of the window. Once it was established in my mind that I wasn't going to be sick, I gave myself up to the recklessness of the ride as you would to a helter-skelter you can't get off.

This is mountain scenery of the most magnificent variety. At Kale stands an old blackened castle in a desperate pass, the rushing river between sheer rock walls, the wild sharp mountains upreared against the sky. From the heights above Torut, in the very matrix of mountains, such a wilderness of peaks and winding valleys as I never saw before lay below us, threaded with rivers gleaming up through the smoky, cloudy light of evening. This is scenery for the hand of the illustrator, and the vocabulary of the narrator, to work upon until they produce together a volume which will satisfy the romantic expectations of the armchair traveller. Here the crags 'beetle', the cliffs 'frown', heights are 'dizzy', chasms 'yawn', and the rivers are all 'cataracts'; a deft exaggeration of heights and depths and verticality, and you have ready-made those engraved illustrations by Allom or Bartlett, or Edward Lear, which depicted what readers wished to see, and certainly expected their story-teller to endure, in the wild regions of the world. It was an odd taste. The poet Gay, after all, had pulled down the blinds of his coach when passing through Cumberland, for the sight of even a small hill offended his ideas of order. Mountains, like earthquakes, were abhorrent to the Age of Reason. Then came *The Mysteries of Udolpho*, and

The Castle of Otranto, Gothick mysteries leaning heavily on cliff and chasm to deepen their horrid effect. Horace Walpole is the first man I know of to have spoken favourably of the Alps. Tourism began with tours to mountains; I suppose such fearful regions, like travel amongst wild tribes, appealed to that instinct in man which values the reverse of what his age is tending to create. So the Victorians pined for beetling crag and frowning cliff. Edward Lear tells of an Italian describing to him a nearby view as 'un luogo tutto orrido, ed al modo vostro, pittoresco'. The picturesqueness of the horrid was the traveller's stock-in-trade.

By these engravable passes through the Pontus came all the men, and all the merchandise, to reach Persia and the East by way of Trebizond. I could follow here and there the old track traversing the precipices, a line scratched into the rockface, now climbing out of the gorge, now falling to the rapid water's edge. It's hard to tell how hair-raising a journey it was: sometimes a traveller would pass over it in a couple of lines, eager to recount direr hardships elsewhere – 'I will not detain my reader with the description of a route now so well known' – sometimes, if the narrative requires it, an author will dwell upon the terrors of a track above the abyss like 'the top of a wall'. It all depends. Robert Curzon, who had lain insensible with brain-fever at Erzurum for twenty-seven days before being restored to consciousness by an earthquake which knocked down half the town – 'The earthquake accomplished its mission: in the midst of terror and destruction, it restored one poor creature to life' – Robert Curzon requires ten pages to tell how he was dragged and carried in a litter, in midwinter, through these passes. He describes how ice had to be cleared off the narrow shelves of rock bearing the path, and how ponies and mules had to be lifted round corners too sharp for them to negotiate, and how they came upon a party of Persians seated in a row on the ledge of a precipice, looking gloomily down at their caravan of pack-horses which had all fallen over it; he describes a spot, a break in the ledge, where a servant had to lie down and act as a bridge over which he in his litter, and the mules and ponies, were carried or pushed. Yet Arminius Vambéry speaks of the pleasure of travelling 'from

Tabreez to Trebizond on a good post road', and all that good Dr Wolff says of a winter journey from Erzurum to Trebizond is that 'the road was so thickly covered with snow that Wolff was obliged to take two Arminians to dig him through it, and the savages scarce gave him anything to eat'. I found myself wondering, as the bus thundered through mist and cloud, meeting on blind corners trucks loaded with firewood from the beech forests which plunged towards us between rockface and precipice, if they lost as many travellers off the footpath in those days as they lose in bus-smashes now.

We stopped once more, at Gümüşane, where in old days there were silver mines whose inefficient working came in for a good deal of sharp criticism from travellers anxious to instruct the Turk in how to manage his commercial affairs after the British model. Passengers well enough to eat took their meal in a café; several now looked really ill, the dentist's daughter comatose with exhaustion, others, too, lying dejectedly about the bus. I found a grocer's shop open, bought some biscuits and dried apricots, and ate them as I strolled about the dark streets, the sound of a river in spate not far off filling the night with its wintry roar. Then we drove on.

The scenes of despair were like those between decks in a slaver, the captain crowding on sail to escape the pursuing man-of-war. At last, through mist and darkness, I saw pine trees lit by the headlights, and shrubs clinging amongst the rocks, and many wild briars. Soon the beeches grew larger, the woods thicker, and our descent towards the Black Sea began.

I've never thought that Xenophon's *Anabasis* is a particularly enthralling work, but there is no doubt of the dramatic intensity of the moment when those lost Greeks, in these hostile mountains, cried out, 'The sea! The sea!' and embraced each other with tears on their cheeks. It is an imaginative stroke lighting up the whole work: that scene is known to thousands who never opened Xenophon. For this reason it was well suited to the kind of classical exegesis with which the nineteenth-century writer (Lemprière's *Classical Dictionary*, and Bishop Butler's *Antient Geography*, to hand) could flatter his own and his reader's scholarship. He would make out a case for this mountain rather than that being really the Mount Theches from which the Ten Thousand saw the sea – and argue learnedly about the route the Greek mercenaries had taken from Mesopotamia – and his readers would relish the feeling of taking part in a scholarly argument, their imaginations still ringing with the echo of that dramatic shout, their eyes still seeing the soldiers stumbling forward towards the shouting and cheering of the van.

I was very glad to reach the Black Sea myself after a journey of seven and three quarter hours. At the Trabzon bus station the passengers dispersed in their usual magical way. There seemed to be no *dolmus* into the town on its hills above us. I took a taxi, the first I had hired since my arrival at the Athens station, and told the driver to take me to a hotel described in my guide-book as 'limited facilities, but interesting nineteenth-century survival'. I regarded the words warily, but still they attracted me. Because guide-books are written by the partial, the horrors of a country which first strike a stranger go unmentioned, overlooked by the guide's accustomed and enamoured eyes. And misnomers in my guide-book – 'simple restaurant', 'nice hotel', 'pleasant tea-room' – continued to delude me by suggesting to my mind their English, not their Turkish, meaning: tea-room still implies Hovis and cup-cakes, and always will. Thus my guide's admission that facilities might be limited struck a dire note.

However, the hotel didn't exist, or couldn't be found, and I was taken instead to the Otel Usta, best in town, where the usual downstairs carpets and greenery petered out above into sparse comforts in narrow rooms. I ran out to eat some supper at once, and was delighted with the steep lamplit streets, the cobbles, the sunken green in the *meidan* containing fine trees. Soft lights on the trees and coloured houses, and the warmth of the night after the Armenian highlands, cast a peaceful glow over the town as I walked about looking into the eating-shops. So this was Trebizond!

I chose a *kebabci* and went in. Staff and customers were grouped round a television set, forks halfway to mouths, spoon idle in the cook's hand, eyes intent on screen. A coup? Entry into the Iraq–Iran war? I pushed into the circle. On the screen, direct from Cardiff, Turkey was playing Wales at football.

2

In the recesses of his imagination everyone, I believe, must carry a secret map given him in childhood with the sites of treasure trove marked upon it where the rest of the world sees only a town's name, and to travel is to try and reach these sites, pickaxe in hand, hoping against hope for the ring of its blade on the buried casket. So, wakening early to the feelings of a boy on his birthday, I pulled open the curtains and saw, beyond the roofs of the town, the shining waters of the Euxine. Trebizond! The pick struck gold.

After breakfast in a café under the plane trees I walked out of the square eastward by a cobbled street which allowed, between houses, a glimpse down steps, or down alleys, or over gardens and red roofs, to the blue sea in the bay below. It was enchanting. Fronting the street were old houses built cheek by jowl in any number of styles, no doubt by the merchants and consuls of many nations when Trebizond regained its prosperity as the port for Persia in the 1830s. There were wooden balconies in the Russian fashion, and rickety-looking structures of timber like the *yalis* of the Bosphorus, and workmanlike stone villas you might see along a riverfront in France, and they had in common the feature that surmounted almost all of them, a kind of rooftop loggia open on all sides to catch every breeze of summer from mountains or sea. Most dignified of the houses was an Italian palazzo glimpsed through ironwork street gates, a noble affair of cut stone and tall windows, whose columned portico hung out dreamily over the bay.

Of course every building was far gone in decay or misuse, some being tenements, some garages, some empty shells with broken windows and boarded door. Yet in the midst of decay I came on an open space where stone blocks had been tumbled into heaps for the building of a new mosque. Amongst them was an old man in a skullcap chipping a smooth face on to each block with hammer and chisel. How that chip and tap, which I now heard amongst the ruins, must have resounded on slopes and shore when merchants were building their houses here. Between

1830 and 1840 the value of trade through this roadstead, in opium and arsenic, and leeches and rhubarb, as well as in Manchester prints and Brummagem knives, increased from £10,000 to £1 million.

The bay now was empty, except for one Russian coaster tied up at the quay. But the dockside, to which I went, was overwhelmed under mountains of merchandise, and cliffs of crates and containers stacked high. The Persian border being closed, here at Trabzon the log-jam of goods piles up. I found that the Russian coaster was taking on grain, otherwise the port was idle as I made my way through the silent labyrinth of canyons between cliffs of cargo, till I came upon the office of Turkish Maritime Lines. In accordance with the promise of the timetable I had seen some months before, in London, the boat for Istanbul was expected at noon next day. The charges weren't high – cheaper in fact than the rate between Piraeus and Rhodes which I'd thought such a bargain at the time – but I found them steep now because I was used to the absurdly cheap bus fares, so I parsimoniously booked myself a second-class berth for the two-day passage to the Bosphorus, pushing from my mind the adage of middle-class travellers, 'First on boats, second on trains'.

I had before me a day and a half in Trebizond; the sun shone, the town delighted me, and my way forward was safely booked. Though I had turned for home, I had still ahead of me the uncertainty and strangeness (to me) of making my way through Eastern Europe from Istanbul to Vienna, so that I didn't have the flat feeling of free-wheeling home you get when you reach an airport and buy a ticket for London – that feeling which is like losing your wicket in a cricket match, and having nothing left but a walk back to the pavilion. Life is not over – indeed it has to be admitted that life proper begins when you leave the playing field – but what matters for the moment, your innings, is over.

I wanted to walk out to the church of Aya Sophia, a mile or two west of the town, so I left the *meidan* by the bridge spanning the gorge which moats the citadel. Under the bridge, in a deep cleft, are hut roofs beside a green stream, and festoons of vines scrambling up the walls of the old town. On a chair outside a tree-shaded café I had a glass of tea amongst old men playing backgammon. Here was an impression, given by the stone buildings, and the narrow streets, and the old men on rush chairs around the café door, which had the stability of a scene in Europe, maybe in southern Italy, unlike the towns in Anatolia, where makeshift contrivance makes you feel that the place is in the hands of transients. The restlessness of Asiatics – their nomadic lack of attachment, most obvious to a stranger in their indifference to buildings – makes the settled peoples of Europe uneasy. 'Where the Turk treads, no grass grows' was a saying apprehensively coined by Europeans when the Turk appeared at the gates of Vienna.

Very quickly, too, I had walked through this little enclave of permanence, under the citadel and towers of Trebizond, to emerge on a straight road driven through dusty wastes of demolition stretching into the distance. On one hand concrete tenements obscured the sea, on the other rose hillsides speckled with buildings. I passed a university, a football ground, and a hospital. From this last emerged a crocodile of nurses two by two, many of them in such fits of giggles as they passed me that companions had to be clutched tightly if nurse was to remain upright. Despite this I walked on, dust and light in my eyes, deafened by heavy traffic bucketing along the gravelly, pot-holed road.

It's sad that there seems to be so much to complain about in Turkey's 'modernization'. Unfortunately modernization, in all but a handful of countries rich enough to afford nostalgia, consists in pulling down just about everything that the tourist from those few rich countries would like to see, and in putting in its place all that interests him least about the provincial cities of his own land. The truth is that few individuals have ever travelled, in modern times, to see what other countries are like nowadays; in general people travel in search of traces of past eras, and they have in consequence almost always been disappointed by what exists when they get there. (The ruinous state of Turkey, for instance, has been frowned at by European travellers certainly since Thevenot in the seventeenth century, provoking that slightly nervous abuse of the nomad which you find in children's stories about gypsies.) I suspect that Turkey has always looked as though it would have been perfectly wonderful if you'd come twenty years ago. The disappointments are brought about by the mis-preparation of your mind for what really exists; yet it's the mis-preparation – the treasure trove buried in your mind under certain place-names in early days – which draws you on to travel in the first place. Perhaps if I'd known what it's really like in most of Trabzon nowadays, I wouldn't have come. Only by not knowing, by refusing to listen, by insisting on setting out with pickaxe and secret map, can you hope to find Trebizond.

It wasn't easy to find Aya Sophia at all amongst the high-rise blocks, but when I did come upon its churchyard gate, I was told that the church was indefinitely shut. Suddenly, though, I had emerged from the engulfing buildings, and the magnificent situation of church and graveyard on their windy headland broke over me like light after tunnel-dark. The sky soared blue over the ancient building, the sea shone beyond it, and not less blue than sky and sea were the flowers in the wind-flattened grass that grew up to its walls. I could not go in, but the place was wonderful enough. Strange to see, in the recesses of the porch arches, those solemn angels' faces from thirteenth-century Tuscany, as they seemed to me, painted in fading colours. Of these frescoes Robert Curzon wrote (touching a peak of casual lordliness hard to match even amongst bibliophiles): 'The only ones equal to them are the illuminations in one odd volume of the Μηνολογία in the Vatican library, *and some in my own*.'

I picked a blue flower from the grass, in which sea and sky seemed to combine, and angels too, for that matter: I sat on the sun-warmed wall of the headland: I looked out into the wind which beat upon me from the sea. Out of the dazzle of light and water, distant and white, appeared a ship coming from the West. She was no doubt the boat I was to catch tomorrow, when she had been to the easterly limit of her run, on the Russian border, and would be returning towards the West. Actually to see a white ship materialize out of the vasty deep – a reality where a mere abstract proposition in a timetable had hitherto existed – was to have the proof of theory thrust graphically into the mind. I could not help looking towards the east, her destination today, where the mountains of Circassia, above the mouth of the River Phasis, and the gate to Russian Asia, made a fragile line of snowy peaks painted in Chinese white above the blue eastern sea, hints of 'that untravell'd world whose margin fades forever and forever as I move . . .'

I looked back at the ship, and she came steadily on like a messenger from the West, her materialization reminding me, so to speak, that the bargain made in the timetable had (on her side) been kept. The snowy peaks of Circassia would have to remain a painted horizon until another journey.

I returned on foot into the town and walked through the bazaars looking for one or two presents to take home, and thinking of Robert Curzon's comment, in the 1840s, that 'the bazaars of Trebizond contain a good deal of rubbish, both of the human and inanimate kind'. (He makes, too, another comment of the superior kind with which travellers like to expose the ignorance of all but themselves on Eastern matters: 'I do not know why Europeans persist in calling these places bazaars: *charchi* is the Turkish for what we call bazaar . . . The word bazaar means a market, which is altogether a different kind of thing.') I was obliged to buy myself a Turkish Donegal cap, far too large for me, because I rashly admired it: the stallkeeper, insisting that I should have what I wanted, sent out for needle and thread to reduce it in size, as well as for tea to pass the time pleasantly whilst he sewed. He had been in Germany, but spoke no more German than I did, so that our conversation was very slow as he cobbled away with large uneven stitches at the hatband. No doubt if I spoke Turkish I would discover a thing or two from people like him; but if I spoke Turkish would I then be able to maintain my view of Turkey as mysterious and hostile territory, which is the tint most useful to my imagination in the task of resurrecting the Turkey of Ottoman rule?

In Trabzon I was very well aware of these threads of uneasiness lying like a network of nerves close under the skin of the place. No doubt I found what I looked for; on the way back from Aya Sophia, for instance, I had passed by a parade of schoolchildren, from five years old up to eleven or twelve, marching in step to a military band, whose martial music seemed to me to be thumping and blowing the little feet along the road like the kicks and cuffs of armed men herding crowds into order. A draught of the tyrant's breath chilled me as they marched by. Then, in the evening, when I was on my way out to supper, a power failure blacked out the town. In that sudden eerie dark, dropped over my head like a bag, tension surfaced. The rattle of running feet – the glimpse of a running figure bent low as he dashed past the flare of an oil lamp in a shop – made me look for pursuit, listen for gunfire. I seemed to be alone in the street.

Then up came the lights, on walked the people, the runner and his darkness somehow vanished together, and I went on my way to the Trabzon Restaurant. It was the first self-styled 'restaurant' I had been inside since leaving Rhodes, so I had put on a tie for the outing. Décor ran to red tablecloths, dim lights, the tangles of a fishing net suspended overhead. These suggestions of the West made it all the more noticeable that there wasn't a woman in the place, and made me realize that I hadn't seen a woman eating out anywhere in Turkey.

Two more power failures before I got back to the Otel Usta didn't catch me unawares, as the first one had done; nevertheless, darkness seemed waiting to well up out of crooked lanes whose mouths I passed in walking about the streets after supper to see the effects of lamplight on the town. I was looking across the gorge at the citadel ringed with towers on its rock table, when the sudden stutter of static made me jump, expecting the 'Dikkat! Dikkat!' I'd heard in the streets of Ürgüp. I found that the crackle, as of a brazen throat being cleared in the darkness overhead, had burst from the necklace of loudspeakers circling the minaret above me. As those black mouths darted down fiery words on the town's head, they looked to me like the skulls strung round Kali's neck, which seemed to shoot out maledictions through the smoke and incense of an Indian temple.

Such views and uneasy feelings I brought on myself, as I say, by holding to the view of Turkey which best fed my imagination, rather as another writer might insist upon low candles and a dying fire before attempting a tale of terror. Turkey was not Iran, where the wretched victims of theocracy might well jump at brazen voices from minarets: nor was it Iraq, where a watcher should indeed shudder to see children stepping out to military music; even the running figure in the dark belonged to the Turkey of two or three months earlier, before the military seized power. Though not averse to atmospherics, I didn't want to start jumping at shadows. But before I left Trabzon I made a mistake of just the sort to be avoided by those with no curiosity as to the inside of a Turkish gaol.

Next morning, intending to visit the shop of an *antiquaire* – the first I'd seen in Turkey – whose window, crowded with oddments, I had passed the day before, I went to a bank displaying a CHANGE sign which I had also noticed on my rambles through the town. (Expecting difficulty in cashing traveller's cheques in the east of the country I had changed enough money in Konya to supply me till I reached Istanbul, so I only wanted cash to buy any small thing that caught my eye in the antiquary's shop, whose window seemed to contain the sweepings of old Turkey, such dusty objects as the tiny brass pattens a Circassian girl might have worn to keep her feet out of the mud on an errand through the streets.) I entered the marble and glass of the bank. A sub-manager, into whose section of the open plan office I was shown, studied my £20 traveller's cheque minutely. Startled eyebrows and an over-large moustache made him look like a shrunken Groucho Marx. He consulted a folder issued by Barclay's International in which my cheque was illustrated exactly. This too he studied with care, sometimes through spectacles and sometimes with the naked eye, the eyebrows doing a good deal of interrogatory work, fingers snapping every now and again for my book of traveller's cheques, or my passport, in order to extend his field of inquiry. I had expected slowness, and showed no sign of impatience. Tea was brought to him, and stood cooling on his desk, in front of which he kept me standing. I was offered no tea. The assistance of a meaty woman was next called for, and a consultation with her held whilst sugar was stirred into tea, and documents rushed to him from other parts of the room were signed absent-mindedly. He at last tapped the place on the cheque where I should countersign my name. This I did.

Now began the scrutiny of my signature. First it was compared with the original signature on the cheque, written in haste whilst signing it with forty others in a bank in Bridport; then it was compared with the signature in my passport. Both Groucho and the meaty woman, who smelt most unpleasantly of prawns, pointed out to me discrepancies in the way I had formed the 'z' in my name. I found my smallpox certificate: the 'z' was different again. On my International Drivers' Licence I showed them the 'z' made in yet another way. To me diversification proved that all were genuine. He preferred to believe, apparently, that all these documents had been signed by different forgers, none of them capable of copying a 'z'. To prove his point he had seized a piece of paper and begun signing his name with amazing rapidity, producing each time an identical hieroglyph. To prove mine, I too snatched pen and paper and scribbled my name a dozen times. The conclusions he drew from this were all that was discreditable, for he caught up my cheques and passport and ran clean out of the bank with them.

Through the window I saw him dodge across the street and dart up some steps into another bank in a building even newer and grander than his own (for banks must be excepted from the general decay of Turkish buildings). Knowing how long the simplest piece of banking business can take in almost every country outside England, I had kept my temper under perfect control for the twenty minutes or so which the man had so far wasted. It used to take almost a whole morning to cash a cheque in Italy when I lived there, though I had an account with the bank, and there I lost my temper every time I required money. Now I continued calm, though vexed, for the quarter of an hour in which Groucho was absent with my most essential possessions. I drank his tea, reflecting, as I did so, on Trebizond's decline from one of the greatest trading ports in the world's history to this nadir at which a £20 cheque in a hard currency took two banks all morning to cash. Worse news soon came.

In bustled the manager, in the very style of Groucho playing a buffoon functionary, and handed back my cheque, refusing to cash it. I lost my temper. In a stern but clear voice (mixing languages as the words occurred to me) I pointed out to him that the cheque, which I had dated and countersigned at his request, was valueless unless cashed by him, today. I found that he turned his back and began tidying his papers. Empty and half-empty tea glasses stood on his desk waiting collection. These I swept on to the floor in a glorious wet smash. Then I took up my cheque and passport and walked rapidly out.

I crossed the street to the other bank, where I found a melancholy-looking manager, as distinguished as the other had been seedy, who spoke a little French. Shaking with rage I told him what had happened. In response, sadly and quietly, he laid on the counter before me a cheque for £200 drawn by a Mr Macmillan, and returned to them dishonoured by his English bank. The nervousness of the Trabzon banking community in the face of English cheques was explained. Though I pointed out the difference between my traveller's cheque, which I had bought from my bank, and a personal cheque which a bank may dishonour, I remained linked to Mr Macmillan in his mind. He did not see how he was to recover his money for the worthless cheque, nor did he seem to grasp the English bank's meaning in scrawling 'Return to drawer' across it.

In his uncertainty and dismay I saw my chance. Calling for pen and paper I said I would write there and then to the embassy at Ankara and ask for their help in recovering the money from Mr Macmillan. Did I know the British Ambassador? he asked. Rather carefully I replied that my name was known to him, as was my presence in Turkey, which I hoped was the case, since he had been told by a mutual friend that I was travelling alone through the country. My credit rose. As I wrote the letter, a sheaf of new Turkish notes (the equivalent of my cheque) appeared at my elbow. Amid as much bowing and hand-shaking as could be managed across the counter – 'It is normal, a normal banking transaction,' he insisted quite correctly – I left the bank and ran down its steps into the street.

The instant my feet touched the street, a hand fell upon my shoulder. I turned. I was surrounded by police. Untrue to claim that my heart did not sink. There were five of them shutting me in against the wall, only one in uniform, the rest a blurred image of weasels in blue shirts and sharp shoes, and of heavy men in leather jackets. One of them demanded my passport, and took it from me. Would I come to the police station and answer some questions? I refused, and stepped back rapidly into the bank, managing rather deftly to recover my passport as I nipped through the ring and up the steps. In the bank I called to the manager. He appeared: the blood left his face when he saw me amongst policemen. Slowly he put down his pen and came over. He translated into French for me the question: Would I go with these gentlemen to the police station to answer a complaint that I had damaged property in another bank? Thugs and weasels took my measure. I took theirs. Like a medieval church, the bank appeared to afford sanctuary; it seemed the police mightn't act so hastily in view of a dozen or so bank clerks, as they might in a police station or on the street. I therefore refused to leave the bank until someone who spoke English was brought to me. At the police station, it was urged, there would be an interpreter. I appealed then to the banker to ring up the embassy in Ankara, to whose chief (I reminded him) I had just written on his behalf. Nobly, if sadly, he took my part. He would go across the street and speak to his colleague who had issued the complaint against me.

Surrounded by police like terriers round the heels of a man going ratting, my kind friend left the bank. Two men stayed to watch me. The style of these premises provided a gloomy pillared space for customers, encircled by counters behind which sat the staff. In this central space I strolled about with as unconcerned an air as I could manage. No pretence of work was kept up by clerks eyeing me with relish, and hoping for the worst.

At length the banker returned, having with him only the uniformed policeman, who dismissed my two guards at the door as he came in. My champion said that all was explained. Cashing my cheque, he had made clear to the police, was a normal banking transaction sadly mismanaged across the street. He too, he added, had a temper; but would I consent to apologize to his colleagues for smashing their tea-set? His refined face, and elegant figure, gave out an air of indifference to us all, like that of a French diplomatist obliged to act in a dispute between fuzzy-wuzzies. With him and the policeman I crossed the street and was presented not to the seedy Groucho, but to an urbane superior in an inner office who waved aside apologies and offers of compensation alike. On my way out I noticed Groucho's desk was deserted, his papers scattered. Attended by thugs and weasels, was he perhaps answering questions at the police station?

Still, I wasn't altogether sure I wouldn't find my escort waiting after all in a side street or shop doorway to take up the tale. I gave up my idea of visiting the antiquary. Keeping well out from the walls I walked rapidly back to the Otel Usta, entered my bedroom cautiously, locked the door and began to pack, for my boat was due to sail within the hour. The sense of precariousness in Turkey – which I had enjoyed and even cultivated – like ice you speed across for the thrill of it, had suddenly cracked. Yesterday, watching the white ship's approach from the west, with the mountains of Circassia sketched in above the eastward horizon, I had felt rather like a child at a party who sees his Nanny come to fetch him home; today I was glad to find the ship tied up at the quay, the timetable's promise kept, when I carried my bags down through the cobbled bazaars and went aboard.

I can see why the first phrase in the Englishman's legendary phrase-book is 'Take me to the British consul'. Like faith in the power of a British passport, and trust in an English policeman to help him out of a difficulty, this instinctual cry for official protection reveals the middle-class Englishman's essential belief in the justice of his own institutions, and in his right to claim their support. The case of Don Pacifico – a Jew with British nationality whose claim against the Greek government for the value of goods lost in a riot resulted in Palmerston sending the Fleet to Piraeus – enshrines such a view. In a speech embodying his ideas of England's magnificence, made on the case throughout a summer night in 1850, Palmerston compared the British subject to the Roman, who 'held himself free from indignity when he could say *civis Romanus sum*; so also a British subject, in whatever land he may be, shall feel confident that the watchful eye and strong arm of England will protect him against injustice and wrong'. See how he slides from 'indignity' to 'injustice', as though any indignity offered an Englishman by a foreigner was, *ipso facto*, an injustice: this is the very heart of the matter. There was the case of a Mr Churchill, a journalist of Galata, who peppered a Turkish boy whilst quail-shooting, and was in consequence seized and bastinadoed by the local police; where-upon the British Ambassador (with Palmerston's support) made such a to-do that policemen were bastinadoed right and left, and the Sultan's favourite himself was dismissed from office for a time. No one pretended that Churchill hadn't shot the boy; it was upon 'dignity' and not 'justice' that the matter turned. In the cry of the tourist, 'Send for the British consul!' an echo of this remained. I myself invoke the British Embassy partly out of Palmerstonianism, partly because I worked for the Foreign Office free of charge for a couple of years, as an unpaid attaché, so that I feel I may fairly claim a favour, if by merely touching the hem of the legation's garment I can help myself out of a scrape.

3

          The ship, a beautiful vessel called *Ege*, was three hours late in sailing. She took on cargo, chiefly grain, and I hung over the side, or walked through the lanes amongst the discharged cargo on the dock, or watched the Russian seamen lounging on their rusty coaster next to us. The dock crane, trundling to and fro on rails, announced from a notice that it had been given by the British government, and the *Ege*, too, is British built, all the notices on board being in English. Palmerstonians are pleased by that kind of thing.

At last, at five o'clock, came the casting-off, the shudder of the screw through every plank and rivet of the ship, the splash of rope ends in widening black water; and we stood out into the evening sea, whilst declining sunlight gilded the town's house-fronts piled up from shore to citadel, and the scene slipped rapidly astern. As we sailed westward the buildings of Trabzon thinned, became few, and rare, then failed altogether into empty mountains and a wild shore. Smoke-blue gorges opened up from the sea-coast into the foothills, whilst the fierce peaks of the Pontus rose behind. I stayed on deck till the light faded, and nothing could be seen but hissing wake on inky water.

The moment I asked my way to the second-class cabins, the staff's contempt for second-class passengers became plain.

Though my bunk in a four-berth cabin looked well enough, and the cabin roomy, I feared the worst like a new boy at school, and was on the look-out for slights. These soon came. Advertised freedom to eat supper whenever you liked between seven o'clock and eight was knocked on the head by a gong beating at six forty-five, and waiters like warders driving the second class into the hold to eat at common tables. I took my book, didn't speak, ate nothing. In the second-class lounge (described in English on its door as 'recreation room') simple families sat stunned into armchairs by the medley of television and wireless both booming in their ears.

As it seemed to me increasingly that the second class was oppressed, so a sense of grievance against the first class grew up in me. I read their menu, saw through their swing door little tables for one laid with snowy linen. Envy of this Eden soon led me to cultivate an active dislike of its occupants. I sat reading amongst them in the first-class bar, darting out furious thoughts of hatred at knitting wives and squabbling children and husbands noisily playing cards.

Yet above them existed another class to envy. Before the ship had even sailed I had been made aware of the existence of an aristocracy aboard. I had climbed a ladder to the topmost deck, hardly more than a platform round the funnel, and there I had seen wine glasses, and a bottle in an ice-bucket, on a table between a man and a woman seated on camp chairs. I had had the sensation of trespass on a private preserve, so had hardly looked at them before clambering down the ladder again. But I knew they were there.

Next morning I came face to face with this couple ashore. I found on waking that the boat had docked at Samsun, so I went ashore to explore for the hour or so we were to lie there. Against the hillside there remain a few apricot-coloured merchants' houses, with tall windows and red roofs, and to look at these I walked through deserted and grass-grown docks, past rusty shunting engines, out of the dock gates and through a confusion of streets under the hillside. The dwellings on the upper slopes stood back in tangled gardens, the colour-wash flaking from their façades, and from the pillars supporting their porticoes. It was hot and quiet in the roads round about them, and I stayed up there for some time, poking about, before I dropped down towards docks and ship again. Crossing a street in the dock quarter I saw the couple from the funnel-deck walking towards me. He was a large man, bald, with a big bare face, who trod along springily and silently, in rubber shoes and a short-sleeved shirt worn outside his slacks. Undoubtedly there was power of some kind at his disposal. The woman was insignificant in herself, though 'smart' in a glittery style. As we passed, the unpleasant lizard's eye of the man confirmed the poor impression always made upon me by a short-sleeved shirt.

On board ship, when we sailed on along the coast, these two disappeared again, though I visited the funnel-deck in search of them, and indeed sat on one of their camp chairs for a time under a rain of smuts. But it was not comfortable; nowhere was quite comfortable, except where I imagined them to be. This is the central problem of life afloat: it is impossible to combine shelter from draught with sufficient air and a tolerable seat, so as to make yourself perfectly comfortable, even though the sun was doing his very best to make the billows smooth and bright. I shifted from deck to deck, port to starboard, sun to shade, windward to lee, but remained restless. There was a plague of children, too, noisy little Turks in miniature grown-up clothes – the boys in bow ties, the girls in high heels and earrings – who clattered round and round the planking, screaming loudly. Their parents had made no preparations whatever to entertain children by bringing toys or games or drawing books to ward off boredom; instead they sat sipping drinks (the first coffee I have seen consumed in Turkey) and knitting complacently, the women in dreadfully high heels and tight sweaters, the men lounging by, paying for fizzy drinks when required, chatting idly amongst themselves. (I thought as I watched them of a description in Creagh's book of a voyage on a Turkish ferry when an Aga's harem was kept on deck in a cage guarded by a Negro eunuch, food being pushed in to them through the slats. These passengers could be the grandchildren of such a ménage, so recent is Turkey's 'enlightenment'.) Meanwhile the children, bored and cross, rampaged in their new shoes up and down the iron ladders and round and round the wooden decks. Spoiled as far as indulgence goes, they were neglected of all interest and attention. I watched a girl of ten or eleven stare down into the seething water from the rail until she could endure her boredom no longer and turned in a kind of paroxysm to kick and punch her brother. Perhaps, however, these children will say when they are grown up that their parents took them everywhere, even on the Black Sea, and that they enjoyed it tremendously; whereas my children will only be able to say that their father went away for months and months when they were little, despite his protestations of affection.

Gloomy reflections and discontent were brought on that day by the recognition that I wasn't well. I had woken up feeling wretched, but had hoped to blame it on a Turk who had snored fit to bust all night in the bunk above, pausing only for a moment when I banged and thumped at him. (I wasn't surprised that he had to spit most of the contents of his lungs into the basin on rising.) By lunchtime I felt worse. That first chill certainty that good health has deserted him is a disagreeable moment for the solitary traveller. I know of no more graphic description of the onset of illness than this account of Fraser's of his plight quite alone in a Persian town in the 1830s:

Till then I had been perfectly well and strong, but on rising I thought I perceived the slightest sensation of a *swim* in the head: on going out, a slight thrill of something between heat and cold, and a little obscure shoot down one leg, gave me a mental twinge, and made me pause and look up to ascertain if the feeling belonged to the night, or to my own frame. Have I caught cold? thought I. On return from the stables the case became clearer. The hot uncomfortable eyes, and one or two thrills in the head, with some other shootings and twitchings about the praecordia, declared the disagreeable truth too plainly for mistake. I was in for a fit of fever. I immediately set to – finished closing my packets; refused all dinner except a cup of tea; took seven grains of calomel, and was in bed by ten.

Because illness was one of the chief dangers to be met with, the traveller uses it, like other perils of the road, to heighten his drama. The difficulty is that he mustn't make himself out a valetudinarian: he must thoroughly alarm his reader without ever

163

letting on that he was frightened himself; he must recount dread symptoms, and the fear of worse, without compromising his hardihood of mind and body. Kinglake, in Cairo during a very severe epidemic of the plague, tells how one day he became too ill to eat and, afraid his servants would abandon him if they knew the truth, how he wrapped up his dinner in *The Times* newspaper and threw it out of the window after dark. He had not in fact caught the plague, but an impression of wonderful sang-froid is created in the reader's mind by the passage, especially since he describes the probable fate of the traveller who succumbs: 'The next night he becomes "the life and soul" of some squalling jackal family, who fish him out by the foot from his shallow, and sandy, grave.'

A stoical attitude towards illness is easy enough to maintain when you are perfectly well, but, once ill, the difficulties of life itself, let alone of travel, grow insurmountable; for it seems that your grip upon events, and upon your own affairs, is utterly loosened so that they may batter you where they will; a kind of general vulnerability, of body and mind, is brought on by illness, and it is not the preceding passages but the one which follows, from Fowler's book, which strike on my ear the authentic note of an account written during illness, rather than long afterwards, in restored health. 'On my solitary mat,' Fowler says, 'I had full time to ruminate on my travelling adventures, finding myself quite alone on the wild Asiatic soil, a prey to disease, wasting by fatigue, with only Mahommedans for my guides and the banditti for my neighbours, feeling gloomy forebodings that I should never more see Ferengistan.' This plaintive tone seems to me the one I should echo if ill and alone in a distant land. As it was, pretty certain that I only had a cold, I took large quantities of vitamin C in soda-water, wore both sweaters, and hoped for the best.

Towards dusk we approached Sinop. I was curious to see the gulf where the Turkish fleet was destroyed at anchor by a Russian squadron which appeared out of the mist one November evening in 1853, sinking every ship but one, and drowning or burning to death 3,000 Turkish sailors. A low headland mottled with scrub shelters the bay, wide and flat, where a few fishing boats lay on gentle ripples which caught the evening light. As the *Ege* was warped up to the quay passengers looked down from the decks on to a great bustle amongst the barrow-merchants awaiting us there. The human drama was not lacking. I watched an agitated little baker arrange the flat loaves on his barrow a dozen times as we approached, before he had them to his liking with the best-baked foremost; then, at the last moment, the ship's gangway already rattling down, a stout coster with a barrow of fruit pushed the poor baker aside and took his place. I should think the same thing happened every time a boat docked.

I bought some roast chestnuts and ate them as I walked into the town at the end of the long mole. It was cold, the autumn air sharp, dusk falling on shore and streets. Square towers of dark stone are joined by walls and pierced by gateways. The Russian squadron bombarded the town as well as sinking the fleet, cutting in half the maidservant of the British consul as she ran across her garden, and obliging the skipper of an English brig to spend the night in a tree to avoid robbery or murder at the hands of any Turkish sailors who had escaped ashore. I walked about the streets eating chestnuts, seeing nothing memorable except the flame of virginia creeper leaping up the chimney-black town walls, and mosque-domes and minarets opalled with the last light of the sky. Nothing happened, there was nothing to record; but Sinop joins all those places I've seen, whose picture may dart at any time into my mind like the burst of a firework for vividness, though years hence, and light up as it bursts ideas it has associated with in the mind's store. It's the famous sights that make you set out from home, but it's the accumulation of vignettes that 'deck our little path with light'. *Haec olim meminisse juvabit* – the day will come when it will gladden the heart to remember this – is a fragment of antique wisdom which reassures me when saddened by the transience and waste of what passes.

The deep and solemn blast of the ship's siren summoned me back towards the seashore and further darkness of the bay. On the quay I came upon an intriguing group. At the centre of a circle of deferential Turks – evidently a delegation of small fish dressed in its best and sent out to do a big fish honour – was the large bald man with the lizard's eye, his lady on his arm. I heard flattering laughter for the words he let fall in Turkish; his complacence, and spacious gestures, showed me that he was used to being toadied. Past the group ran many a humble passenger towards the bellowing ship, and scampered up the gangway. The Lizard and his lady came aboard last, not troubling to return the obsequious bows of the delegation, and the gangway rattled up behind them.

On the boat, as before, they vanished. Was he a director of the line? A merchant? That he was in origin English, or part English, I was certain. Of course he had a state room. That there existed, in the background, such superior accommodation as I conceived this man to be enjoying, made me less appreciative than ever of the second-class dining saloon in the vibrating depths of the ship when supper came. I could eat nothing, feeling distinctly unwell, my symptoms distressing the kind little waiter and earning sympathy from the two young encyclopaedia salesmen sharing my table. Both were pleasant, and one spoke good French. They had been selling encyclopaedias to the inhabitants of the mountains between Trabzon and Erzurum, a difficult task I should say, but the solace of their lives was photography. All day I had watched them lugging tripods and haversacks of equipment about the ship, setting up at one place only to discover that the ship had changed course before their arrangements were complete, so altering the light that all must be removed, with whatever girl they had secured as a subject, to another deck where the sunshine fell to their liking. They were friendly, but the food was poor stuff and the saloon a wretched hole. Worse conditions, bare planks, are tolerable if you have made the best arrangements possible; but travelling second class on the *Ege* was not making the best arrangements. That was my complaint, exacerbated by sore throat, aching eyes, light head, and all the horrid legion of miseries which now attacked me.

I was walking round the decks before going to bed when I came upon the ship's upper crust once more. Six or seven of them sat in a sheltered corner of the boat deck, the lamplit table between them littered with the wreckage of a rich meal – lobster claws, wine bottles, peach skins – all the tanned faces inclined towards the corner seat, the choice spot, where the lamp's rays illuminated the Lizard. He spoke English, but not with the accent of an Englishman. They listened, leaning towards him. Two were American, a cumbersome elderly couple, the man in a plaid jacket, whom I had noticed sitting glumly on deck with a bottle of whisky between them all day. Two were swarthier than Europeans, no doubt Levantines of the mixed races – Greeks, Armenians, Jews – which have controlled trade in these parts since the fall of Troy. One was a solitary man in his thirties leaning back in his chair, smoking thoughtfully, his hard, dark face the only one not bent to catch the Lizard's purring words. I watched only as I passed. I can describe it clearly because I saw it clearly, framed in the void of night and water, like the glimpse a passer-by has through the window of a rich man's house. I should have liked something to have happened which would have developed what seemed to me the potential of the picture, but nothing did. I walked on.

You are very open to the suggestive in scenes of travel when you are on your own. And suggestiveness of that sort, striking you forcefully, tempts you to invent, or at least to embellish, so as to convey to others the force of what you have felt yourself. The impulse to write fiction is felt strongly, I think, by travellers. 'Literal accuracy is immaterial,' says Walter Houghton in discussing Newman's *Apologia*, 'because autobiography is an art. All that Newman's words have to do is to convey the essential quality of his past experience.' Incidents need to be developed or run together, events shaped, characters touched up, drama heightened, if the reader is to appreciate what were the traveller's real feelings at the time. For the reader's appreciation of the reality of travel, it is more important that the book's author should be a born writer, than that the events narrated should be the literal truth. A capacity for graphic description anyway shapes incidents into stories in the telling of them. A single event, thus shaped by two men, may be made to serve two different purposes, and so emerge in a different form in each of their accounts: yet neither lies. Here is the account of an incident in the mountains of Luristan, described first by Layard, who was riding with a party of marauding Bakhtiari:

It was scarcely dawn when we saw in the distance a company of horsemen. We could not make out whether they too were marauders, or peaceful traders on their way to Shuster. My companions made preparations to fall upon them. Hidden behind a rock, I watched the party as they drew near, and thought that I perceived among them a European wearing a cap with a gold lace band. I begged my Bakhtyari friends to remain concealed until I could ascertain who this European might be. Approaching him, I called to him in French. He was not a little surprised to be addressed in that language by a Bakhtyari, for whom on account of my dress he at first mistook me. I found him to be the Baron de Bode, whose acquaintance I had made in the Shah's camp at Hamadan.

Layard warned his wild comrades of the inadvisability of robbing a Secretary of the Russian Embassy, and they let the Baron pass. 'It was only some years after,' Layard finishes, 'when I met him in a London drawing-room, that I informed him of the danger he had run, had I not restrained Au Azeez and his followers.'

So Layard describes it, making a picturesque and telling point, which informs us of his easy intimacy with Bakhtiari camp and London drawing-room alike. But the Baron de Bode, too, wrote a book. As concerned as Layard to paint scenes in which his courage and hardihood will shine out, the incident as Layard tells it obviously won't serve de Bode, and he merely mentions in an aside how his suite mingled with some down-at-heel horsemen on the road, amongst whom he recognized an Englishman who had once been presented to him at the Shah's court. No; the bold Baron, to get his effect, and to show how dangerous to himself was the ground he intended travelling over, must look elsewhere. He therefore begins his book with as gloomy a passage as ever I read, even in Russian fiction, in which his suite passes, as he sets out from the Russian Embassy at Tehran, the very spot on which the entire Russian diplomatic mission had been murdered a year or two before.

I don't at all object to this. The narrator must turn himself into the Hero, if readers are to follow his adventures sufficiently eagerly, and to achieve this requires selection and embellishment, even invention, so long as verisimilitude – dramatic truth – is the aim. Created in this way, the Hero is the narrator's alter ego, rather than his own self. Into his creation the writer builds, out of his own experiences, the heroic attributes which society extols, and expects from the adventurous traveller.

I was thinking about this, whilst the ship slid softly into the night, and I watched from my seat at her stern the wake which glimmered away behind her into the eastern darkness of the Euxine, when I was made aware by the glow of his cigarette of a shadow leaning on the taffrail not far from me. A man stood smoking, elbows on the rail, looking back eastward into the darkness like myself. There was an impression of power in the way his light suit seemed strained to contain his physique. His easy stance at the rail had the assurance, even complacence, of a man who wins fights. When he lit another cigarette I recognized in the match-flare the individual who had sat with the upper crust at their supper on deck, without toadying the Lizard as the rest had done.

As a heroic alter ego for a book of travels he could hardly have been bettered. In the darkness of the Black Sea he gleamed with the attributes of the Hero. I might have invented him . . . I was wondering idly what to do with the ideas he put into my mind when I suddenly saw, very clearly, why it was that there had been two horsemen, not one, riding ahead of their servant over the seven-arched bridge of stone across the Araxes at Horasan. One was the narrator, the Traveller who was to be the protagonist of my novel; the other was his alter ego, the invented companion whom he would make into the Hero of his travels.

That the protagonist should invent a hero who would accompany him on his travels struck me as one of those brilliant ideas which, to the writer, galvanize the matter gathered together for a book, but whose force cannot well be explained to a reader except in the finished work. I don't expect anyone else to think it was a brilliant idea. But I sat enthralled: even ill-health receded for a while. The traveller's impulse to shape events, to heighten drama – to write fiction telling the real truth – would have its outlet in the fabrication of this heroic alter ego. The gap between literal truth and dramatic truth – the gap between the two men on the bridge at Horasan – would be the device by which I would frame the characteristics of the Traveller I wanted to depict . . .

When I became aware of things around me again – the shudder
of the boat, the gently surging wash, soft sea, soft dark – I found
that I was alone. The shadow from the taffrail had gone. Rather
stiff and cold, I, too, went below.

4

We didn't reach the mouth of the Bosphorus
until three o'clock next afternoon, steaming all morning within
sight of low flat land which had succeeded the mountain ranges
to the east. As usual with a cold – for cold it was – I had the
muffled and watery sensation of inhabiting a diving-bell at the
bottom of the sea.

For thirty years or more I had been eagerly looking forward
to seeing the Clashing Rocks which guard the entrance to those
straits between the Euxine and Byzantium which we now
approached. In *Fabulae Faciles* there is a picture which shows
Jason, hero of his travels, standing upright if apprehensive in the
bow of the *Argus*, dove in hand, whilst behind him the rowers
roll nervous eyes upward at the frowning crags and gloomy sky
which threaten their destruction, and around them an inky sea
licks inkier rocks. Of these rocks the text warns: *si quid in medium
spatium venerat, incredibile celeritate concurrebant. Easy Fables* – ! I
was profoundly intrigued by this image of the Clashing Rocks
from early days. Now I looked out eagerly from the prow of the
Ege for black moving cliffs wreathed in cloud at whose base the
sea moaned. Notoriously difficult to find, though its headlands
are capped with squat castles, the straits at length opened before
us. Alas, the Symplegades are a ledge, a reef, black indeed but
low, not cliffs at all, though the sea managed a little snarl of
white fangs as it dashed over them in spray. *Easy Fables* had
misled me. But I was not disappointed: here I saw the source of
the myth, like the source of a great river in a spring under a
muddy hedge, which doesn't in the least diminish your awe of
the rolling waters which that spring is to become.

The wooded winding channel of the Bosphorus which you
first enter from the Black Sea soon degenerates, I'm afraid, into

shores littered with buildings and bays made ugly by hulks rusting at anchor. Three winters ago, living alone for six weeks in St David's in West Wales, I imagined these romantic shores so vividly to myself (when I was writing a novel set in Constantinople in the last century) that I painted in my mind an image of the place which eclipsed what I really remembered of it. Not this, but the Bosphorus of Bartlett and Allom's engravings, were the waters I had set my tale beside. Never mind, I'm used to wrecking the magic of things by writing about them: very little of the mystery of a place or an idea survives the scrutiny required to sort out and to put into words what it was about that mystery sufficiently intriguing to have compelled you to write about it. The spell you have parsed works no magic on you: 'when the clouds are scattered, the rainbow's glory is shed'. Knowing this, I expected to arrive in Istanbul where I had imagined Constantinople.

However, the last grand sweep of the Bosphorus past the marble splendours of palace and mosque and water-stairs, when you first see the hoary old Tower of Galata rise above Pera's terraced roofs, and the Golden Horn busy with ferries opens before you as watery foreground beneath Stambul's domes and minarets – that arrival has an inextinguishable magic. It has a dreamlike quality. It intrigues and beckons and, like a mirage, disappoints. It dissolves the minute you land. The approach by water is a fiction, which you can spend the rest of your visit hunting for. This dissolution of the distant magic of an Eastern city into dirty lanes between blank walls, and heaps of offal poisoning the air, has been the subject of complaint from Western travellers since Marco Polo. 'But whoever would paint the horrors of semi-barbarism in their most vivid colours, has only to land and wade through the abominations of this den of disease,' wrote Edmund Spencer. We feel tricked by the veiled city which shows us her beauty once, and never again.

I hated the place when I first went there. Innocents abroad, we had booked a hotel without knowing its situation, and the bus we took from the airport drove us into Istanbul – it was at night – and then slap through it and out the other side, to our surprise and dismay, as if the city really was only a mirage. The one solid fact we had to hang on to from the middle of the illusion was the moment when the bus had stopped outside the Pera Palas Hotel, and we had seen through massive doors the indisputable reality of marble and mahogany. To this we clung. Next morning our hotel floated in a mist, nothing was visible save flat water, a jetty, boats occasionally materializing out of nowhere; but we clung to that glimpse we had of certainty in the midst of flux, and, navigating through the mist by telephone and taxi, we fetched up before noon at the Pera Palas, and based our feet at last on solid rock amid shifting eastern sands. We still disliked the city, though the hotel was our solace. There seemed to be none of the superficial attractions which make a tourist's stay pleasant: no proper restaurants or cafés that we could find, no elegant streets or shops; in stumbling about the steep broken pavements we saw nothing but shabbiness and confusion, eyes full of dust, interest baffled and rebuffed. We almost left in disgust. Then one day on a Bosphorus ferry an old man in a long snuff-coloured overcoat came up to me on the rail and spoke to me in French. Other impressions accumulated: a villainous cook in a skullcap carving *doner kebab* in the Egyptian Bazaar and laughing to himself as he forced his wares upon us; the courtyard of the Imaret Muzesi; certain glimpses of Bosphorus villages; a nightingale singing in the cypresses of a burying-ground; walks I took through the streets at night, and the crowd upon the Galata Bridge. I began to catch behind all this the siren song, and in the plane on the way home I scribbled the outline of *Byzantine Honeymoon*. Whilst I was writing the book, in the cottage of a friend in St David's, I came across a copy of Layard's *Early Adventures*, and with that my real interest in Near Eastern travel began.

Now, to me, the *Ege* steaming into the Golden Horn from Trebizond, and tying up at the honey-coloured façade of the Customs House by the Galata Bridge, fulfilled a good many of the rules of romance. Still, I was anxious to be sure of a room at the Pera Palas. It had, I knew, been closed down because of a strike by its staff, but my friendly encyclopaedia salesman told me it was open again and promised, what was more, to drive me there and insist on them taking me in, for his wedding reception had been held there and he counted on his pull with the management. Since his car was aboard the ship I had to wait till its turn came to be lifted ashore by crane.

From the deck I watched the boat unload on to the cobbled quay. It was a swarm of individual activities. First ashore were the upper crust, the bewildered American couple and the Levantines, followed down the gangway by blue-jacketed *hammals*, bent by the weight of suitcases into the attitude of slaves in an Assyrian carving, their thin stalky legs working away like pistons attached by straps to bulky loads. Cars waited for them. In piled the baggage, in climbed the powdered American woman without a glance at ship or quay or Stambul across the water, in piled her husband in sky-blue slacks and tartan jacket, pushing away the porters' appealing hands angrily, and away they drove. I felt anxiety to get ashore and get on with life on terra firma, for activity on the quay made the idle ship seem abandoned, and myself left behind amongst stewards with their feet up and piles of dirty linen in the passages. The rattle of passengers' feet shaking the iron gangway mixed with the clatter of the crane and the stevedores' shouts. But the crane's claws selected cars out of the hold in so inconsistent an order that only a bribed crane-driver could have explained it, and my friend had evidently not bribed him. It seemed that every car would be chosen before his.

I watched peasant families unload piece by piece, armful by armful, journey by journey, every item of a household dismantled a week or so before in an Anatolian village. Children lugged bedsteads, men staggered under cookers, women hauled sacks, or carried jars of food between two, young girls slaved to and fro under load after load, carrying so painfully such heavy burdens, their feet clicketty-clacketty on the metal gangway against the ship's white side; and all the time cars and cargo, swung out on cranes, came lurching and spinning down on their heads till a casual shout from dockers in heavy gloves scattered them to safety. The peasants removed their possessions from the boat with the intentness of ants removing eggs from a smashed nest. They were embarked on a great adventure, and families threw themselves into this work of emigrating, glad no doubt to have work to do which quieted fears and sorrows.

One thing I watched which I have thought of often since.

There was a mother in her thirties already established in Istanbul whom I saw reunited with her son of eight or nine, who had arrived with the rest of the family on the *Ege*. The strength of their love impelled them towards each other, the boy running over the cobbles of the quay, face uplifted, throwing himself into the kept promise of her arms. But the minute he was sure from her touch that he possessed her love I saw him shun it – turn his face from her kisses – go limp in her hug as if love was a bore. She knew the need which had driven him over the cobbles into her arms, and she feasted in her heart on that. She had brought him a magazine which he took eagerly, and sat down then and there on a heap of belongings to look through its pages, whilst she turned to organizing the rest of the family. The magazine was *Stern*; no doubt they were going to Germany, Istanbul only a first step into the unknown. Whatever the uncertainty, or stress, or tears for their far-off home, I was sure that her cheerful round face burnt by the sun, and her plump hands with the silver wedding-ring indented in her finger, would supply the strength the family would need. I was glad of the chance which had delayed me on deck and let me see them. You can feel sorry for people submitted to an ordeal; but the moment you understand that they are equal to the test, then it is admiration, or even envy, that you feel.

In watching them I had missed my friends' car being swung ashore. They waved, and I ran down the gangway and got in, and the old jalopy was soon rushing uphill through tall stone-grey streets towards the Pera Palas, my heart in my mouth in case those Americans with their taxi had bagged the last room. From envisaging first-class life on board ship I was used to Them having what I wanted; I'd forgotten that, ashore, thank goodness, there is the Hilton for them and the Pera Palas for me.

VI

❖❖❖❖❖❖❖❖❖❖❖❖❖❖❖❖❖❖❖❖❖❖❖❖❖❖❖❖

I

I don't believe there were more than half a dozen people staying at the Pera Palas, and none of them looked as though they were enjoying it anywhere near as much as I intended to. At dinner, in vast arched recesses of the gloomy halls, there sat at widely separated tables three Turkish soldiers whispering together and an elderly single American who looked, I must say, like a man who would change his hotel next day. Soup, fish, mutton, pudding, were carried gravely towards us across tracts of carpet by waiters obliged suddenly to dodge and hop out of the warpath of a swarthy little girl on a tricycle who rode out at them from behind a pillar, pedals whirring, plaits flying. She rode up to each table, too, and stared long and hard into the face of each diner. Meanwhile another girl, a teenage sister, trotted across the carpeted and columned horizon in jeans now and then to change one tape of rock music for another. The music beat the air faintly; or perhaps its loudness was extinguished in the heights and distances of the dining-room, which extended into such dim regions that mist seemed really to have formed beyond reach of the lamps which lighted that fraction in which we sat.

When you find that your own idea of perfection in the hotel line is shared by so few, it isn't surprising that there are only a handful of hotels like the Pera Palas left round the world. Hotels are built, after all, to make the tourist feel at home, and that, nowadays, means that the home of the mass tourist and of the commercial traveller must be copied, whereas, when the Pera Palas was built (or any of the magnificent monuments to the *belle époque* of hotel building), 'home' to a majority of visitors was a

Victorian country house – or, if it wasn't, they would have wanted the hotelier to think it was. So, at the Pera Palas, once behind your mahogany door off the long dim corridor, what you have is the bedroom of a Victorian country house with an Edwardian bathroom added to it. When the porter had gone, leaving me master of solemn wardrobes and chests of drawers, of plush curtains and Turkey rug, of broad white bed and comfortable white space in the bathroom, peace entered my soul. Home at last!

Though the comic element is part of the treat, I have to admit that I laugh ruefully. Such gravity and dignity make a solid floor underfoot which I stamp upon, even while laughing at it, and recognize as reality – I mean 'reality' not quite as it exists in everyday life, but a copper-bottomed standard of Reality (rather like *Coronation Street*) once known and now lapsed from. I suppose a Victorian country house probably is my idea of home. In which case to find here beside the Bosphorus such a matrix – such a chunk of Reality set down in this doubtful shadowy city – is wonderful luck. I made a tour of its public rooms to digest the sombre pleasures of the place. Lights glittered dimly in huge looking-glasses: huge pictures, huge portraits, enormous palms in brass pots, sofas so uncomfortable, and so exposed, and so very large, that nobody ever sits in them; the forbidding ponderousness of all this didn't at all make me feel that I was mistaken in feeling at home here. The idea of home transcends aesthetics and mere discomfort of an earthly sort; the grass and leaves of Paradise were no doubt softer to Adam than the downiest mattress thereafter. By way of baroque lift, by marble stair and dusky corridor, I mounted contentedly to realms of bliss.

2

Still, wonderful as the shell of the place is, in fact because the carcase of the hotel is so splendid, I felt it my duty next morning to declare war on management and staff to prick them into keeping up the standards within. I refused to accept that I couldn't have breakfast in my room, or that they wouldn't do my washing. Soon breakfast appeared at my door, delicious as ever, and my washing I deposited tied up in a dirty shirt on the foyer desk as I went out. I was determined to use the solid floor, which the hotel put under my feet, as a base from which to extend my acquaintance with the city, until I had faced out what I had felt before to be its hostility, and strangeness, and confusion. I hoped to make myself as intimate with the streets as I felt with the corridors of the hotel.

So I set out my first morning through steep streets twisting down to the Golden Horn under a warm misty sky. There were two unusual factors about Istanbul at that time. One was the curfew, imposed from midnight until five o'clock in the morning, which had a strangely silencing effect on the town at night – silence isolating the quarrelling of dogs, which was heard far and near throughout the hours of curfew; the other factor was that the three-day holiday of Kurban Bayrami had begun, closing and quietening the city by day. I didn't want to shop, so I welcomed the leisurely uncrowded streets I followed towards the Galata Bridge, on my way first (of course) to the station to lay plans for leaving Istanbul by train to Sofia or Bucharest.

To me the streets and buildings of Pera looked magnificent. The mighty banks, the stone façades, how imposing and sturdy they were, how European was the severe dark architecture shutting out the sky! Could these be the same streets I had thought so shabby and broken-down when I first came to Istanbul? The streets in which I had felt myself lost in a dismaying Asiatic city? The difference was, that then I had come by air from England, and juxtaposed Istanbul with London. Now I set Istanbul beside Trabzon, Kars, Kayseri, Konya – I saw the capital in the context of its provinces, as all capitals should be seen.* No judgement of a country's capital is worth a straw that isn't made by eyes and mind conditioned by the sights and experiences of its villages. Air travel has pushed this principle aside – you judge one capital by another, and both by the one you started from – but it hasn't invalidated it. Fly to New Delhi from London, and the place is a joke, a muddle, a collection of drab little suburbs

* I know that Ankara is officially the capital of Turkey.

straggling round the shabby colonnade of Connaught Place; come to the same town from the villages of Mysore, and you gape and gasp at the pace and glitter and dash of capital city life, and the great shops and hotels, and the leafy 'Colonies', and the gleaming cars. This is what Vambéry says of Tehran:

The Persian capital appeared to me, when I saw it again, as the very abode of civilization and culture, affording to one's heart's content all the pleasures and refinements of European life. Of course, a traveller from the West, on coming to the city for the first time, is bitterly disappointed in seeing the squalid mud hovels and the narrow crooked streets through which he must make his way. But to one coming from Bokhara the aspect of the city seems entirely changed. My first ride through the bazaar made me feel like a child again.

There is no more important effect of travelling by land than this fact, that you approach the principal cities by way of their own provinces, and accordingly do them greater justice.

As I crossed the bridge towards Stambul I felt that this fresh judgement of mine about the city – made more humbly and a little less from the outside than before – already helped put me on terms with it. Respectful awe is the proper emotion in face of so ancient a seat of power. On that first morning, when all difficulties of onward travel had dissolved in the discovery (made in an empty and peaceful station) that a through-coach ran once a week on the train to Bucharest, I thought I'd walk myself into knowing the city.

My view is that you have to drum a town into your head with your feet. You have to walk till you're lost, and then slog on till you're lost no more, and at last the plan of the city, and the relation of one quarter to another, and the distances and gradients between them – and the very street corner where one quarter changes into another – is mapped out in your mind. I used to hate standing on corners consulting a dog-eared street-plan with that forlorn look of the tourist, but I've got over that now. I sit on a bench in a park if I walk through one, or at a café table if I pass one by, and I mark down the places I'd like to have dinner, and the streets I might come and window-shop in, but I keep on walking till my feet have flickered over the town the way a snake flickers its tongue all over its food before attempting to eat it. You have to be alone to walk. Two abreast is too wide a front for an old city's pavements, and Indian file breeds impatience in leader and resentment in follower. Alone you can nip through crowds, and take short-cuts without explanation, and retrace steps when lost without apology. Nor are the distances in any town (except Los Angeles) considerable if you're used to walking in the country: three miles will carry you from one side to the other of the centre of most cities, so that if you're prepared to walk ten miles, and you don't mind your feet hitting pavements, you can knock the plan of the place into your head in one easy day.

Mass tourism makes no inroads into Stambul. The old town of khans and cobbled alleys is too baffling and dismaying to be sacked by tourists *en masse*. Ranks of coaches wait in the outer courts of the Topkapi Palace, more ranks are drawn up outside Santa Sophia: upon them are concentrated all the peddlers of souvenirs and ices, who line with their stalls the short walk which is all a coach-party is encouraged to take, the few hundred yards between Santa Sophia and the Blue Mosque. In the environs of one or two other mosques, and in the Grand Bazaar, you meet with parties of tourists, but in the streets and lanes of Stambul (by calling it that I mean to distinguish it from Pera, across the Golden Horn, always the Feringhee or Frankish quarter) I rarely met a single tourist walking alone like myself.

It takes time to walk, which few tourists seem to have, and walking shows you not famous sights but an accumulation of detail of your own noticing, which perhaps few tourists care to trouble with. No one can tell you where you'll find an illustration for the ideas dormant in your imagination. You have to look for that yourself: the façade of an old house, a child on a step, the barred window of a khan, a wooden house blackened by fire, the many details you can't take a bus to, which act as so many piles driven into a morass, each one helping to carry a yard further the solid road you are hoping to build into the heart of the city. By chance you see an incident which sharpens your focus, some graphic scene or occurrence which illustrates the text of streets and people. I can think of a couple of examples I saw that day, of striking little pictures which I would have been pleased to have invented, in order to express the characteristics of place and people.

I was admiring one or two of the old timber houses, fantastically carved, which still persist here and there, salt and sun whitening their starved planks, to give a country air to certain parts of the town, when I saw a young man labouring up the sloping street towards me under an enormous load of cardboard boxes. They were strapped and strung to him like the loads of firewood you see almost hiding the donkey carrying them, boxes of all sizes, the stock no doubt of a stall in one of the markets, which sell socks and plastic toys and nylon shirts, and a lot more gaudy things as well. As he passed me, the whole load fell off his back. Some vital knot had parted. Boxes cascaded to the ground, bursting open on the cobbles and scattering goods far and wide, some of the wheeled toys speeding away downhill, white shirts spilt from their boxes like corpses from dropped coffins. I looked down, horrified. He met my eyes and smiled. He shrugged resigned shoulders, parted resigned hands, sat down on a house-step, took out cigarettes and matches and lighted up. There were a number of people wandering up and down the hill. Most of them were young men, and most of them kicked a box or two out of the heap as they passed by, hands in pockets, and sauntered on after an incurious glance at the sufferer of the misfortune. Nor did the unfortunate resent their kicking his boxes. He had sat down upon the carpet of acceptance to smoke the pipe of resignation. To have done as I would have done in a Christian country, and helped salvage his load, would have been absurd. *Mashallah!* He and the passers-by could both mutter that sentiment (as no doubt did the passers-by in the case of the man who fell among thieves on the road to Jericho) which has no equivalent in the Christianity of the man-in-the-street – though Christian martyrs have given utterance to its equivalent at stake or cross. *Mashallah!* I saw it in action, that distinct idea of conforming to God's will without complaint, which is central to the Mussulman's character, and I walked away up the street myself, though I did not go so far towards Islam as to kick a cardboard box.

The second scene I saw that day, which struck me as an

illustration of Istanbul's remoteness from modern Europe, came about on the patch of grass outside an eating-shop where I had stopped for a meal in the middle of the day. I ate out of doors at a wooden table and chair set in the dust under a plane tree, where a tourist was evidently a less common sight than he would be in any small village near the Aegean coast of Turkey. Between my table and the street was a patch of grass enclosed by low railings, and over the grass coiled a dribbling black hose attached to a stand-pipe. Its free end was in the mouth of a large brown bear. He was asleep on his tummy, rather sadly, a shabby old bear, the chain round his neck attaching him to the railings, his paws reaching out for the hose which dribbled into the corner of his mouth like the flexible stem of a hookah. No doubt his owner was eating at one of the tables beside me. Water was a good deal in demand amongst passers-by, more so as the hour of the midday meal passed, and men leaving the eating-shop, who needed to rinse out their mouths and spit, or to dash water over face and hands, jerked the hose away from the grumbling old bear and tossed it back to him when they had done. I see the scene in my mind's eye when people complain about Istanbul, for it seems to me to illustrate, as I say, the city's Asiatic remoteness from the spot on the modern map which Western visitors expect it to occupy.

The city is less friendly than it used to be. Certain factors – the rise of Islam, a despotic government, decreased tourism – have created in the famous mosques a less warm welcome for Christian tourists than there was a year or two ago. Fences now keep us separate from the Faithful, notices prohibit this and that in sharp tones; we enter very much on sufferance. This seems to me right. Division should be visible, where deep divisions exist. The crass trespassing of the ignorant on to holy ground builds up a great head of animosity amongst the simple believers. Notices and barriers help prevent the ignorant from trespass, and remind visitors of their low standing in a temple.

To have your eyes widened, and your organ of belief stretched, whilst remaining discreetly submissive, seems to me a faculty the tourist ought to cultivate. If you look at the jewels in the Topkapi Museum you must at least keep a straight face when told what the 'emeralds' and other brilliants weigh. If you are not prepared to believe the literal truth of what you are being told about jewels, you should listen carefully to what the message is telling you about Turkey: laugh at the literal message, and you don't hear the coded one. Look at the 'jewels', and remember that the Baghdad of Haroun al Raschid, and of the *Arabian Nights'* entertainment, lay within the old Turkish Empire. Go then to the Room of the Mantle of the Prophet, and look at his gigantic footprint. It is very large indeed. The personal reaction, though, needs to be guarded against in case it blots out what is more interesting than your own affront – or should be more interesting to anyone who has taken the trouble to come to Turkey – which is, that you are given a window into men's hearts when you are shown the objects they venerate. Look through the window; if you snigger, you mist up the pane. When you have submitted to looking about you discreetly, and to observing with as little prejudice as possible those objects which the people who lived here wanted to believe in – or were required to believe in – then you are in a proper state of mind to walk about Topkapi Serai and learn from what you see.

To me it is the most oppressive of palaces. Indeed I hadn't meant to undergo another visit on this trip, but had walked in one day because the Archaeological Museum at the gate was shut. I hate its crooked passages and grim courts. The very plane trees, cheerful enough in the Gulhane Park outside, lose spirit and become sombre pyramids of whispers above trunks riven and shattered as if by torture. In and out of those latticed kiosks – up and down those marble stairs – at the mercy of unhappy kings – with what hopeless slippered footsteps must the inmates of this labyrinth have shuffled to and fro, their lives lit by uncertain glow-worm joys, and overhung by awful punishments. But if you criticize the way the place was run it must be remembered that the Ottomans developed their own system of government and court, which was not a tyranny imposed on a subject race but a system freely developed out of their own history. (Recent history shows that other forms of government imported from outside, parliamentary democracy, for instance, have insufficient authority to direct the contrary impulses of Turkish politics.)

Foreigners' criticism, and their shivers in depicting what they find tyrannical, are as supererogatory as the strictures of an African on the architecture of the Eskimo.

Many visitors to Turkey at all times have been concerned (as I am) to feel as strongly as possible the alienness of the place, not its familiarity. It is to feel the outlandishness of abroad that I leave home – to feel the full strength of its distinctive foreign character, and to come to terms with that. So I value the barriers I come upon which mark off my home ground from foreign territory. Emeralds and footprints of vast size, intimations of tyranny, the fearful courts of the Sultan – all serve this purpose of travel, all mark boundaries as deep and wide as the pool of the Danube between Semlin and Belgrade. I grow to like Istanbul more and more as the first hot breath of my resentment and perplexity clears off the pane, and allows me to look distinctly at the strange city I see.

In the evening of the first day I was there I walked back to the Sirkeçi Station, having decided that I'd go to Adrianople in a few days' time, and from there take the through-train to Bucharest, missing out Sofia, about which I did not have any very great curiosity. The station, so empty in the morning, now held a seething mass of travellers. Crowds overwhelmed the information office. When I fought my way to the guichet an indifferent girl made me understand that the through-coach was booked solid for weeks. It seemed that to try and see Adrianople (Edirne) was to invite misery, for the only train onward to Sofia leaves it at two o'clock in the morning. I couldn't follow my original plan, which had been to take a boat from Istanbul to the Romanian coast, for no boats ply upon that route. What should I do?

I hung about the station. The unwisely opened window of indecision let in the flies of worry. At such moments I know I'm capable of abandoning plans to see a city I've longed to see for years, for the sake of a ticket onwards, and for the peace and quiet which possessing a ticket brings. There is a danger of buying a ticket back to London. I left the station, and walked to the quay where the Bosphorus ferries depart, and bought myself a fish sandwich from one of the cockleshell boats bumping the sea-wall, in which they cook up fish in a black pan over a kerosene fire flaring away on the boat's bottom boards. The fading light on this fabled water – the smoky ferries slapping through waves tinged with sunset – myself in the midst of it fish sandwich in hand – the scene regained for me at once my delight in travel.

3

On my way home to the Pera Palas that evening I noticed, as I've often noticed before, the sign to the Tünel, which is an underground funicular railway carrying passengers up the hill from the waterfront to the heights of Pera. I had never taken it. I had only once ever taken a bus in Istanbul, when I was here before, and that had been disastrous because we had caught one saying 'Topkapi' on the front, intending to go to Topkapi Serai, and had found ourselves whirled far away to the Topkapi Gate . . .

It is true that walking about a town serves a distinct purpose – a preliminary purpose – but you aren't on intimate terms with the place till you can hop on and off its public transport. I know this, and I know my disinclination to take buses and subways in strange cities, which is rooted in a dislike of looking helpless, and of needing strangers' aid to understand what is so simple to them, the system of tokens or pre-purchased tickets or whatever method of paying your fare which is in use. I'd rather walk. But as I plodded up the hill to the Pera Palas – a hill I would have been wafted up if only I'd braved the Tünel – I knew I'd have to come to terms with Istanbul's transport system in the next few days. Taking taxis, and travelling first class if the train was at all crowded, were part of an aloofness I'd indulged in when young – the whole four or five years I lived in Italy I never took a bus or a subway – but which would seem now, even to me, as archaic an attitude as wearing none but handmade shoes.

So, next morning, I took the Tünel down the hill – you buy a token which opens the gate – and walked over the bridge to the station where I bought myself a second-class couchette to Sofia.

No extravagance could buy me what I wanted – a first-class sleeper on the old Orient Express – so I took what was available. Facing thus cheerfully in the direction of reality, I set out by bus for the Church of St Saviour in Chora beside the distant Adrianople Gate. Making use of any means of transport new to you abroad – borrowing a bike or a boat or a car – adds length to your stride, and when I jumped out of the bus at Edirnekapi I felt on more equal terms with the size and spread of Istanbul.

There are two sorts of freedom when you're abroad. One is the 'freedom of the like', the freedom of anonymity which you achieve by mastering the system used by natives – manners, public transport, language, clothes – in which you aim to be one of the crowd, and enjoy the crowd's liberties. The other sort you might call the 'freedom of the unlike'. In this the traveller is the solitary stranger passing through, detached, aloof, car-key in pocket when he steps off the plane, gang-plank only waiting till he has crossed it before the yacht sails for distant havens where no ferry calls. Crowds and timetables are avoided as a seabird avoids fouling his wings with the tar which hampers flight. I suppose most people would choose this freedom first; doesn't everyone who has the chance pick a seat to himself on the bus, or an empty compartment on the train, which gives him the illusion of private arrangements?

'You ride your own horse, and a servant with a pair of saddle-bags, and some rough and ready bedding, rides a strong pack-horse; and thus you may travel the wide East, from Constantin-ople to the Wall of China.' That was true independence, the means of travel recommended to the adventurous. Through country too dangerous or unsettled to travel by this means, disguise could be worn and a caravan of merchants joined, the equivalent of public transport; or, for a man with the Sultan's authority to hire post-horses, a very fast journey across the Turkish Empire could be made with the Tatar postmen and their escort of yelling *surijis* who kept up a desperate pace for days on end, as did Colonel Townley in a famous ride from Belgrade to Constantinople, a distance of 800 miles which he covered in five days and ten hours.

At this very gate of Constantinople where I now stood had

ended a ride with the Tatars which Layard made (in faster time, so he claimed, than Townley) from Belgrade: 'I reached Constantinople before dawn,' he says, 'and as some time was yet to elapse before the Adrianople gate would be opened – the gates of Stamboul were then closed between sunset and sunrise – I dismounted, and lying on the ground, slept until I could enter the city.' I climbed on to the ruinous walls and hollow towers beside the gate, and looked down on the spot where he must have slept. It isn't so much the extent of modern Istanbul beyond the walls which surprises me, as the vast extent of the old city within the walls. When the size of, say, London in the early nineteenth century is considered, Constantinople must have seemed a megalopolis to travellers.

Opposite this gate, under five marble slabs, were buried the heads of five Albanian rebels, and N. P. Willis, an American, was examining these marbles when

four men, apparently quite intoxicated, came running and hallooing from the city gate, bearing upon their shoulders a dead man on his bier. Entering the cemetery, they went stumbling on over the footstones, tossing the corpse about so violently, that the helpless limbs frequently fell beyond the limits of the rude barrow, whilst the grave-digger, the only sober person, save the dead man, in the company, followed at his best speed, with his pickaxe and shovel.

Willis then walked back through the city, which, he says, 'though in a city so thickly populated, was one of the most lonely walks conceivable. We met, perhaps, one individual in a street; and the perfect silence, and the cheerless look of the Turkish houses, with their jealously closed windows, gave it the air of a city devastated by the plague. The population of Constantinople is only seen in the bazaars, or in the streets bordering on the Golden Horn.'

He proceeded to visit the place pretty vigorously. An early priority was the mad-house: 'I have visited lunatic asylums,' says Willis with an air of self-commendation, 'in France, Italy, Sicily and Germany but, culpably neglected as most of them are, I have seen nothing comparable to this in horror. We entered a large quadrangle, surrounded with the grated windows of cells. In every window was chained a maniac. "Are they never unchained?" we asked. "Never!" And yet from the floor-ring to the iron collar there was just chain enough to permit them to stand upright. There were no vessels near them, not even a pitcher of water . . .' His description then becomes too distressing to read.

Everyone visited the mad-house, and everyone visited the slave-market, trying by bribery to catch a view of the white girls, Circassians or Georgians, whom the *giaour* was supposed neither to see nor to buy. Accounts of the slave girls, in the context of Victorian writing and painting, seem to me definitely salacious – whether the style is romantic or poke-in-the-ribs jocularity – as indeed is the habitual tone of travellers' accounts of harems and of encounters with women in the East in general. There are hints of intrigue covered by *chaddar* and veil, and enthusiastic appraisals of 'forms' and 'figures' revealed by bodice or shalwar or chemise, and accounts like this one by a fisherman of 'falling upon a fine bevy of Koordish damsels, clothed much in the original dress of Mother Eve. One or two plumped into the water, others tried to shuffle on a pair of inexpressibles whilst taking a good glance at the intruder.' It is the inexpressibles which turn the girls into Victorian misses, and the reader into a voyeur (who runs the risk of suffering what the Reverend T. R. Jolliffe, a sprightly clergyman, describes as 'the Thessalian sportsman's chastisement' for watching Diana bathing).

Yet Englishmen abroad were perfect tigers for condemning moral lapses where they could contrive to light upon them. On a Danube steamer Pridham of *The Times* reports that 'a portion of our female society gave unmistakable proof of frailty'; and the 'frailty of the fair sex' at Angora caused Captain Burnaby to shake his head. Murray, in his handbook to Northern Palestine for 1858, finds it necessary to animadvert against 'an unhappy Englishwoman whose sad plight garnishes travellers' books' for her connection with an Arab at Damascus;* and Lady Sale, who escaped the massacre of the English army in Afghanistan in 1842, cannot forgive 'so incorrect a personage as Mrs Wade' for her

* This was Jane Digby who, after enjoying three husbands and the favours of three kings, was married to the Sheik of an Arab tribe employed by travellers to safeguard the desert journey to Palmyra.

moral lapse during imprisonment by the Afghans. Even a puppet show – 'a beastly exhibition, from which we immediately retired in disgust' – deeply offended Colonel Stuart in Brusa, though slave-market and mad-house in Stambul left him unmoved. Worse even than a puppet-show, in the Colonel's eyes, was what threatened him in Persia when 'a youth with a smooth face and long hair, in woman's clothes, began to dance. We immediately ejected the brute.' (Mitford, on the contrary, says that these *luti* and *nautch* dancers are decent beside 'the gross indecency of an English ballroom where women half-naked to the waist dance polkas and waltzes in men's arms in a state of wild excitement'.) References to homosexuality are of course veiled and rare, the most open discussion of its prevalence in the East being in Palgrave's *Arabia*, where 'the nameless vice and "disgrace baboons are free from" ' is blamed upon Muhammad for creating a society in which women, 'too degraded for respect, may be also too despised for love'.

Having read no private diaries giving an account of such things, I've no idea how possible it was for a traveller to have affairs with Eastern women, but it must always have been dangerous work to 'pick the rose from the encircling thorns' – far more dangerous than to have homosexual relations – and it seems that the Russian Ambassador and his entire suite were murdered at Tehran in 1829 by a mob persuaded that Persian women had been decoyed into the embassy.* On the other hand Layard gives an account of himself and a friend being decoyed into a palace in Stambul by a mysterious woman who turned out to be the Sultan's sister; so like an *Arabian Nights* tale is the adventure, with veiled beauties beckoning from caiques and go-betweens hastening through midnight streets, that it doesn't quite have the ring of truth about it. It certainly could not be used in a novel.

I had come out to the Edirne Gate to see the church of St Saviour in Chora, and I walked down by steep cobbled streets

* Griboyedoff, the Russian Ambassador, a writer and an intellectual, harboured as political exiles the Royal eunuch and two Armenian odalisques, whom he refused to give up. The caravan conveying his corpse to Tiflis was met in a wild region by Pushkin, who wrote of him: 'I know of nothing happier or more enviable than the last days of his storm-filled life.'

from the walls to the church's forecourt. I had not seen the mosaics here before. Hard to think of a more stubborn medium to work in than mosaic, yet its flexibility in the hands of the men who decorated these walls is amazing. The range of expressions found in the faces, and their subtlety, seemed to me to match anything in fresco; and mosaic contrives an illusion of depth beyond what paint can do.

Very much struck by the beauty and gravity of those Christian faces, I began to consider what range of expressions it is that you find in the Saints. There is the wisdom of St John, the combative fierceness of St Peter, fortitude and resignation in many a martyr's steadfast eyes; then there is the meekness, and sorrow, and sweetness, of female Saints. In these faces there are many emotions given expression, but one above all is lacking, and it is a lack which strikes you with particular force if you have been looking much into the faces of antique statues, as I had done in Athens and in Caria, as well as in the Archaeological Museum here in Istanbul: in a medieval Christian face you never see that look of amused irony which distinguishes the portraits of antiquity, and culminates in the expression of Marcus Aurelius. Amused irony: perhaps the most refined mark of ancient civilization (and the one which appealed so strongly to the men of the eighteenth century, and set the tone they aspired to); such detached equilibrium was never to become a Christian virtue. Fervour is required of Christians.

I went to the Archaeological Museum several times whilst I was in Istanbul, and on my next visit, after seeing the Kariye mosaics, it occurred to me to look into those antique faces for the Christian virtue of Humility. It is not to be found. Humility was not a virtue in the ancient world. The only humble people you see portrayed in pre-Christian art are people obliged to look humble, against their will, by force of arms. On grave stelae you see often enough the marvellous calm acceptance of death, a noble sadness, but you see neither contrition nor humility, let alone the abject self-prostration common in Christian art.

This idea interested me for its relevance to the extremely humble and submissive role played by the Christian native of Eastern empires in the nineteenth century, a humility which aroused, as I've said, distaste in the Christian gentleman at finding himself linked by faith with such an inferior breed in the lands he travelled through. Only Dr Wolff, a German Jew converted into a Christian missionary, shines on every page of his crazy narrative as a traveller of pure humility in whose eyes every man he meets is equal. It was the rulers, not the oppressed, with whom travellers apart from Dr Wolff found themselves in sympathy, whether the ruler was a Sultan in Stambul or a Caesar Augustus in Rome. He would have dined with Pontius Pilate, not in that Upper Room, on the night before the Crucifixion.* Certainly it was the amused, ironic detachment of the Roman governor, and of Augustan Rome, which was the style he admired, and hit off in his narrative. The truth is that the virtues of the ancients – valour, temperance, wisdom, justice – must always have been admired by a ruling class above the specifically Christian qualities of long-suffering, charity, faith, hope and humility, which are the virtues of the oppressed. It is the central difficulty, which so worried Gladstone and many another Victorian scholar-Christian, of how to reconcile Homer with the Bible. I went and looked into Marcus Aurelius' face in one or two of the fine busts lurking in the museum's recesses. He is indeed a model for the Victorian gentleman. That look of ironic inquiry lights up his intelligent face just as it illumines his *Meditations*. Is he, I wondered, the only Roman emperor whose head was too large for his body? In most the reverse is the case – pea-head on vast torso, as with American footballers.

If ever you complain about overlit, overcleaned, overcrowded museums nowadays, as I often do, you should remember the Archaeological Museum in Istanbul. It is an untreated case. Dingy, chilly, damp, the dust and dirt mantling the marbles, statues not so much displayed as given house-room in the half-dark, attendants bent over feeble heaters like soldiers picketed by watchfires in a petrified forest, the stone vaults echoing your own footsteps alone: since the 1950s no European gallery has preserved such an atmosphere, once traditional for museum

* Lord Elgin is quoted by Laurence Oliphant as having said (in 1857), 'I have seldom since I came into the East heard a sentence which was reconcilable with the hypothesis that Christianity had ever come into the world.'

basements holding 'the marbles'. In Europe and America you get used nowadays to seeing objects of less than the highest excellence brilliantly displayed, showmanship outpacing worth. In the case of antiquities the fashion for this sort of showmanship amongst museum directors has coincided with the whittling away of their collection by scholarship – especially in America, where 'Greek statues' were collected at a rather bad time for fakes – so that you may find a brilliant light shone on a caseful of Greek fragments, and too brilliant a light altogether showing up the defects of Roman copies which ought properly to be covered in lichen, and discreetly closing a vista under the ilexes of an Italian garden.

In Istanbul the opposite of this trend towards showmanship is the case. Here are matchless creations you can hardly see in the gloom. Dust has greyed the whiteness of marble. Figures loom above one another in a confused crowd. I should think the place is unchanged since it was built in the 1890s, when the Turk had first cottoned on to the value of classical remains buried in his soil – their value, that is, in foreigners' eyes, not in his own, for only when the Sultan saw the museums of London and Paris and Berlin filled with objects he had given away to the first comer, did he commence collecting on his own behalf. No doubt the indifference to antiquity which delayed him so long in building a museum has kept him from modernizing it. The race of Osman, after all, is not descended by blood or by culture from the Greeks, as Europeans are, so it isn't surprising that Turks don't instinctively revere classical remains. All the upper floors of the museum were closed, as they had been the last time I was there three years before. The building appears to be falling to pieces.

But it is full of marvellous works. I walked about in the gloom for hours together, staring at things, and wondering why it is that I stare at them, these fragments of antiquity. What am I looking for? The open window, the sudden staggering view through it which exalts the mind. It is so rare. Here, for instance, is one figure only which threw open the window for me and let in the divine light, a nude of perhaps the fourth century B.C., its stone vibrant with every aspect, good and bad, of the female life force. All the rest is only interesting, only beautiful; if there was nothing else, nothing more, I would hardly cross the road to look at antiquities or art of any kind. Take the great sarcophagi in this museum, the Satrap's and those from Sidon: marvellously skilful as they are in craftsmanship, virtuoso carving, they exact from me the admiration you feel for a miniaturist, a maker of dolls' houses, something exquisite and perfect; I look and peer and try each side in turn, like a bird in a room fluttering at the glass between himself and freedom, but the window does not fly open. I look at such works, and I've come to love them and to learn a little about them, not because they are the objects of the search, but because I pass them in the search for something else, something more, like the two pilgrims I met in Caria who had hoped the ancient site would be 'something else', but who had hurried on elsewhere when they found that it was not.

Amongst the works of man, Christian mosaics and pagan marbles touch high points of achievement, but Santa Sophia compared to such things impresses its visitors like a phenomenon of nature which transcends human architecture altogether. Marbles and mosaics depend to an extent on the knowledge the observer brings to them; if they open a window, it is a library window. Such a place as Santa Sophia, on the other hand, engulfs mere knowledge like an earthquake swallowing the library whole, books, reader, windows and all, so that what you know seems very insufficiently puny compared to what you feel. In this Santa Sophia possesses the power essential to any of the man-made Wonders of the World that I have seen, which is the power to sweep aside all preparations made in your mind, and to hit you amidships with an original force which makes you stop and stare. The Grand Canal does that, and the Taj Mahal, and the skyline of Manhattan seen from Central Park; and so does Santa Sophia. First there is the hint of vast internal space glimpsed between massy columns, the effect of its magnitude broadening upon you as you advance under shadows in the half-domes like clouds, under gilt like dingy sunlight, until you are far from shore in the midst of the place, exposed to the total blow it deals you. Reverberant, multitudinous, the crowds with their many-echoing voices pay homage to the building itself, prayers of Muslim and Christian alike arising into those dim muttering domes like the smoke of incense mounting into the cranium of an indifferent god. On myself the solemnity and magnitude bear down with such weight that history and aesthetics are absolutely crushed out of me. Thereafter the building's presence up there on the skyline dominating the city – knowledge of what those domes contain every time I look up and see them there – has made me feel that I have identified the genius of the place, much as you feel that Vesuvius brooding above Naples is that city's *genius loci*.

My days in Istanbul went by. For a time the Pera Palas brought breakfast to my room, and did a little light washing for me; but one morning no breakfast appeared despite pleas and harsh words on the telephone, and when I went down to blow them up in person they pointed to notices printed in the night and plastered up askew on the columns supporting the cupola above the foyer, which announced the End of Room Service. It was like the work of the Jacquerie desecrating the pillars of Church and State. The Reality of the Pera Palas was cracking up. Perhaps it was time to go.

The way I had come to Istanbul, from the east of the country, and the time I had spent alone in the city, gave me a fitter appreciation of the place than I'd had before, and I was sadder at leaving than I had expected to be. When I had taken my bags down to the station, and had paid my bill at the Pera Palas, I returned to the old Tower of Galata and took the lift to its highest gallery. From the windy ledge I looked down affectionately at the city, quarter by quarter. Wrongly, but fondly – the delivery boy claiming friendship with the *grande dame* who has tipped him – I felt that I knew it well. I never used to wonder whether or not I would see again the place I was leaving, but I wondered now, rather sadly, how long it would be before I looked out next over this extraordinary view, or indeed if I ever would again. The light was beginning to go. There across the Bosphorus lay Asia fading into dusk, and there below lay the busy confused city on either side of the Golden Horn. I descended the tower, and the steep streets, and began to cross the Galata Bridge for the last time.

By quitting Turkey, and 'the free world', for the countries of Eastern Europe I felt I was taking a step out of what is familiar into what is strange – out of the light into the dark. My fears were that I didn't know what to expect of travelling alone through that dark segment of the map until I should emerge into the light again at Vienna. I had been to Czechoslovakia, but not alone, and not travelling independently; apart from that I had always kept clear of frontiers with Russia and her satellites, not knowing how long a memory the Bear possesses. Any worries I had, except one, were to do with the other side of the Iron Curtain. This one concern I had about the Turkish side of the crossing involved the intaglio I had bought from the grave-robber in Caria. Should I declare it? Would it be taken from me? When I had been looking out my visas for Eastern Europe at the Pera Palas I had taken the intaglio, still wrapped in its rag, out of the lining of a jacket where I had hidden it. I had not looked at it since M. Mestan had dropped it into my hand in the lamplight. Now I held the gem up against the light of day at the window of my room. It was a fake. The stuff was glass, not crystal, and the profile cut into it was that of a modern girl.

Everyone has had the experience of walking on a beach by the breaking waves, foam and watery light flooding the seashore, and of picking up from the sands a shining stone, whose loveliness holds within itself all the transient beauty you see and hear, the tide and light, the very sound of the waves and the crying of the gulls. You put the stone into your pocket because you wish you could put the scene whole into your memory. That night a dry, dull pebble is amongst your small change. You throw it away or keep it – are sad or amused – according to temperament. Something of the seashore stays in your mind, and no stone helps you keep it all. So, as I crossed the Galata Bridge to catch the train into Eastern Europe, I threw the fake intaglio into the Golden Horn. Crowds were hurrying to and fro densely over the darkening water, ferries dashed through choppy waves, smoking blackly into the evening sky. The dogs which spend the day sleeping were beginning to make themselves heard from courts and alleys, and no doubt the cats and kittens you see everywhere by daylight were making themselves scarce on walltop or roof.

The Sofia Express stood ready in the Sirkeçi Station. On the platform lamps were lit which glowed on the long curving train. I went on board. There is no telling in advance whether you're going to be comfortable or not on a journey: expecting that this fourteen-hour stage to Sofia would be made in a carriage packed tight with Turkish workers going to Germany, I found myself instead alone amid snowy sheets in a six-berth compartment. I walked about the platform, and drank the last of the many hundreds of bottles of *maden sodasi* which had sustained my Turkish travels – delicious water prickling the tongue and cleaning away dust and heat from the mind like a sponge on a windscreen – and ate a sandwich. A few rooks tumbled across the darkening strip of sky above the train. At seven o'clock, its departure announced in Turkish and English, the Sofia Express drew out. The last sound of Istanbul I heard before closing the window was the watery hoot of the Bosphorus ferries.

VII

❖❖❖❖❖❖❖❖❖❖❖❖❖❖❖❖❖❖❖❖❖❖❖❖

I

A few evenings later, sunset found me on a bench amongst the trees and quiet paths of the Cismigiu Park in Bucharest, where I had sat down to consider my first rather surprising view of Eastern Europe. Amid the rococo glories of the Hotel Bulevard I possessed a room – full of white and gold furniture, with French windows giving on to balconies above the streets – of the style into which Doris Day used to be shown in Hollywood comedies; all day I had been walking through sunny streets strewn with chestnut leaves, and ornamented with houses and villas in the frivolous taste of the eighties and nineties of the last century; at the edge of the park I had passed a church from which chanting and lamplight spilled out into the dusk, and now, from my seat by the water under the trees, the presence of a city was hardly to be heard. Sitting there in perfect security, though it was almost dark, I compared this spacious park and the handsome streets which surrounded it with the armed soldiers and the sense of danger ever present in Turkey. I had expected, as I said, to step out of the light into the dark during those two hours of midnight banging and shouting which it had taken to hammer the train through the Iron Curtain into Bulgaria from Turkey. But that wasn't the effect I felt as I sat in the peaceful park. Bucharest didn't seem to be 'the dark'.

Waking at seven in the morning on the train from Istanbul to Sofia I had eagerly pulled back the blind for my first glimpse of the cramped miseries of Russia's satellites. What scene of collectivist tyranny would meet the eye accustomed to the freedom of Turkey? Under a grey sky, in a low dark landscape, I saw an old man with a bald white head standing up in his cart in blue overalls to drive his donkey through the fields. I recognized in him a European – *mon frère, mon semblable*. I was home from Asia. The train crept through wide flat fields of maize stubble, or passed the fenced gardens and paved streets of villages, of a landscape which, though very distinctly un-English, was yet 'homely' to me in the way that all of Europe is, and isn't, home to an Englishman. I was surprised by the affection I felt for it – for the fine single walnut trees, for instance, which a careful hand had planted and brought to maturity beside the track or here and there about the fields. In Turkey and the Turks I had felt interest – deep, unflagging for weeks – but interest only, never affection. Neither NATO, nor the EEC, nor the self-proclaimed Europeanization of Atatürk, could ever make a Turk *mon frère, mon semblable*. Nor did I want him to be. From Turkey and the Turks I wanted something else, perhaps the antithesis of the 'homeliness' of Europe.

When the Turks were a force in Europe, until 1914, all Europeans were obliged to take a line, and recognize whether they were pro-Turk or anti-Turk. The government position shifted with political expediency – the Turks being on the whole a useful bulwark against Russia and a tiresome presence in Egypt – but for private Englishmen the issue was an emotional one. People were enamoured of the Turks, or loathed them. The Bulgarian Atrocities divided England. On a hillside about twenty miles to the west of my train, in the May of 1876, Turkish irregulars butchered or burned five thousand men, women and children as a measure to suppress a Slav rising at Batak. England separated into Atrocitarians behind Gladstone, and Antiatrocitarians under Disraeli (who maintained that the whole thing was much inflated, a handful of peasants perhaps ill-used by our Turkish allies, the Batak incident probably devised by Russia as an excuse to invade Turkey's Danubian provinces to 'liberate' the Christian population). In England it was a significant division. Gladstone's fervour harnessed the interest of the small-property-owning, church-and-chapel-going, shopkeeping class which had built up for itself the castle-home of the Englishman whose existence – the existence of a bourgeoisie – the very idea of Turkey threatened as the tide threatens castles of sand. In no province of the Ottoman Empire did a respectable middle class ever exist. To the bourgeoisie of Victorian England, the Turk flourished every weapon of Genghis Khan. 'Turkey,' said Miss Skene in her *Wayfaring Sketches*, 'is a despotic and corrupt government, hand in hand with a vile creed, working upon a people whose natural propensities render them singularly apt for the reception of evil.' Two nervous clergymen travelling on a Danube steamer reported to the papers dreadful atrocities on every hand, a perfect forest of Bulgar Christians impaled on stakes as far as the eye could see, and much fury against the Turk was expended until it was pointed out that the 'Christians' were more probably bundles of fodder spiked up out of reach of the stock, as had been the Balkan way of doing the thing for any number of centuries. The English upper class, on the other hand, rather pooh-poohed Turkish atrocities, and don't seem to have felt themselves threatened by Turkish manners and morals.

Between bourgeoisie and upper class come the travellers who interest me. I would invent a man rooted in the middle class, but rejecting its limitations and aspiring to hold upper-class ideas of liberty and independence. Formed in this way, he would have a fundamental dread of the Turk bred into his bones, which he would take pains to overlay with jaunty insouciance towards Turkish manners and morals, and even massacres, in his anxiety to place himself in the company of the Asiatic ruling class.

On the Danube, not far from my train, making slow progress through Bulgaria that morning, there occurred in the palace of a pasha in the 1850s an evening's entertainment which shows the travelling Englishman in a wonderfully clear light. He was a man named Skene, son of a consul in Malta – a relative of the Miss Skene quoted above – and he was dining with the pasha when a storm broke upon the palace, causing tiles to tumble about the party's ears, rain to lash the river, storks to flap heavily through the building seeking shelter. The pasha obliged the narrator to sit on one side of him, and on the other a dismissed official who was made so extremely nervous by this proximity to the tyrant that a shaking hand could convey no dinner between his chattering teeth. First the slaves lost their heads in face of the storm's fury and ran about in packs screaming with terror; next the guests began to hesitate miserably between fear of the elements and fear of the pasha, until one by one they had shuffled away into recesses of the rickety old building where lightning whitened tatters of curtain and the moaning of the wind was engulfed in long passages and empty halls. 'Amid all these majestic convulsions of nature, and weak trepidations of men,' says Skene, 'the pasha sat calmly smoking his pipe, a faint smile lighting up his features; and he cast quick glances of intelligence at me, expressive of his contempt for others and of his fellow-feeling with me because I did not show alarm.' Thus the portrait of himself the traveller wished to present to the public. No Atrocitarian he, if such ideas meant censuring the manner in which his friend the pasha chose to keep in order the miserable Swabian Christian rayahs, whose villages Skene dismisses as 'huts lower than any human habitation save the cabins of Connaught'. Indeed Skene describes his dissatisfaction with the tower of skulls at Nyssa in these robust terms: 'I was much disappointed with this relic . . . not more than fifteen feet high and ten feet square . . . not built of skulls but of stone and lime, a number of skulls having been merely embedded in the plaster.'

But that dark tower is part of the furniture of a Turkish landscape, frightening to the reader if not to the narrator. Scenes of terror and tyranny, through which the traveller strolls with an amused smile, is how the English reader expected the Ottoman Empire to be depicted. The Turkish Tourist Office still has a hard time eradicating from the landscape the shadow cast by that tower of skulls. And so I found it hard to convince myself, on entering Bulgaria from Turkey, that I had left the free world and entered a tyranny.

Sofia, like Bucharest, only existed as a dirty village in the times which chiefly interested me. Finding myself obliged to spend the day in Sofia until the Bucharest train left at ten at night, I stood outside the station with no clear idea of the city's identity to grasp at or to make for. 'A Balkan Capital': the words suggested a vague *fin de siècle* picture to my mind, but nothing definite enough to take a taxi to. Trams threaded amongst concrete islands and bore away passengers towards the tall, pale tower-blocks of the city. Their destinations, and everything else written in Bulgarian, was shrouded from me in the mysteries of the Cyrillic alphabet. But I had put my bag into the left luggage, changed some money into *leva*, and needed now to find the railway office in the town where a seat reservation – in effect a permit to leave the country – must first be made before a ticket to Bucharest could be bought at the station. I took a tram into the blue.

It wasn't until the afternoon, when I had suffered the usual trials in extracting what I needed from a bureaucracy, that I stepped through an arch into the very picture which 'A Balkan Capital' had suggested to my mind. Away curved a broad carriage-drive of ochre-coloured cobbles. Under steep mansard roofs, nestling amongst their trees, charming little residences, and chancelleries and embassies in the same icing-and-marzipan style of architecture, were grouped by the carriageway. Filigree railings contained gardens and park, and under a blue sky the scene gleamed with a kind of theatrical gaiety. It was Strelsau, capital of Ruritania! I knew it well. In a green hilly park sparkled the royal palace, a sugar confection in ochre and white like the rest of the buildings, and I could see the very elm trees at its windows in which Rudolph Rassendyll heard the wind sough as he declared his love for the Princess Flavia, and was interrupted in this indiscretion by Colonel Sapt. I went in. It was sadder now, of course, rather shabby and dim, the creaky parquet and tarnished pier-glasses holding the ghosts of waltzing countesses, the head of the double staircase empty without Rudolph V of Ruritania (or his impostor) to stare coldly at you through his monocle, no warm champagne presented by a footman in powder. Instead the art gallery (which the palace now houses) was showing a Lenin exhibition, and it was a hundred versions of his mountebank face which stared from the walls. The palace chandeliers, which had tinkled uneasily to the Bear's approaching tread in the 1880s, now shone upon the Bear himself.

Out in the winter sunlight again I noticed, above the steep-pitched roofs of the residences flanking the palace, the gilt onion-domes and green paint of a Russian church. On my way towards it I passed under the gigantic equestrian statue of the Tsar. Across this sunlit little kingdom, from the moment of its first emergence after the Russo-Turkish War of 1876, had lain the shadow of the Bear. In 1946 Stalin only completed the Tsar's plans for Bulgaria when he made it a People's Republic, and popped the bell-glass over the sugar-icing heart of the capital of Ruritania.

The streets and houses which I had admired in Bucharest, and was thinking of in comparison with the dilapidation of Turkey as I sat in the Cismigiu Park, date from the same Ruritanian interlude in Balkan politics, when the action of Russia appeared to free these Danubian provinces from the Ottoman Empire. In Bucharest, as in Sofia, a German princeling was sent for, a fanciful little capital built in place of the Turkish village, and the nobles and their king set up shop as a Balkan Power. It was the instability of these provinces, between their domination by Turkey and their annexation by Russia, which gave rise to the First World War. Had the Balkans had no period of freedom from foreign rule, perhaps Europe would have remained at peace. Signs of de-stabilization in these lands now are not good news.

I tried to think, as I sat in the Cismigiu Park that evening, of a time in history when Romania has been so politically stable, and so peaceful, as it has been in the forty years since Russia annexed it. Certainly not in the nineteenth or twentieth centuries: quarrelled over by Turkey, Austria, Russia and Germany, she had suffered as much as any country in the world. Now the pleasant streets under the chestnut trees, and the music spilling out of the church, and the security of this dusky park, gave an impression (after the harshness and dangers of Turkey) that an agreeable life could be led in this city, more agreeable than could be led in Turkey. Then I wondered what Turkey would lose, which she now enjoys, if Russia annexed her. I understand the ideological gulf, I know what NATO would lose; what I wondered was, what would a poor Turk lose, that he now possesses? – what practical freedom has he, that a poor Romanian has not? As I say, I couldn't at that time honestly feel that I had left the 'light' of Western freedom for the 'dark' of Russian tyranny. It would, after all, be possible now for a man with the proper visas to travel across all Russia and her satellites in peace and security which no amount of visas could guarantee him in a trip across Central America or Africa or many another part of the 'free world'.

For a European traveller in these provinces the plunge into the dark used to come, in the days which most interest me, when he left Transylvania (under Austrian rule) and entered the Turkish-dominated principality of Wallachia, whose capital was Bucharest. He came by the Tamesche Pass through the Carpathians, from Kronstadt (which is now Brasov) into the Danubian plain, thirty hours in a springless diligence drawn by 'seven dirty little ponies' from Brasov to Bucharest. James Creagh's account of this passage of the mountains separating Christendom from Islam – the plunge into the dark – is like the 'threshold incident' in a novel which presages events to come. The road was at times a ledge cut into the side of a precipice, at times crossed torrents on creaking timber bridges. On one of these bridges Creagh's diligence began to slide backwards, dragging the seven ponies after it towards the abyss. All jumped clear save Creagh, who had taken the coupé for himself and was now stuck fast in its window. 'I tried to get out through the window,' he says, 'but it would have been as easy for a camel to get through the eye of a needle . . . my feelings were like those of a Turkish woman in a bag about to be thrown into the Bosphorus.' All was well – 'an angel in the shape of a long-haired Wallach peasant wrenched open the door from the outside' – but the similes Creagh used to describe this adventure on the threshold of Islam and the East, are lights into the English traveller's mind. Here, on quitting Christendom, is the Pass he must undertake, the 'eye of the needle' he must squeeze through at great peril, leaving much behind; beyond the Pass lies the dread East, with its frisson of licence and cruelty, where women in bags are thrown into the Bosphorus.

Behind him, in Brasov, lay a diligent and respectable community of 'Saxons' whose neat houses, and Lutheran churches, and bourgeois society, typified what a middle-class Englishman was leaving behind him to travel into the East. I was very much struck with the streets of fine houses in Brasov, and in Sibiu a few days later I was able to examine the inside of one such town house, which holds the Brukenthal Museum. There were fine rooms on the first floor with windows of wrinkled glass through which you could see the heavily enriched façades of your neighbours' houses curving away down the street, their roofs pierced for dormer-windows like sleepy eyes lidded with slates, and a glimpse of the green country at the street's end. Inside was the creak of parquet, faded silk covers, the smell of dust; they were rooms for calling in, gloves in your hat on the floor by your French chair, when taking leave of the solid European bourgeoisie which did not exist beyond the Tamesche Pass. Here my picture of my Traveller became clearer. If his position at home was safe and stable – if he was the son of a rich and established family in England – then he'd take leave of this society with some uneasiness for what lay ahead in the East. But an adventurer, or a young fellow who fancied himself undervalued in England – repressed indeed by an established bourgeoisie squatting on the ladder he hoped to climb – would find these dusty, airless rooms, and the need to be polite to their owners, just what he wished most fervently at the devil about the society he was quitting in order to try his capabilities in the wide free field of the East. I saw the contrasted characters of a pair of friends I would have setting out together for an Eastern tour, as they sat together in this room. One looks quite at his ease chatting in German, gloves in hat, to the ringleted daughters of the household, conscious of his ability to beat such a family at its own game by wealth and prospects superior to their own; the other sits by impatient of drawing-rooms, eager to reach scenes beyond the border of Christendom and of gentility, where he believes that his abilities, rather than his companion's advantages, will come into the ascendant. 'In the Caucasus,' says that deplorably bloodthirsty sportsman, the Old Shekarry, 'a man's worth is not estimated by the length of his pocket, but according to the gifts bestowed upon him by Nature . . . a bold spirit, a cool head in time of danger, a good shot, a skilful horseman, and a strong arm that can defend his own . . . is a rich man in Circassia.' Such a house as I was in, at Brasov, belonging to a prosperous Saxon, would have been the last outpost of genteel society before such altered ground-rules as the Old Shekarry describes gave back Sir Gawain his ascendancy over Galahad.

I came to Brasov the other way, from Bucharest where I had hired a car for my spin through Transylvania, and the Germanic atmosphere of the town – that sensation of being once more in the North which greets you in, say, Milan Cathedral after months spent in southern Italy – made a most profound impact on me. The day was dark, an easterly wind bending the poplars of the low wintry landscape north of Bucharest. Rènting a car in a foreign land gives you back the boundless freedom of first owning a car. The bonds of timetables are snapped. You are master of your destiny. Freedom so wide, so sudden, is tinged with alarm, like the freedom you feel when the wind tugs suddenly hard at the sail-sheet in your hand, and the sea ahead flows dark. With these feelings I had driven into the Carpathians, and stopped at Sinaia to walk uphill through the trees to the monastery. Damp white walls rose against misty pines, and against gloomy wooded peaks wound through by scarves of mist: beyond those forests and precipices lay Transylvania. Because of the ring of the name, and because I had reached my view of its frontier by lands and seas steeped in romance for me, I felt sure I stood in lonely isolation amongst crag and mist at that monastery gate. With a hiss of airbrakes two charabancs stopped behind me. Out poured a torrent of English tourists. Not the wisps of gentlefolk I'd seen stumbling after their Serenissima professor over the ruins of Asia Minor – not young like the Enid Blyton pilgrims – not in the least adventurous-looking – they had comfortable faces and thick figures, and descended rather reluctantly from the warm coaches, zipping up anoraks or tying plastic hats under chins. 'No photos today,' said a man looking doubtfully at the mist.

The Englishman's view of his countrymen encountered abroad is an interesting theme running through travel books. With the development of tourism (and the simultaneous decline in national self-confidence) it has become the fashion to mock compatriots seen in foreign parts, as if contempt elevated the writer into a swan amongst geese; but an English traveller writing for English readers in the nineteenth century needed only to describe an Englishman, warts and all, for these readers to stand on their chairs and cheer. James Creagh writes in Rustchuk on the Danube:

It was in front of the Pasha's house that I saw in the distance two men, and one of them belonged to that type of mankind which some people admire, and look upon as the masterpiece of the creation; and which others regard with the greatest aversion, considering him a mixture of ignorant pride, stupidity, and rudeness. As to the type there could be no mistake, and the man, who, with his hands thrust into his pockets and his head rather bent down, was wading through the mud in the Pasha's square, jostling everyone who came too close out of his way, and caring very little if he upset the Pasha of Rustchuk, tails and all, into the gutter, was of that type which people mean to explain when they say 'a regular Englishman'. I hailed my compatriot and accused him of being a countryman.

Indeed the difficulty in those days was to insert any criticism of the English whatsoever into a book, and keep your readership. Arthur Conolly uses a sly artifice; he inserts a 'comical' story giving the view of a Persian traveller upon the English he had seen at Ludhiana; the Persian says,

The English are by no means a pleasant race to be among, for they have nothing to say for themselves and, considering they are unbelievers, have more pride than enough. I saw a great little man who was very civil, but as dry as a stick . . . he gave me tea, which they make deliciously; asked me questions, and when I answered 'Bulli' said only 'Ha!' First came in one captain and then another; they looked at me and at each other, and every now and then delivered themselves of a syllable or two; while one man was pacing up and down as if he was possessed. Formerly the English were a small tribe of merchants, servants to the Kings of Hindoostan, but now they have it all their own way. If two men quarrel about a country, they step in to adjust the dispute, and turn both out . . . soldiers the Inglis are not.

This satirical treatment of so solemn a matter as the empire, and the English character, is rare in the books I've read. It is other European nations, even more than the natives of the East, who are slighted at every opportunity. 'Some travellers (says Palgrave) have said that the Persians are the Frenchmen of the East; perhaps they said it in haste, indeed I hope so; for to compare Europeans with Persians is but a bad compliment to the former. If, however, such like vague assimilations can bear a real meaning, I would unhesitatingly affirm Arabs to be the English of the Oriental world.' He goes on then to describe Arab characteristics, giving as he does so an idealized picture of the English race as he wishes it to appear before the world:

A strong love and high appreciation of national and personal liberty, a hatred of minute interference and special regulations, a great respect for authority so long as it be decently well exercised, joined with a remarkable freedom from anything like caste feelings in what concerns ruling families and dynasties; much practical good sense, much love of commercial enterprise, a great readiness to undertake long journeys and voluntary expatriation by land and sea in search of gain and power; patience to endure, and perseverance in the employment of means to ends, courage in war, vigour in peace, and lastly, the marked predominance of a superior race over whomsoever they came in contact with among their neighbours, a superiority admitted by these last as a matter of course and an acknowledged right.

Arab readers, if he had any, might have been surprised by this catalogue of their virtues; English readers would not. And yet Palgrave chose to pass his life almost uninterruptedly out of England, away from this race of paragons. The traveller is a strange mixture of love and hate for his fatherland.

I reached Brasov in another hour's drive and parked in a broad medieval square through which crowds were hurrying. A thin cold rain fell, darkening the buildings. But through the rain, through the dimness, the town's distinction immediately made itself felt. Venerable old roofs of stone slates rose against misty steeps of crag and pine. Above roofs and wet cobbled streets hung the bulbous steeple of the Lutheran Church. It was clear that I had arrived somewhere most unusual.

As soon as I'd found a hotel room (curiously fitted up with two beds head to head, no curtains on the street window, and a bentwood hatstand in the bathroom) I set out to put my first impressions to the test. Used to hunting in the rubble and cement of Turkey for one glimpse of what I wanted to see, I found here more gladdening vistas, on turning a street corner, than in any town I was ever in. Street after street of handsome town houses face one another across the cobblestones with a pleasing complexity of architectural detail. Some are washed lime-green, some eau-de-nil, others the colour of a pistachio ice; on one façade there is baroque plasterwork, on another a row of pilasters, on a third elaborate window architraves, all this richness of ornament filling the curving street front with light and shade. All are capped with steep slate roofs, and behind them rise the wooded mountains. Here, as I say, is the setting for the society of provincial gentry and bourgeoisie described by Mrs Gerard (in *Land Beyond the Forest*) which the Carpathians protected from the Turk. All the advantages of European stability and order – and the drawbacks of such a society, too – might have been recruited within the walls of Brasov.

I left the town by one of its gates and followed the old grey walls on their outward side. Across a rain-filled stream rose immediately the steep wooded heights disappearing into mist. So close is wall to hillside that a buttress of one springs across to a crag of the other, arching the rushing stream where a gorge confines it. The falling water – the deep and mossy arch – the steep dark crags – I was aware of receiving those especially sharp sensations which at rare moments assail you like a shower of sparks. A painter makes his sketch, a poet writes his line, but what can an ordinary person do at such a moment, to catch the water as it curves over the brink of the fall? I looked round for something to catch at. By the water's brink grew a Wayfarer's Tree, the polished scarlet of its berries, the fragile strawberry-red of its leaf, glowing in the mist. Having learned my lesson from the fake intaglio I'd bought in Turkey, I picked neither berry nor leaf, but dropped the tree whole into my memory, where it flourishes still.

Dusk was falling. I entered the town, and walked back through wet streets and squares, splashes of lamplight gleaming in puddles, or brightening the colour-wash of a façade, or glinting in the crinkled glass of old windows, until I came to the Black Church. Past the statue of Honterus, and the thin saints on thin high buttresses, I went in by a low doorway which seemed to bear the church's full weight on its shoulders. Stone and oak, and carved saints with earnest faces, supplied the atmosphere with Northern severity familiar to Protestants, proper to worship. A dark aisle led the eye to the altar, where a light burned in the stilly way of a candleflame unruffled by draught. By the gleam of that light the crucifix hanging in the darkness looked not like art but like the simple truth. The simple truth! *And the light shineth in darkness; and the darkness comprehended it not.* That happy spark of light, added to the glow of the Wayfarer's Tree by the water, lit a picture of Brasov which I believe won't fade from my mind for many a year.

2

The dominance in Transylvania of this 'Saxon' culture, which makes itself felt in the architecture and atmosphere of the towns, is an ingredient in the uneasy mixture of races which has made Transylvanian history so miserable, and which I became aware of when I left Brasov in a day or so and drove north-west. On the road to Sibiu I stopped at Fagaras, where a castle ringed by its moat stands at arm's length from the town. In a country where nobility and peasantry are of one race, as they are in Italy, you find that the castle walls encircle the town too, and protect the townspeople, as do the walls of Italian castles. Here, on the contrary, the castle behind its walls and moat stood where it could threaten or defy the town. And that is the whole history of Transylvania.

The ingredients of this polarized society were Magyar land-owners, a German or 'Saxon' bourgeoisie, and a Wallach peasantry. The whole province has been handed about between Hungary, Austria and Romania, and whichever group has found itself in the ascendant has behaved with the utmost savagery towards the others. The so-called 'Saxons', who were brought in to settle the country in the twelfth century, survived the wars of the sixteenth century by siding with the Turkish invaders, and the revolution of 1848 by inviting the Russians into the country to fight the Hungarians, so that it is not surprising to find them welcoming the Nazis in the 1930s. 73,000 of these 'Saxons' joined the SS rather than the Romanian army. 'In Sibiu alone,' says Professor Wolff, '300 girls proudly had illegitimate children by German soldiers.' After the war all German males between seventeen and forty-five, and all females between eighteen and thirty, were deported to unknown destinations by the Russians, and the 'Saxons' of Transylvania were broken.

With them was broken the prosperity which the little towns, and the Lutheran steeples, seem to suggest. Instead of well-to-do farmers, a most miserably primitive and debased set of creatures inhabit the land. Ox-carts lumber about the fields, and I even saw a cow harnessed to a cart. Such horse-drawn traps as there are, with wicker sides and rubber wheels, look dingy and rickety, like the possessions of gypsies. In them, and by the roadside, I never saw so many base and brutish faces, or pig-fat trunks on little legs, or such heads like thick squashed fruits gashed for eyes and mouth in the way of Hallowe'en masks. These are the Wallachs. It was with a shudder of horror that I remembered the fate of many Magyar nobles and their women and children who fell into Wallach hands in the 1848 revolution.

The walls of the castle of Fagaras defy the Germans of the town and the Wallachs of the country alike. The castle's attitude to its surroundings reminded me of the relationship of the Party Headquarters building in Bucharest to its surrounding streets, and to the people in them. One Sunday evening I had been walking about the streets of Bucharest through dense crowds and noise – drunken chanting from cafés full of sottish youths, rock music leaking from radios people carried, or spilling from open windows overhead – when I had suddenly stepped out of the crowd on Calea Victoria into hushed isolation. The vast pale block of Party Headquarters loomed in its pool of silence. Like a crocodile in a backwater it lay in wait. I was challenged by a sentry, and stepped back from the short cut I had meant to take under those silent walls. Better any crowd than that emptiness.

Magyar castle, German king's palace, Party Headquarters – I don't suppose a crowd of Romanians ever felt happy too near their ruler's walls. Despite ideological revolutions, despite mass murder and deportation, despite the abolition of an entire ruling class – despite all that has been done so violently and radically in this country – the number of peasants living out lives almost identical to the lives of their great-grandparents is infinitely greater here than it is in England. In England nobody's life, duke or labourer, at all resembles the life lived by his great-grandfather. In England it would be hard to convince a returned Victorian that there had not been a revolution; in the Eastern Bloc it might be hard to convince his counterpart that there had.

I ought to know more about ordinary life in Romania than I do, or at any rate ordinary urban life, because I had been asked to a birthday party in a worker's flat in a suburb of Bucharest by a young couple who picked me up one evening on the Bulevard 1848 with the excuse of asking me the time, and with whom I spent a good many hours of earnest talk over white wine in a dirty underground café. The young man was a welder, married for sixteen months, who lived in a distant flat with his widowed mother. He spoke good Italian, not uncommon in a Romanian, and was sharp and bitter. I talked to him at first with the idea that he might be a snare set for me, with his foreign language, and his superiority to the usual run of welders, and his lack of caution in accosting a foreigner in the street; when his wife ran out for a large bottle of linctus to soothe a cough I developed from the smoke and the talk, I couldn't help laughing aloud at the idea of the *agents provocateurs'* anxiety lest their victim lose his voice, and with it the clear diction necessary to incriminate himself on their handbag tape-recorder. But they set no traps, unless asking me to the girl's birthday party in a day or two's time was a trap. Instead Nello talked mockingly himself of the *pezzi grossi*, the corrupt rich, whom he blamed for all that was wrong with Romania and with his prospects. This is a tale you can hear in any land. Like M. Mestan asserting his independence far away in Anatolia, Nello was a malcontent, who would have resented any form of government he might have lived under. Because malcontents tend to unburden themselves to foreigners, tourists can easily gather the impression that foreign countries contain more dissatisfied citizens than is really the case. Everyone else in the café was perfectly happy, and blind drunk. Should I go to the birthday party in his mother's flat, taking with me (they begged) a present bought in a Tourist Shop which would impress the guests, and Nello's mother, with my genuine status as a foreigner?

I felt when the day came that I could sufficiently well imagine the cramped flat in the concrete block, the rusty railings, the dead trees, the crying children, the blocked lavatories, and the stultifying interchange of sign language with mother and her guests. The shortcomings of Romania were already making themselves felt by that time through the gilt and the curlicues of Bucharest's façade, which had so impressed themselves upon me that first evening in the Cismigiu Park.

In fact Romania began to depress me altogether as I drove through the disappointingly mild landscape of Transylvania by way of Sibiu and Alba Iulia towards Cluj Napoca. Instead of the mountains I had pictured, there were undulations. Instead of forests there were mere copses of beech or russet-leaved oak, and instead of torrents there were sluggish streams. It wasn't the landscape I had expected.

From Brasov I had driven one afternoon out of the town, meaning to visit the castle at Bran out of my old affection for Count Dracula, and the scenery in which I was soon lost (going to Poiana Brasov rather than to Bran) was steep and wild as I'd thought all Transylvania would be, mist and crag and the trackless forest of the wolf-hunt. To travellers in the old days, before the Forestry Commission put down squares of evergreens in Britain, such wildernesses of pine forest were the very heart of Gothick darkness, haunt of vampire and wolf, setting of German tales. The forest pressed in on Poiana Brasov, which is an entirely new skiing resort. In its chilling emptiness, across vast car parks between half-built hotels, East Germans with red noses could be seen going for mass walks, whilst all around them the huge dark candles of the pines burned silently with inextinguishable hostility. It was in hopes that all Transylvanian scenery would strike this note that I had rented a car to drive through it, but it did not.

I found, too, that travelling by car encouraged me into a supine attitude towards the country I was driving across. What had seemed freedom to go exactly where I liked, when I first stepped into the car at Bucharest, soon became the freedom to go directly to Cluj Napoca without bothering to turn aside. If you have to fill in time between bus or train or boat schedules, you're obliged to jump in wherever you happen to be stranded, and make the most of it. Timetables discipline you. Driving a car there is no discipline, you please yourself, and are soon discontented by finding nothing sufficiently pleasing in your surroundings to seem worth the trouble of getting out of the car. The cocoon of privacy in the car is like a warm bed on a cold morning, and in it I dozed on from town to town across Transylvania, glancing at one or two, my sense of dissatisfaction growing as the day passed.

Although I don't set very great store by food when I'm travelling, the nastiness of Romanian food had begun to irritate me. Nor was there much choice. A Romanian waiter conceives of no higher pleasure than to lean over your shoulder and strike out with his pencil whatever dish you have just ordered from the menu. In Sibiu, for lunch, I tried the dining-rooms of two large hotels without finding anything eatable, and ate in the end a foul mess of meat in a café. In the dark dining-room of the hotel in Brasov, that morning, I had sat for twenty minutes watching an old woman in hat and overcoat rolling up the carpet, a Herculean task, whilst other guests, their faces clamped into expressions of unswerving joylessness, waited for breakfast in their black leatherette coats and small round hats. In Bucharest, too, the food was rotten. I had not eaten a decent meal, it seemed, since my rather good dinner long ago at the Hotel Bulgar in Sofia, where I had sat next to a tableful of 'intellectuals' puffing at their pipes with an air of furious discussion (and had read in the *Sofia News* an article eulogizing Mr Gladstone at the expense of the disreputable Jew D'Israeli). Now the menus and manners of restaurants in other lands began to haunt me – particularly Italian food, and the manners of Italian waiters. Indeed, could I have opened a door out of Romania, it was into Italy I would have liked most to step.

No doubt it was in part because I was on my way home that I found bad food and rudeness such a bore in Romania. On an outward journey you are more likely to 'support the bad without repining' for fear of worse ills ahead than poor food and disagreeable people. Like the first touch of the dentist's drill, which sobers you into preparation for real pain, the lack of lunch at Sibiu would have reminded me, if I'd been going the other way, that it was still a very long way to Kars. Instead it added to my dissatisfaction with Romania and with myself. No doubt the old quarter of Sibiu is as striking as that of Brasov. According to Mrs Gerard, Doctor Faustus was a resident of the town remembered by the older inhabitants; and there does seem a continuity with the Middle Ages in these German towns, as if those magical days had not ended, but had disappeared to continue in hidden ways, as the waters of a river may sink underground, to be heard still in certain caves. Sibiu, however, didn't strike me as Brasov had done. Instead I noticed what fed my dislike.

For instance, there are females in Romania condemned to live in hutches on the pavement made of wood and glass. To sell tickets of all kinds (for lotteries as well as for buses and trams) they pass their life in their miniature lounge in full public view, like a mouse in its nest watched through a pane of glass. In Bucharest I had seen the fearful and repulsive effects of this life on an old woman who had limped out of her booth as I passed, on swollen legs patched with scotch tape and brown paper like parcels fallen apart in the post. Now, in Sibiu, I watched a young woman embarking on this miserable existence. She was settling in with sandwiches and a calendar, trying her stool against one glass wall after another. Once when I passed she was out cleaning the glass; later she was knitting, a smile still dispensed with each ticket she sold; but the life she faces is truly awful, or seemed so to me, and her compliance, even eagerness, in taking it up somehow condemned the régime more effectively than Nello's malcontent mockery I had listened to in the Bucharest café. It is sadder to see a man holding out his wrists for the handcuffs than to see him resisting arrest.

In general, though, the women who front the bureaucracy of Eastern Europe do not arouse the tourist's sympathy. Whatever you need you are confronted by them, grim wardresses in museums, gaolers with power to issue or not to issue the ticket permitting you to travel – but on the train from Sofia to Bucharest I had been unluckier than that. This comfortless journey had started at half-past ten at night, sitting up in a darkened and unheated compartment shared with a Polish woman and her son, but I had contrived to settle myself in a seat (tying my feet by a stroke of genius into a plastic bag for warmth) and, until Pleven was reached at about four in the morning, I had dozed restfully enough. But at Pleven a horde of these harpies invaded the train, and for six hours, until Bucharest ended my tortures, they never ceased from screaming at each other for a single moment. The smell of their meat-breakfast filled the train, which for an hour and a half was stationary at Ruse, the Bulgarian border-town on the shores of the Danube (it was a misty morning, and when at last, with infinite caution, the train rolled forward on to the rumbling iron girders of the long, long bridge into Romania, to my great disappointment only a ripple of dark water showed below). Evidently these women were a group on an outing, for a leader more terrifying than the rest came round with a bag of buns, and sat on a friend's lap in our compartment whilst she handed them about amid a crescendo of screeching and tickling. She shook the bag under my nose, her face close to mine. I would have taken one had she not exposed the interior of her mouth in a grin: planted in her gums was a set of metal teeth, cheap metal, dirty as café cutlery, which caused my hand to shrink back in horror from the buns. I found it hard to face such women after that without experiencing a twinge of the alarm which that mouthful of weapons had put into my mind.

But you have to face them all the time in Eastern Europe. In order to leave Romania I had to spend a morning in Cluj Napoca extracting from women who almost certainly had metal teeth a ticket to Budapest. In their battles with the Amazons – as in their battles with Centaurs or Giants – the Greeks saw themselves as defenders of the true line of life against a race of aberrant monsters, rather as the human race is shown in sci-fi defending itself against freakish invaders; and the tribe of women who infest the bureaucracy of Eastern Europe seem to me Amazons in this sense, especially since those monstrous females were known to inhabit lands bordering the Black Sea. I can very well imagine them fitting themselves out with metal teeth in the same spirit as an Amazon cut off her breasts the better to wield her weapons of war. To run up against them in battle, in the many offices which must be visited for chits and permits, is an everyday occurrence; but to have had a glimpse into their recreations, as I had done on those six hours on the train, added (like my glimpse into that metal-lined mouth) a dimension of horror like a *Doppelgänger* lurking behind each one of them.

My growing dislike for Romania culminated in a series of rows in Cluj Napoca. I had arrived at dusk, in the rush hour, and had got hopelessly lost. Hours later I took a room in the only hotel I could find in the town, a concrete and glass monster glittering on a hilltop, which turned out to be the worst hotel I have ever stayed in. Here, in the morning, I fell out with the desk-clerk over returning my hired car. To be confronted with my own extravagance always makes me angry, and each extra charge the clerk loaded on to my bill – petrol, mileage, insurance – made me realize the more clearly that renting a car had been a costly mistake, and so infuriated me further. Moreover the clerk in his little leatherette jacket had a cold, and snuffled and sneezed over me and his sums. Presented with the grand total I refused to pay in foreign currency, offering only the large quantities of *lei* I seemed to have collected. The more he huffed, the more my accumulated grievance dissolved into satisfaction. When he reached for a telephone to call the police, I walked into the dining-room to have breakfast, confident that little peccadilloes of his own would enter his mind at the prospect of an interview with the police. I prolonged the game until I had recovered my temper, when I paid up and walked down flight upon flight of steps, beneath chestnuts rusting into autumn colours, until I crossed a shabby river at the foot of the hill, and entered the sunlit town to buy my railway ticket to Budapest.

Tramping from office to office, and Amazon to Amazon, I thought of Laurence Oliphant buying a rail ticket in 1852 in St Petersburg: having arrived at the station an hour early, as the government required,

we rushed to show our passports for Moscow, to procure which we had been to three different offices the day before. Here the descriptions of our persons and our reasons for travelling being copied at full length, we were hurried to another counter, where we got it stamped; whence we sped to the ticket office, and went through a few formalities which ended in receiving a ticket to add to the number of those with which our pockets were pretty well filled. Ladies do not think in Russia of trying to carry their tickets in their gloves.

There was here an example, like the Wallach peasantry's unchanged degradation, of methods and mentalities of government surviving the revolutions intended to sweep them away; I couldn't have persuaded Oliphant, had he been with me trying to buy a ticket that morning in Cluj, that the Tsar no longer ruled the Russian Empire.

The scene at Cluj station next morning, a cold, dark, crowded scene, typifies, when I look back on it, rail travel in Eastern Europe. It was 5.30 a.m., an hour at which more journeys seem to begin in the East than in the West. Buses constantly arriving in the yard delivered more and more people into the swarming station, which was meagrely lit and very cold. On my platform passengers stood shoulder to shoulder. In the dark waited men with briefcases, children, women amongst bundles of seedy luggage, all of them just doggedly there, waiting, with the air of people used to being sent elsewhere. At six o'clock a giant locomotive came pushing slowly through the darkness and the crowd, drawing a long dark train behind it. I looked for wagon 78, and my reserved seat, sure that the efficient numbering of coaches which I remembered from other journeys would make it easy to find. I looked harder, began to hurry, realized that the coaches weren't numbered in sequence. I ran. I reached the end of the train. There was no wagon 78. I ran back, my luggage impeding my way through the frantic crowd. The train was on the point of departure, immensely long, crammed to bursting at doors and windows. I struggled aboard, and continued fighting along a corridor in which a jam of passengers elbowed and argued, newcomers disputing seat-numbers with those already installed. Thrust by pressure behind into pressure in front I forced a path for myself and my luggage through coach after coach until I came to the first class, empty, and threw myself into a seat. I was exhausted. The Hotel Belvedere had failed to wake me as they had promised, failed to produce any breakfast, failed to send for a taxi. Waking by chance I had left them in no doubt as to my opinion of their hotel, rung a taxi myself and demanded bread and water whilst I waited for it to arrive, Italian making it possible to believe that I was communicating my views to them. As I watched the light of morning begin to strengthen on the lean hills and forests of western Transylvania, I hoped for better things from Hungary.

In that landscape thoughts of home suggested themselves to my mind. A beech-hanger on the flank of a down, a highland river flowing fast and clear over its stones, willows and alders crusted with old man's beard – even a gorge where the river deepened, its black water reflecting crags and leafless beeches – made me think of scenes at home in a way that no landscape I had passed through until this had done. Maybe on a homeward journey your mind runs home ahead for its comparisons, whilst the excitement of being outward bound makes you anxious that all things should be new. Soon, however, the sun rose, the mountains ended, and the train began to cross an enormous plain whose flatness and extent washed all comparisons with England out of my thoughts.

To cross the border between one of Russia's satellites into another, as I'd done from Bulgaria into Romania, and did again now into Hungary, seems to me lacking in the significance and excitement of frontier-crossing between independent nations. But a long line of neatly dressed policemen standing by the track with clipboards, who threw away their cigarettes and prepared to board the train as it slowed down at the border, showed how distinct the Romanian government believed itself to be from its fellow-satellite. In the next couple of hours, on both sides of the border, eight men at least scrutinized my baggage and papers: I don't know whether such overkill shows efficiency or incompetence. One, a jaunty Anglophile who clapped me on the back for being English (and so, by descent, in part responsible for inventing football), promised to exchange the large quantities of *lei* for which I seemed to have no documents; but never returned. I read, and looked out at the sheds, and wrote, and looked out at the sheds again. At last the train crawled forward into the enormous flatness of the Hungarian plain. Dreariness was relieved by the sunlight and cloud-shadow which sailed across the whole vast level of grass and maize-stubble, and by plantations of poplar and oak, and by wind-scudded water amongst bending reeds, and by the occasional gaunt outline of a well-pump. In winter, in an easterly gale, I could imagine the dread with which travellers viewed a crossing of the *puszta*'s undrained marshes, at the mercy of its brigands and its abominable *csárdás* where the innkeeper clattered about in spurs and national costume, kicking those he took against into the surrounding mud. In these wastes of marsh and of mud, dragged day after day over the plain in a rattletrap carriage by what was known as 'fast peasant', or ponies supplied by the peasantry, a first taste of the hardships of travel came to an Englishman of 1850 fresh from England by train and steam-ferry as far as Budapest. He could have gone on by Danube ferry and Black Sea steamer to Constantinople in modern comfort; but if he was impatient with modern comfort, and bourgeois society, as I imagined one of my pair of Travellers to be, against this landscape he could first test out the superior resolution and independence over his companion on which he had prided himself, in theory, whilst enduring his companion's superior sparkle in the salons of Vienna and Pesth.

When the train arrived at the Keleti Station in Budapest I went straight to the Ibusz Tourist Office and asked the girl for help in finding a hotel room, which my guide-book had warned were always in short supply. No, she said, there was a different Ibusz office far away in the town which dealt with hotel reservations. My heart sank; this was as bad as Romania. Could she not call the Hotel Gellért for me, I asked, as I had heavy luggage for tramping about the streets looking for a room? She looked at me, and I at her. There was no reason except official policy why she should not help me. In Romania official policy would have won; but she picked up the telephone, and with relief I knew that Hungary would be different from Romania.

3

In the ways that matter to a tourist Budapest certainly is different from Romanian towns. You have only to walk down Vaci Utca, that elegant street, as I did in the dusk the day I arrived, to feel delight, and relief, in the evening bustle and the lighted shops. The crowd is an assortment of individuals going different ways at their own pace, instead of the lemming-horde which pours by you empty-eyed on the pavements or underpasses of Bucharest. Cheerfulness abounds. Shop-windows are arranged to attract individuals, not queues. In bookshops there is a stock of foreign titles which you can look through and replace; in Romanian bookshops the books are kept in bays only to be entered under the supervision of a female guard, and the only foreign-language titles are translations of the works of little Mr Ceausescu, whose cocky face shines up from the covers with the complacence and vanity which even Renaissance princes made some attempt to conceal.

Because Budapest is outwardly so cheerful it appears to be free. From the station I had been driven through the city to the Gellért Hotel by a jolly taxi-driver who roared out affection for England. 'You know Brentwood? Chequers – White Horse – very good pub!' he shouted, leaning back almost into my lap as I tried to peer past him at the bright city we were dashing through, 'Very fine pub! Drink! Girls! Yes, Brentwood is tops!' He had been exiled in England after the 1956 rising; but the dark side of this experience was easy to forget in the gaiety with which he spoke of Brentwood's pubs, just as Budapest's history of countless destructions at the hands of Turk, Austrian and German is easy to forget in the bright air sparkling on hills and roofs and river. Because it is a city apparently familiar to Western eyes – shops, restaurants, traffic, buildings, are all on the plan of Western cities, or at any rate on the plan of Vienna – it is easy to make further assumptions of familiarity which are probably not true. You think you know all about what appears to be familiar; particularly if you've come from lands where everything is evidently strange. The people dining at the Gellért brasserie, or drinking coffee at Vörösmarty's, were not opaque to me, as had been my fellow-diners for so many weeks in the Balkans and in Asiatic Turkey, so that I was tempted to imagine characters for them which probably didn't sufficiently allow for their foreignness. There at one table sat a young man dining with his father who became so oppressed by the silence between them that he took the back off his watch and spread its innards about the cloth as a topic for discussion: I knew the workings of his mind, or thought I did, just as I knew the mind of the elderly sportsman, at another table, who was dining with a young girl and who had drunk deep enough of old Tokay to persuade himself that he was young again, so that he leaned forward forgetful of specs and bald patch to clasp her hand with a rattle of cutlery. It was like returning to a country where I understood the alphabet, if not the language. Outside Sofia station the destinations of the trams had been encoded in Cyrillic; in Budapest I soon took trams, and trolley-buses and subways, too, in the confident style of someone who thinks he knows his way about.

The same confidence would have been true of an Englishman in Budapest in the 1850s, when I pictured my mismatched pair of English Travellers pausing here on their eastward journey. In the preceding decade almost the whole of Pesth had been rebuilt in the Western European style, so that now a succession of white stone neo-classical façades along the Danube quays greeted the arriving traveller. An Englishman who had built the Hammersmith Bridge, Mr Clarke, had recently finished the Chain Bridge here with British workmen. Count Szechenyi had put English steam-ferries, with British captains and engineers, on to the Danube between Vienna and the Black Sea; he had also opened a casino on the lines of a London club, to which the traveller might stroll from the Queen of England Hotel next door on the quay, and look over the English papers which were taken in. The theatre was apt to be giving a representation of *The Old Curiosity Shop*. Although the town was a little raw – 'Even now,' says the *Times*' correspondent, 'the croaking of the frog may be distinctly heard, as evening sets in, from the Joseph Platz' – the society of Budapest was racy, and horsy, and Anglophile (shifting its allegiance to the Irish for a time after the 1848 rebellion, in which the Magyars considered that the English should have helped them against Austrian rule). A well-connected young Englishman would have found that he had fallen unexpectedly on his feet in the capital of Hungary, and might have required a good deal of tugging by his sterner companion if he was to be dislodged and placed in a miserable diligence en route for the *puszta* and the terrors of Transylvania.

Intending to set a scene or two here, what I wanted from Budapest was sufficient knowledge of the fundamental topography of the town to enable me to write about its features, and their relation to each other, with the same confidence as I would set out to walk about them on my feet. I'd always known that the Danube separates Buda from Pesth, but I needed to see the way it flowed with my own eyes, and to see how the Blocksberg stands in relation to the Castle Hill, before I felt the confidence you need to use topography as background to action in a novel. Who is there, for instance, who has ever understood the relationship of the Golden Horn to the Bosphorus, and of Pera to Stambul, without having seen Istanbul for themselves? To rely on maps or photographs is to have to write about a town with the wariness of a blind man walking through it. Once the topography is clear to you, though, you can deploy it with confidence on the page, no matter whether the year is 1980 or 1850, and hope to transmit a little of your confidence to a reader.

In making myself familiar with Budapest, however, I was making myself familiar with an illusion. In 1980, as in 1850, the Westernized façade of Budapest is a mask stitched over its reality. Look into the National Museum, as I did at dusk the first evening I was there. Here are rooms filled with fragments of Hungary's fragmented history. Of the many different strands which make it up, few, if any, are taken from Western Europe. In one room are relics of the Magyars, in the next are books from Matthew Corvinus' library, in a third stands a Turk's campaigning tent of faded old stuff into which you could look and see, by the light of a lantern hanging within, the piled Eastern arms, the divan, the wonderful colours of Eastern rugs on walls and floor. Very late in the day came the 1840s, and Count Szechenyi, and the façade of fine stone buildings along the quays of Pesth to patch over all that went before. The new streets and squares which looked so familiar and reassuring to an Englishman were scarcely built before the confused Civil War of 1848 destroyed half of them, and reduced the Palatine's castle in Buda to a heap of rubble. Clarke's Chain Bridge, on its opening day, was first used by the entire Hungarian army (6,000 troops and 270 cannon) fleeing across it before a small Austrian force – and they would have blown the bridge up after them, too, had they possessed sappers skilful enough to destroy the Englishman's engineering. Then, as now – 1850 as in 1980 – it was probably mistaken to suppose that you could read much of Budapest's character in its most pleasing face.

It seemed to me as I walked through the museum that evening that perhaps Hungary's crown, or at any rate Hungarians' attitude towards that nebulous circlet, best represents what a foreigner should try to grasp as an aid to understanding. The National Museum's largest room, its grandest and most reverent display, is reserved for showing off the Hungarian crown. In a lofty chamber, dark as a chapel, shafts of light sparkle down on to the brilliants of the Royal regalia, which are guarded by Communist soldiers. On the walls enormous blow-ups of medals or prints show the crown playing its part in Hungarian history. At vital moments in the tale, however, the crown has gone missing – once after the 1848 rebellion, when it was buried and lost for many years in Turkish soil, and again when it was taken to America after Hungary's defeat in the Second War – but no matter, St Stephen's crown links and unifies the fragments of Hungary to the fragments of her history, so that now Communist soldiers form a guard of honour round the relic of kingship. 'They set a preposterous value on the "golden round of Holy Stephen", and precious little on aught else,' observed J. G. Kohl with Germanic lack of feeling in the 1850s.

I came out of the museum into the dusk and walked back towards the Gellért Hotel on the Danube's other bank. In the middle of the bridge I stopped. A bitter wind blew under a starlit sky. Clanking and groaning trams twinkled with lights along the embankments, cars shrieked on the cobbles; but traffic and all the works of man seemed stilled out here above the mighty river. The bridge was as cold and remote as a raft on the sea. The stars gleamed in the ruffled water, and the wind sang in the bridge, and the Danube sucked and pulled and glistened below my feet. Impossible to gaze into the Jumna or the Tiber, or the Thames or the Danube, without feeling that you have been offered a glimpse of understanding into the mystic relationship between what passes and what remains. To me it is the Danube, rather than the golden round of Holy Stephen, or the Castle Hill which has so often been laid waste – for me the Danube, if I was Hungarian, would flow like ichor through my heart.

4

None the less, though it may be a mistake to suppose that familiarity with Budapest is anything other than superficial acquaintance with a mask, you can have a perfectly delightful time there. It was the nearest I came to having the 'holiday' which inquirers on my return always suppose I have been abroad to take. The Gellért is a magnificent hotel in the best tradition of European hotels, comfortable, discreet, the staff reserving to themselves that faint air of disdain essential to grand servants, which in no way impairs their courtesy, but stiffens it with that touch of starch which formalizes a head waiter's shirt front, and dispenses with any obligation on the customer's part to apologize for giving trouble. The foyer bustled with different nations, rascally, grey-haired, flirtatious Italians from Turin, likeable because they were enjoying themselves so much; Americans in spanking new tweed with leg o' mutton guncases on their mountains of luggage; refined elderly Europeans whose attenuated figures in dressing-gowns might be glimpsed passing along corridors on their way to the thermal bath the hotel contains; and a group of English trade union officials, one or other of whom was permanently lodging a complaint at the desk. After the shadowy crowds thronging the hotels of Sofia and Bucharest, I felt I was back in the land of the living, amongst people I understood. In the morning, from my room whose windows looked on to fiery autumn trees on the flank of the Blocksberg, I sent out for the largest breakfast the hotel could supply.

It's remarkable how consistently well I had felt throughout my trip. Waking usually between four and five o'clock – travelling all night now and then – eating sparsely and missing many meals altogether – I had never once woken without zest for the day ahead. This is wonderful to someone who would describe his spirits at home (though not his health) as middling.

The cold I caught on the Black Sea, for instance, I shook off as I used to do when I was young, in five or six days, instead of suffering a month's misery as I've done for ten years past. How long, though, would travel continue to outpace weariness and torpor? The overfed Victorian middle class ascribed the health and vigour felt by Eastern travellers to a leaner diet, to early rising, and to exercise for long hours in the open air. But travel killed more than it cured. In reality the wandering life itself – the detachment from whatever is normal – the dependence upon self rather than upon system or fixed position – unearthed high spirits in certain temperaments otherwise morose. It must remain an aberration from normality for the prescription to succeed. Mere lean diet and exercise at home do not suffice. Satisfied on this point, I sat at the window of my room and ate a breakfast of orange juice, yoghurt, eggs and bacon, croissant, apfelstrudel and coffee, amongst the most delicious breakfasts of my life.

There is no doubt that good meals in pleasant restaurants make solitary travelling a great deal more enjoyable. Where bad food and bad service encourage you to fill the silence at table by brooding on your injuries, a friendly atmosphere and decent food set the mind free to float off on a warm updraught into higher realms of general ideas, which is a rest from the little worries and short views of the traveller's day. Every meal I ate in Budapest seemed to me a feast, and each one increased my affection for the place. One day I had lunch at Szentendre, on the shore of the Danube a short electric-train ride from the city, in a neat little pine chalet warmed by the sun and by a large glazed stove, where two kind girls brought me the very food I wanted on that bright cold day – thick spicy soup, and wine and bread and coffee. Before lunch I had been wondering why I had troubled to come to Szentendre, which didn't seem to amount to much, but when I stepped out into the wintry sun afterwards, it was as though a magician had rearranged the village specially to charm me. I walked by narrow streets between gardens and cottages, and old shops and old houses, to a cobbled square high above the rooftops where a yellow church stood amongst leafless trees, with a view eastward over the broad hurrying Danube, and westward into low sunlight colouring the Buda hills.

Just as good food counts for more than the stern-minded traveller might allow, so also with the contacts you make willy-nilly with people along the way when you're travelling alone. The two girls in the Szentendre restaurant – the clerk from whom I bought my ticket to Vienna – the girl in the main post office from which I rang up a friend in Zurich – all the people I ran across in these ways in Budapest presented a human face susceptible of a relationship of some kind, which I have learned (by its absence in Romania) is more necessary to me than I think when I claim to shun all contact with the indigenes whilst touring.

I soon had the topography and public transport of the town at my fingers' ends, or so I thought, undertaking wide casts about the city to visit its museums and other lions, but whenever I found myself near Vörösmarty's café, in the square of that name, I took a gilt chair at one of its elegant tables and treated myself to coffee and Vienna cake. Not lugubrious and smoky and filled with gypsy music, which is another café tradition in Eastern Europe, Vörösmarty's has the sparkle and glint of gilt and glass – the men in long dark-blue overcoats and silvery hair – the women in hats putting their heads together over China tea – which refreshed me with a draught of what the countries I had been travelling through most lacked: style. Here was the society which should occupy the rococo brasseries of Bucharest, but doesn't. The style of Vörösmarty's – of Budapest altogether – banishes all that pinches the traveller's soul in Romania, and I took it like a medicine whenever passing.

Maybe I took too large a dose. There is a danger in travelling alone – as in living alone – a danger of constructing a windowless tower of opinions based on premises which a companion would question. You begin to think your opinions are facts because no one disputes them, whereas in truth the brain occupies itself only in developing prints from the snapshots sent down to it by chance and partiality. Out of the snap-perception, for instance, that Budapest's tube stations are furnished with a row of individual seats rather than with benches, I had developed the picture of an authority caring for the sensibilities of its citizens, single girls perhaps, who prefer a seat to themselves rather than to be crushed against strangers. And there I sat in the warmth and glitter of Vörösmarty's, charmed by it all, charmed by the waitress kind enough to come out with me into the square to show me where nearest I could buy a foreign-language newspaper – and determined to insist, because I was charmed, that Hungarians live in tolerable freedom under a liberal régime. I had in my hand the newspaper, the *Daily News*, which is published in English by the authorities. I read it, and was aware of the temperature sinking to zero despite the elegant café around me.

The language used by the *Daily News* for reporting Eastern Bloc affairs is the doublespeak nullification of language – the silencing of the Word – which affects those who utilize language only as a vehicle for doctrinaire ideas. The style and the vocabulary of all who have been indoctrinated by study of Communist theory are infected in this way, by the paralysis of gobbledegook. Listen to one sentence from that day's *Daily News*, under the heading POLITBUREAU APPRAISES NORMALIZATION PROCESS: 'Initiatives, taking shape in the form of the establishment of democratic frameworks necessary for the solution of the problem of workers' collectives, have special importance.' Clang! The portcullis of Kafka's Castle has dropped shut behind you. Words hurry along dark corridors from one meeting to another. Due to shortages of clarity there is insufficient light to read the noticeboards on which directions are constantly being changed. It is very cold. Isn't this, rather than Vörösmarty's and the Gellért, the truth about Hungary?

There is a painting of Rembrandt's in the museum in Heroes' Square. Joseph is shown being poked awake by the angel, who tells him he must fly for his life into Egypt, whilst Mary is still asleep with Jesus in her arms. He looks at her. She does not yet feel the wretched cold of the night which chills him; she is warmed in her cloak by her love for Jesus, warmth which Joseph cannot share. It is his rest which the angel disturbs, he who miserably chafes his hands. But he must break in on her completeness asleep with her son, and drag them awake to fear and cold and flight. In the Castle Museum there is another object, a carved figure from the fifteenth century, full of the loneliness and dejection of Christ in Pilate's hands. Despair in the set of the neck, the gauntness of ribcage and collarbones, make his body defenceless to his torturers. Nose and beard have the sharpness of a death-mask already. In his eyes, besides weariness, and tolerance of the pain of the thorns tearing his forehead, you can see the expectation of pain to come. He knew it was not finished yet.

I did not know why these two images had struck me so forcefully until I was in the train leaving Budapest for Vienna. When you have clanked out of the Keleti Station through the suburbs the train gathers speed, wheels, and makes a fast swoop back over the Danube, crossing it below the Blocksberg, allowing you a kind of curtain-call of river, domes, hills and monuments before the whole theatrical scene is extinguished by the Buda hills. Into my mind came not Vörösmarty's or the Gellért, or good food or cheerful people, but those two bitter images of cruelty, and the threat of exile and death. Never mind the cheerful little electric train rattling through the sunlight to lunch at Szentendre, or the people playing tennis in the park on Margaret Island, or the crowds and lighted windows of Vaci Utca, or the teeming food-market at Batthyany Tér – never mind these pictures which also crowded into my mind as the Vienna train crossed the Danube and gave me a last view of the city I'd enjoyed so thoroughly because I so thoroughly needed enjoyment – remember instead that there are few walls in Budapest more than twenty years old which don't turn out to be pitted with bullet-marks if you look at them closely.

Remember the bullets as well, anyway, I thought to myself as Budapest fell behind and the train hurried towards the frontier with the West. Leaving Istanbul for Eastern Europe I had supposed that I was taking a step out of the light into the dark; then the Cismigiu Park in Bucharest hadn't seemed like the dark after Turkey's rather fitful illumination; now images of Budapest, light and dark, jostled for place in my mind as I sat at the train's window speeding west.

You might think that midnight searches of the buses in Eastern Turkey by armed soldiers showed me how closely the West can seem to resemble the Eastern Bloc. But in Turkey, though there may be danger and dilapidation and armed roadblocks, there still exists, even under a military dictatorship, the Principle of Freedom, individual freedom to come and go, which the government has not denied or abolished, only suspended; whilst in Eastern Europe there is its opposite, the Principle of Constraint, to which exceptions may occasionally be made. Different intentions of government exist. The governed, too (it must be said), have different expectations. If you read the speeches of the leaders of the Eastern Bloc, you find that they use the words 'peace and security' about as frequently, in depicting their goal as governments, as Western democratic politicians use the word 'freedom'. This distinction would, I think, always have been discernible: 'peace and security' what Central or Eastern Europeans desire and are promised by their rulers, 'freedom' what Western rulers claim to provide, and Western people believe that they possess. Maybe the majority of Eastern Europeans have too intimate and harrowing a knowledge of the opposites to 'peace and security', war and chaos, to risk a return to them by desiring 'freedom'. Given peace and security, perhaps the majority don't expect what the West calls freedom. To disregard what another group or race or nation regards as normal – the degree of freedom a nation expects, for instance – is intellectual colonialism quite as bigoted as that which imposed unsuitable religions, languages, political systems and clothes on three quarters of the globe in the last century. Perhaps the Turk isn't really free, and the Romanian isn't really secure, but you may be sure that they wouldn't be happier if they changed places.

On dashed the train. It would take me not only to Vienna, but on to Basle, so that I could land on the English coast within forty-eight hours if I wanted to. I wondered if I should stop at Vienna, or if such a stop would only be the protraction of a journey that was already over, now that no strange countries or cities lay between myself and home. 'When your journey draws near its close,' advises Galton in his *Art of Travel*, 'resist restless feelings.'

I didn't decide. I just sat on at the window of the rushing train and watched the light fade on Hungary, on wide darkening fields, on the black tracery of forest against evening sky, until there flashed in the landscape the broad cold waters of the Danube where it forms the frontier with Czechoslovakia. I wasn't crossing that frontier. Neither the black poplars outlined on its further shore, nor the country beyond, made my heart sink as it had sunk in the train drawing into Belgrade from Paris that first wet night I had started out. Missing the apprehension, the nervous darts of excitement at what lies ahead – even though what lay ahead was the Iron Curtain – I knew the trip was over, and I might as well go home.

Buying a ticket across the Iron Curtain, in Budapest, hadn't been by any means the tiresome business it had been to buy tickets between Russia's satellites in Sofia and Cluj Napoca. I remembered the rail office in Cluj – associated in my mind with grim frontiers such as the broad Danube forms here with Czechoslovakia – and the female clerk's hands which I had watched through the guichet as they moved from pen to date stamp to pen again in checking my papers. On the wall a clock ticked, and a murmur of Romanian came from the queue behind me. I watched her hands unlock the cupboard of tickets, and thought what my feelings would be if those hands of hers were building me a bridge to escape over into freedom, each step they took a stone added to the span, my heart fluttering with fear that they would hesitate, stop, and that I would hear her voice grate out, 'Mais monsieur, pourquoi vous n'avez pas le permis . . .' – and in place of her hands there would appear through the grille an Amazonian face armed with metal teeth. Down would go the bridge into the river, and my chance of freedom with it. She would reach for the telephone – not as the hotel clerk's did when I refused to pay my hire-car bill, but in real earnest. I wouldn't get as far as the street before the dread hand fell on my shoulder with that touch of ice to the heart which I remembered from Trebizond. Though only a clerk, to the Secret Agent such a woman would appear as a creature pitted against him by the Adversary. Such views – the spy's eye view – enable you to see your life in heightened colours, heightened drama, which is no small thing, especially to the young and bored. There is probably an element of the spy in the make-up of anyone who loves travelling alone. The excitement and apprehension I had imagined for myself in the Cluj rail office came back to me when

I looked out on the cold dark Danube separating me from the trees and buildings of another country on its further shore. Over there lay Bohemia. Frontiers are among the 'ordeals' of romantic travel, or should be. To achieve a proper relationship with them – to promote frontiers from mere lines on a map into real barriers which require penetrating – maybe it's necessary to cross them secretly, with false papers if not a false nose.

On the train, signs of activity showed that we were approaching an ideological frontier: a woman cleaner came by, sweeping up rubbish, wiping lavatories, laying out paper and soap with a prodigal hand, working to turn this Eastern Bloc donkey of a train into an Ambassador's palfrey fit to send into the West. Such simple-minded propaganda reduced the Iron Curtain to a hedge between housewives' back gardens. As I say, to buy a ticket into the West, instead of tramping the streets of Cluj or Sofia between queue-filled offices, I had sat reading travel brochures for twenty minutes whilst a kind Ibusz girl looked through my papers and issued my ticket. Pleasant memories of Budapest came back to me. Next to the Ibusz office, in a restaurant the girl recommended me to try, there had been a distinguished elderly woman eating alone, a book on the table, who had left after her coffee without being given a bill; in looks and style she had reminded me of the wealthy widows you used to see dining alone in the Queen's Restaurant in Sloane Square on cook's night off, so that from her example I had constructed in my head a whole comfortable middle class to inhabit the pleasant houses on the slope of the Gellért Hill, if not with cooks at any rate with accounts at a comfortable restaurant. If you see substantial houses in a well-to-do quarter of a foreign city – as I had found in the charming streets of Bucharest – it is hard not to people them with the kind of person who would live in them at home. 'Pezzi grossi', as Nello the welder had described them when I asked who lived in such houses; well, there are *pezzi grossi* in Eaton Square, too. As I had felt that evening in the Cismigiu Park, so I was tempted to feel now, with those prosperous and peaceful memories of Budapest eclipsing its bullet-marked walls; was the approaching Iron Curtain really so harsh a division of light from dark?

The door of my compartment was flung open. A tall, powerful man came in swiftly on his own. He was wearing a sweater, loose trousers, gym shoes, and looked like a boxing instructor. He signalled to me to get up and stand in the corridor. He dropped on the floor to look under both seats, scanned roof and rack, glanced out of the window. Then he was gone, window and door left open, dark and cold rushing through the carriage, the noise of the flying train tearing harsh ideas out of my mind. Yes, it is the dark. The image of Joseph awakened by the angel came back to me; darkness, cold, fear, flight. The sense of security I had felt after Turkey in the Cismigiu Park was similar only to the fly's feeling of safety when standing on a spider's web after the rough and tumble of bird-filled skies.

VIII

✦✦✦✦✦✦✦✦✦✦✦✦✦✦✦✦✦✦✦✦✦✦✦✦✦✦✦✦✦✦✦✦✦✦✦✦

In Basle next day I felt that the journey was over, my bags booked through to Calais, the train due to leave at midnight. For the second time in my life I spent the morning at Basle Zoo. I walked down to the Rhine. There it flowed deep between the flat façades of a European town, grand and green, swirling under an old dark bridge. I found a restaurant overlooking Rhine and bridge, where I ate a leisurely and comfortable Sunday lunch. The current was flecked with leaves, and on to the cobbled walk by the river shabby leaves fell thickly from the chestnut trees.

Switzerland is a wonderful country to arrive in from a journey through less tidy lands. Vienna station – which might seem overlit and heartless to someone accustomed to the dusky stations and hastening crowds of Eastern Europe – had struck me as the very model of reason and order when I changed trains for Basle there, with just what I wanted to know written up on the noticeboards, and just what I wanted to buy on sale in the bright shops; but my memories of Vienna station were positively alien and Eastern compared to the conditions I woke up to in Switzerland in the morning. Where, for instance, was my travelling companion? In my couchette at Vienna there had been on the top bunk an infinitely gloomy presence muttering to himself in an unknown tongue, an elderly bearded student in pea-jacket and peaked cap after the style of Lenin, who had now and then clambered down to drink a bottle of beer at the window with many deep sighs. By morning what had become of him? He was nowhere to be seen in the train running briskly through sparkling Swiss scenery, though I had the feeling that he had joined that underground presence of which reading *Under Western Eyes* made me aware in Switzerland at a time when I was in Geneva a good deal. I had slept so soundly that a Swiss policeman had been needed to rouse me at six o'clock; perhaps the Conradesque student had been removed from the train at an earlier hour. Anyway, in his place was a deft steward, an excellent breakfast, ordinary Western passengers like myself to eat it, and an arrangement of scenery at the window which unreeled like a travelogue. We passed by huge grey lakes at the foot of solemn mountains, the train taking care to remain in the foreground of meadow and orchard, and not to stray into those savage and picturesque 'views' we were shown with the croissants and the cherry jam. In Swiss scenery a lake turns up just as you begin to yawn at mere mountains, and an island just as you weary of water, and a tea-shop just as you feel like stopping: expeditiously, and agreeably to himself, the traveller is helped through Switzerland and pushed politely outdoors again into one of the draughtier countries sprawling round its borders. In Basle station I was rapidly sold a ticket for the night train to Calais, and was able to trundle my luggage from country to country on a handy little trolley, for France and Switzerland share the station. Nothing could be more unlike the East.

In Switzerland, for the first time since entering Yugoslavia on my way eastward, I was in a land which had never fallen under Turkish rule. Not only when the Sultan's outlandish armies welled northward to the walls of Vienna, but also in their long outflow which left first Hungary, then Romania, then Bulgaria, under the debris of fallen buildings, and corrupt government, and oppressed peoples – during all those centuries, since the fall of Constantinople, the Turk had been the ogre of Europe's nightmares. Everything that the educated European valued – all that his civilization was based upon or had produced – was regarded by the impassive Turk with indifference, and was allowed to become a heap of ruins. The Turkish language contains no word meaning 'preservation'. Whatever fell into their hands became 'the undrained marsh, the sand-choked river, the grass-grown market-place, the deserted field, the crumbling fortress, the broken arch. Stagnation, death-like stagnation, has ever characterized the rule of the race of Othman.' These indignant words preface one of Edmund Spencer's books of travels in the 1850s. The very buildings and ornaments which Pericles had set up at Athens to celebrate Europe's turning back of the invading tide of Persia at Plataea, in the fifth century before Christ, had tumbled into ruins under the sway of another Eastern invasion by the Ottomans. Lord Elgin rescued for Europe the Parthenon frieze with the feelings of a man rescuing his own ancestor from the flames of destruction, as Aeneas by carrying Anchises from burning Troy had set in train (according to *Sir Gawain*) the founding of Britain on 'bluffs abounding and broad'.

Underneath the scolding and the disdain of Europeans for the Turk there remained, I think, a little flutter of fear that would not quite go away. It was not only that Europeans took affront at Turkish peasants feeding the works of Praxiteles into their lime-kilns, and at tribesmen throwing down the columns of Palmyra to get at their clamps for a supply of bullets, and at bashi-bazouks stabling their horses in the libraries of Christian kings; the Englishman's denunciation of the Turk has a ranting tone which suggests fear – fear of darkness, of unreason, of evil powers.

You may remember that when I was sailing along the Turkish coast before having set foot upon it, or was looking towards its stony ramparts as they loom above the eastern horizon from the acropolis of Lindos, I found that I was frightened, and dreaded what lay ahead. I believe it is an ancient fear. Out of Asia by way of Turkey have come not only the Persians turned back by the Greeks, but Attila and Timur the Lame and Genghis Khan, forces of darkness and disorder which threaten the stability of the European world. To the Victorian traveller the reservoir of such malevolent powers lay in the hidden khanates beyond the Kizil Kum, behind Bukhara, beyond the Oxus and Kashgar, in a howling wilderness of dust and sand to be pictured something like the smoking rent in the earth's crust from which arose 'the gloomy monarch of the realm of woes' – the Lord of Tartarus, a domain confoundable with Tartary, whose ravishing of Perse-phone laid the land under blight of perpetual winter, just as the lords of misrule rode out of Russian Tartary to waste the West. Turkey is the western outpost of this adversary. Entering Turkish territory, an English traveller braved the destruction of all that he valued in this world and the next. He crossed the Danube to Belgrade in the spirit of Sir Gawain leaving Camelot for his journey through lands haunted by enchanters and ruled by wizardry, to keep his tryst with the Adversary. To scold the Turks for letting their houses fall down, as Europeans always have done, is to fix upon a superficial aspect of an elemental dread, like complaining of the sea for destroying sandcastles.

The Turks themselves would probably prefer it if their houses didn't fall down. Swiss scenes at the train window reminded me of the pictures on the wall of the eating-shop in Kars, of views Swiss in their neatness, amid all the shabbiness and disintegration of Turkey at the door. Had the Turk invader ever reached Switzerland he might have altered, like the pilgrim reaching the paradise whose picture he carries in his heart; on reaching his goal he might have given up his nomadic ways, repaired his house, mended the clock, settled down. But it appears that the Turks were doomed only to rule over lands racked by earthquake; at the Swiss border, where neatness and order begin, the threat of the Turks and the threat of earthquakes run out together, as though the power of the race of Othman were indeed linked in some sense with the forces of the underworld.

When I had eaten my Sunday lunch by the Rhine I walked through cold, still sunlight to the Kunst Museum. Despite Galton's advice, the end of the journey had made me restless. I walked through the gallery impervious to most messages from its walls. But a picture which pierced my self-regard – pierced through my feelings almost of panic that the journey was over and nothing decided by it – was a drawing by Holbein of Erasmus. There are a number of Holbein portraits in the collection, and they show you (what those mosaic saints in the Kariye in Istanbul had shown me) a wide range of the medieval face and character. With that portrait of Erasmus, though, the Dark Ages are over. In his expression, lost since it shone in the face of Marcus Aurelius, there was kindled again that amused indwelling irony which had illuminated the best works of antiquity. This quality — fastidious, patrician, tinged with a certain wise disenchantment — the influence of Christianity had extinguished, as a virtue, under the snuffers of guilt and humility brought in by its Judaic ancestry. With the Reformation the element contributed to our civilization by Hellenism was restored. The Dark Ages ended: that was what I saw in the face of Erasmus. Since the Reformation it is that uneasily yoked pair of Judaism and Hellenism which has pulled the cart along together, to the dismay of so many of its occupants. 'Why,' complains Cardinal Newman –

> Why, wedded to the Lord, still yearns my heart
> Towards those scenes of ancient heathen fame?

Homer or the Bible? The dilemma exercised the best minds, obsessed Gladstone's. Put them in joint harness, as was made possible by Erasmus' Reformation, and the pair would pull an Englishman inevitably to the Middle East, where both horses in the team found grazing and water. That the fearsome Turk had so recently ruled Athens as well as Jerusalem, glossed the journey with the Mysteries and Perils of a Quest through lands enthralled to the Evil One.

It was dusk when I was turned out of the museum, and very cold. For a long time I walked here and there through darkening streets which gave glimpses of the Rhine down steep slopes, or glimpses of old German courtyards and of lamplit corners. From the Anglican church resounded hearty hymn-singing behind doors on which was posted a notice forbidding entry. Everything seemed significant, but I couldn't see what anything signified. The trip was over; this was the last foreign town I would walk through alone at dusk: if there was any meaning in making the trip, now was the moment for it to step out of the shadow and let me take its dimensions. I walked and walked, getting colder and colder. There were lots of scenes in my mind, but no patterns. In Kars the cold by now would have frozen solid the mud of the streets. I thought of firewood coming down in trucks from the mountains to be sold on the pavements, and of the huge glowing moonlike melons hoarded on Anatolian housetops. I wondered if the very last strawberry-red leaf had fallen from the Wayfarer's

Tree into the stream which washes the walls of Brasov. Winter would have come, on the Black Sea, on the Bosphorus, to the dusky green park in Bucharest, to the cold spaces of the Black Church in Brasov, to the Danube – winter following me like a succession of curtains dropping over the scenes behind me, as you sometimes see rain-columns of an advancing storm blotting out the mountains with giant strides marching after you, till the curtain falls on the very slope you have just climbed, and isolates you with only the rocky steeps which lie ahead.

No finished ending or meaning proclaimed itself to me as I walked about Basle. Past all the glistening jewellers and patisseries, which enrich Swiss streets at night with ideas of self-indulgence, I walked to the station because I had nowhere left to walk to. There I took a table in the restaurant. The place had a suitably eleventh-hour atmosphere of imminent departure for me to concentrate my thoughts. The truth was, I had had the fun, now came the hard part. It was necessary to think, after all that looking and feeling. The novel I intended to come out of the excursion was not going to write itself now I was back. I am always hoping that I've stumbled on a system which will produce a book without as much hard work as the others have cost me; and I'm always wrong. What I had hoped would step out of the shadows as I walked about Basle was the postman with page proofs of the novel my outing had written of itself. Instead, the curtain dropped behind me over pleasant scenes, and I was isolated with only steeper and rockier ground ahead.

I ordered my dinner and a bottle of claret. Before the meal came, and whilst I ate it and drank the wine, I set myself to answer on paper, by light of what I had seen in these months away, the question I had framed before going: What was the impulse which drove middle-class Victorians to leave the country they loved chauvinistically, and the society of a race they regarded as God's last word in breeding, to travel in discomfort, danger, illness, filth and misery amongst Asiatics whose faith, morals and habits they despised, in lands which, at best, reminded them of Scotland?

A waiter uncorked the bottle. Travel (I began) gave opportunities lacking at home to deploy the magnificent armoury of attributes possessed by a cultivated man of the mid nineteenth century. His knowledge of ancient history and the classics, his practical curiosity as to politics and military matters, his resourcefulness and enterprise, his sensibility to antique art – all these, allied to courage, and sang-froid in face of danger, could be exercised by their possessor in the course of a journey.

The soup came, and between sips I continued: The traveller chose countries familiar to him from the Bible and the classics, where he could usefully copy inscriptions and make his skilful drawings of ruined temples – or of prophets' tombs or merely of the scenery – and take bearings and map routes, too, at the risk of his life from suspicious *wallees* or *wuzzeers* to whose ears had come tales of how Hindustan itself had fallen to just such a handful of Englishmen as now prowled about the Sultan's domains.

The peculiarity of the times was this (I wrote whilst waiting for my entrecôte to be brought): that just such an armoury of attributes as travel put into play was inculcated by English schools – indeed was supposed to be the object of education – yet once the boy who had acquired such capacities left school, he found that the English middle-class society he entered offered no chance to use them. He had been fitted out for one era, and found himself in the midst of another. As an apprentice in business or trade or the law, where was the use of valour and a knowledge of Xenophon and all the rest of the accoutrements? He had put on knight's armour to play croquet in.

The claret, I could see, was having its effect on my prose. I ate the entrecôte before resuming: Worse still, the school-leaver discovered that the world he was apprenticed to paid only lip-service to school virtues anyway. Well enough for children in schools, such a farrago of old-fashioned ideas had no place in the modern world which the nineteenth century was busy creating. They belonged to the past. The new man of the nineteenth century, the prosperous tradesman or manufacturer, in the main only pretended to admire the ideals of the eighteenth-century upper class, and the classical tradition: true, he wanted what had once been an aristocrat's education for his own son, but only to break down the palings into an aristocratic preserve, not so that his son should truly emulate the ideals of a nobleman of, say, Lord Chesterfield's time and temper. Such an education had more effect than the parent intended. Schools cast out upon the English world young men who found it a disappointing place. The abilities they had been taught to admire, and to acquire if they wanted to succeed at school, were in reality neither admired nor rewarded. They must look elsewhere for the rank and honour they thought their capacities deserved. In the Middle East, in the stagnation of the Turkish and Persian Empires, an older world still existed: the past for which his education had prepared our Traveller. Wherever Shah or Sultan ruled, Europe's Middle Age had not ended – the picturesque Middle Age imaged into nineteenth-century minds by Strawberry Hill and Tennyson and Walter Scott. He had read Kenelm Digby's *Broadstone of Honour*: all the trappings of such romantic medievalism were there in the East of those days. In place of wizards there were double-tongued pashas in latticed kiosks beside the Bosphorus, for intrigue there were veiled odalisques, for enemy kings there were barbarous chieftains in chain armour dwelling in stone castles on the crags of Circassia, for repose there was the sheik's bivouac in the ruins of Baalbec, for challenge there was the ambushed river-crossing – and over the traveller's head hung at all times, or so he could make out, the executioner's knife. In the Turkish Empire, as nowhere else, both the classical and the romantic appetites of the educated Northern European could be sated – Homer, the Bible, and Walter Scott as well. Quickness, hardihood, self-reliance, courage to face odds: these points of character learned at school, as well as the romantic and classical temper of the mind, were all again of vital use in the arena these adventurers jumped into when they crossed the Danube from Semlin to Belgrade, and left counting-house and croquet-party behind them.

It must be said, too, that in England there was readier appreciation of the returned traveller than in any other country. Here a reputation could be made by a bold journey or by an entertaining book of travels. 'Go straight forward to London,' the Austrian Ambassador at Constantinople advised the Hungarian Vambéry when he emerged from his adventures in Central

Asia, 'you will have there a good reception; but you must not forget to style accordingly the account of your travels.'*

My coffee had come, and the claret bottle was empty, by the time I had written this. The train might by now be at the platform. I read my answer through. Probably I could have written it without leaving Dorset, except to travel to the London Library. But as I read through the points I had written down, scenes to illustrate them glowed in my mind, figures rode through landscapes, incidents unfolded, voices spoke. I had that sense of buoyancy again, like a boat the incoming tide floats free of the mud-bank.

> There lies the port: the vessel puffs her sail;
> There gloom the dark broad seas . . .

The journey ahead was writing the book. That was the real journey. Enthusiasm for it filled my heart, and overran all melancholy feelings of 'journey's end'. I drank my coffee, paid my bill, and made my way to the darkened, waiting train.

---

* In Budapest it took Vambéry ten days to raise sufficient interest amongst his compatriots to collect the £15 he needed to travel to London, where he was at once lionized by scientific as well as by fashionable society. His debt to the English he repays with this impenetrable compliment: 'The liberal institutions in which the Englishman is brought up have made him straight-forward and open-hearted; the damp and foggy air in which he lives has made him stern and reflective; and the continually increased struggle for existence has strained his nerves to an unexampled activity and to that perseverance called "British Clamminess". He is therefore the real embodiment of the European spirit – the rightful civilizer of Asia.'

CONCLUSION

❖❖❖❖❖❖❖❖❖❖❖❖❖❖❖❖❖❖❖❖❖❖❖❖❖❖❖❖❖❖❖❖❖❖❖❖

I always turn up the last paragraph or two of a book of travels, even if I've only read bits of the book itself. When the traveller we've followed through remote scenes takes his latchkey from his pocket and runs up his own front steps, I want to know what is his view of his native land, how do things at home look to him through those eyes which have seen such events and adventures as he has recounted? Does the dingy snugness of England irk or gladden him, when he lands at Dover after months in such un-snug lands? Having crouched with him in the caravanserais of the East, I would like to sit beside him poking a coal fire in the waiting-room at Dover station, till a train takes us away up to London through the landscape of fields crowded in upon by fat trees, and watched over by thick-towered churches, so that I can hear his comments upon these homely scenes.

But he has given us the slip. Sometimes there is an off-hand dismissal of the reader, as of a servant engaged for the journey only: 'Shaking hands with the faithful little Tartar, who had accompanied me to the last, I said goodbye to him, and, as far as my travels are concerned, must say farewell to the reader.' Sometimes the journey continues without us: 'Affairs of a private character took me from Baku to the Russian capital, but I will not invite the reader to accompany me thither, leaving him to his library chair and cheerful fire, whilst I make ready to encounter the perils and hardships of winter travel upon the Volga.' Sometimes, again, the book peters out amongst appendices tabling the volume of trade through Bushire, or in an addendum of 'hints to travellers'. All these disappoint me. I want to follow the man not only into England, but in through his own front door, to see him greet wife and family, and take note of how he settles himself back into the domestic circle. For when you put down your bags at last, you shoulder a different load. After months of depending on what you carry – and of the satisfaction of needing nothing more – it is dismaying to see how much more you seem to possess. All those trunks NOT WANTED ON VOYAGE reappear from the hold at journey's end. Travel is (amongst other things) the accumulation of instances of self-sufficiency; and self-sufficiency is not a domestic virtue. I want to see how the man we have watched coping with his travels copes with his homecoming. Was Tennyson right to attribute to Ulysses, after his return to Ithaca, only the restless desire for further wanderings? Will Captain Abbott now enjoy what he thought never to know again, during fearful nights under the freezing Khivan stars, 'a bed smoothed by a mother's hand'? Will the trees James Fraser inquired after in letters from the Elbruz have survived the winter storms at Easter Moniack? – and will he not now compare them unfavourably with the *chenars* of Persia? The man has told us so much about himself – or, rather, the form of 'personal narrative' has revealed so much more than he may have set out to tell – that I long to eavesdrop further in nursery or boudoir. But he has created for himself the personality of the Hero, and he has no intention of letting us in to confer with his valet. He recollects himself and sends us packing. It is because he is contemptuous of people like us that he left England in the first place. He only pretended to have taken a liking for our company.

'Reader!' exclaims Eliot Warburton at the end of his book (having revealed that a fever, caught in the marshes of Butrinto, had 'terminated my wanderings'), 'you have been my fellow-traveller through many lands; wherever I have wandered you have been; whatever I have learned you have known; yet I scarcely venture to hope that you will share in the regret with which I say – Farewell!' But I do, Eliot (if I may call you that), I do! For Warburton had achieved what Seneca advised, and had made himself a delightful companion. I don't want the intimacy to end. What happened when he recovered from the fever? But his protestations of affection were a ruse, his front door closed in my face, and I am obliged to kick my heels and watch the Channel ports until I catch him setting out once again with his battered luggage, and some remote destination before his eyes as a goal.*

---

* Warburton's next journey, alas, was his last: seven years later, at the age of forty-one, he was burned to death in the shipwreck by fire of the *Amazon* steamer on a voyage to the Isthmus of Darien.

BIBLIOGRAPHY

I have listed below the books which I have mentioned or quoted. The date of publication is not necessarily that of the earliest edition.

ABBOTT, Captain James, *Journey from Heraut to Khiva, Moscow and Petersburg*, 2 vols (1843)

BODE, Baron Clement de, *Travels in Luristan and Arabistan*, 2 vols (1845)
BURNABY, Captain Fred, *A Ride to Khiva* (1876)
  On Horseback through Asia Minor, 2 vols (1877)
BURNES, Sir Alexander, *Travels into Bokhara in 1831*, 3 vols (1839)
  Cabool (1842)

CARLISLE, George, Earl of, *Diary in Turkish and Greek Waters* (1854)
CARNE, J., *Letters from the East* (1830)
CONOLLY, Lt. Arthur, *Journey to the North of India*, 2 vols (1838)
CREAGH, James, *A Scamper to Sebastopol and Jerusalem in 1869* (1873)
  Armenians, Koords and Turks, 2 vols (1880)
CURZON, Hon. Robert, *Armenia* (1854)
  Visits to Monasteries in the Levant (1849)

DIGBY, Kenelm Henry, *Broadstone of Honour*, 3 vols (1829–48)

FOWLER, George, *Three Years in Persia*, 2 vols (1841)
FRASER, James Baillie, *Winter Journey to Tehran* (1838)
  Travels in Koordistan, etc., etc. 2 vols (1840)

GALTON, Francis, *The Art of Travel; or, Shifts and Contrivances Available in Wild Countries* (1855)
GERARD, Mrs, *Land Beyond the Forest* (1888)

HOUGHTON, Walter, *The Art of Newman's Apologia* (1945)

JENKYNS, Richard, *The Victorians and Ancient Greece* (1982)
JOLLIFFE, Rev. T. R., *Letters from Greece*, 2 vols (1827)

KINGLAKE, A. W., *Eothen; or, Traces of Travel Brought Home from the East* (1844)
KOHL, J. G., *Austria* (1843)

LAKE, Colonel Atwell, *Kars, and our Captivity in Russia* (1856)
LAYARD, Sir Austen Henry, *Nineveh and its Remains*, 2 vols (1849)
    Monuments of Nineveh, 2 vols imperial folio plates (1849–53)
    Discoveries in the Ruins of Nineveh and Babylon (1853)
    Early Adventures in Persia, Susiana and Babylonia, 2 vols (1887)
LEAR, Edward, *Journals of a Landscape Painter in Southern Calabria* (1852)
LEVESON, H. A. ('The Old Shekarry'), *Hunting Grounds of the Old World* (1883)
    Wrinkles; or, Hints to Sportsmen and Travellers on Dress, Equipment, and Camp Life (1874)

MACGAHAN, J. A., *Campaigning on the Oxus, and the Fall of Khiva* (1874)
MADDEN, R. R., *Travels in Turkey, Egypt, etc.* (1833)
MALCOLM, Sir John, *Sketches of Persia*, 2 vols (1828)
MITFORD, Edward L., *A Land March from England to Ceylon 40 Years Ago*, 2 vols (1884)
MONK, Charles J., *The Golden Horn*, 2 vols (1851)
MORIER, J., *Haji Baba*, 3 vols (1824)
MURRAY'S HANDBOOKS, *Greece, Turkey, Constantinople, Asia Minor* (1845)
    Syria and Palestine, 2 vols (1858)
    Southern Germany (1858)

NEWTON, Charles T., *Travels and Discoveries in the Levant*, 2 vols (1865)

O'DONOVAN, Edmond, *The Merv Oasis*, 2 vols (1882)
OLIPHANT, Laurence, *The Russian Shores of the Black Sea* (1853)
    Episodes in a Life of Adventure; or, Moss from a Rolling Stone (1887)

PALGRAVE, W. G., *Narrative of a Year's Journey through Central and Eastern Arabia*, 2 vols (1865)
PFEIFFER, Ida, *Visit to the Holy Land, Egypt and Italy* (1852)
PRIDHAM, C., *Kossuth and Magyar Land; Adventures during the War in Hungary* (1851)

RICH, Claudius James, *Narrative of a Residence in Koordistan*, 2 vols (1836)
    Narrative of a Journey to Babylon and Persepolis (1839)

ROSS, H. J., *Letters from the East, 1837–1857* (1902)

SALE, Lady, *Journal of Disasters in Afghanistan* (1843)

SANDWITH, H., *The Siege of Kars, and Narrative of Travels in Armenia* (1856)

SCHNEIDER, D., *The Traveller's Guide to Turkey* (1975)

SHAW, Robert, *Visits to High Tartary, Yarkand and Kashgar* (1871)

SKENE, Miss, *Wayfaring Sketches* (1845)

SKENE, J. H., *The Frontier Lands of Christian and Turk*, 2 vols (1853)
  With Lord Stratford in the Crimean War (1883)

SPENCER, Captain Edmund, *Travels in Circassia*, 2 vols (1839)
  Travels in European Turkey, 2 vols (1851)
  Turkey, Russia, the Black Sea and Circassia (1854)

STUART, Lt.-Col. W. J., *Journal of a Residence in Persia* (1854)

THEVENOT, J. de, *Travels into the Levant* (1686)

URQUHART, David, *Spirit of the East*, 2 vols (1838)

VAMBÉRY, Arminius, *Travels in Central Asia* (1864)
  Life and Adventures, written by Himself (1884)

WARBURTON, Eliot, *The Crescent and the Cross*, 2 vols (1846)

WILBRAHAM, Captain R., *Travels in the Transcaucasian Provinces of Russia* (1839)

WILLIS, N. P., *Pencillings by the Way* (1839)

WOLFF, Professor Robert Lee, *The Balkans in Our Time* (1978)

WOLFF, Rev. Joseph, *Narrative of a Mission to Bokhara to Ascertain the Fate of Colonel Stoddart and Captain Conolly*, 2 vols (1845)
  Travels and Adventures, 2 vols (1860)

WOOD, Captain J., *Journey to the Source of the Oxus* (1841)

YOUNGHUSBAND, Sir Francis, *From Peking to India in 1887* (1939)

A CHOICE OF PENGUINS

☐ *Small World* **David Lodge**   £2.50

A jet-propelled academic romance, sequel to *Changing Places*. 'A new comic débâcle on every page' – *The Times*. 'Here is everything one expects from Lodge but three times as entertaining as anything he has written before' – *Sunday Telegraph*

☐ *The Neverending Story* **Michael Ende**   £3.50

The international bestseller, now a major film: 'A tale of magical adventure, pursuit and delay, danger, suspense, triumph' – *The Times Literary Supplement*

☐ *The Sword of Honour Trilogy* **Evelyn Waugh**   £3.95

Containing *Men at Arms, Officers and Gentlemen* and *Unconditional Surrender*, the trilogy described by Cyril Connolly as 'unquestionably the finest novels to have come out of the war'.

☐ *The Honorary Consul* **Graham Greene**   £1.95

In a provincial Argentinian town, a group of revolutionaries kidnap the wrong man . . . 'The tension never relaxes and one reads hungrily from page to page, dreading the moment it will all end' – Auberon Waugh in the *Evening Standard*

☐ *The First Rumpole Omnibus* **John Mortimer**   £4.95

Containing *Rumpole of the Bailey*, *The Trials of Rumpole* and *Rumpole's Return*. 'A fruity, foxy masterpiece, defender of our wilting faith in mankind' – *Sunday Times*

☐ *Scandal* **A. N. Wilson**   £2.25

Sexual peccadillos, treason and blackmail are all ingredients on the boil in A. N. Wilson's new, *cordon noir* comedy. 'Drily witty, deliciously nasty' – *Sunday Telegraph*

A CHOICE OF PENGUINS

☐ **Stanley and the Women** Kingsley Amis £2.50

'Very good, very powerful ... beautifully written ... This is Amis *père* at his best' – Anthony Burgess in the *Observer*. 'Everybody should read it' – *Daily Mail*

☐ **The Mysterious Mr Ripley** Patricia Highsmith £4.95

Containing *The Talented Mr Ripley, Ripley Underground* and *Ripley's Game*. 'Patricia Highsmith is the poet of apprehension' – Graham Greene. 'The Ripley books are marvellously, insanely readable' – *The Times*

☐ **Earthly Powers** Anthony Burgess £4.95

'Crowded, crammed, bursting with manic erudition, garlicky puns, omnilingual jokes ... (a novel) which meshes the real and personalized history of the twentieth century' – Martin Amis

☐ **Life & Times of Michael K** J. M. Coetzee £2.95

The Booker Prize-winning novel: 'It is hard to convey ... just what Coetzee's special quality is. His writing gives off whiffs of Conrad, of Nabokov, of Golding, of the Paul Theroux of *The Mosquito Coast*. But he is none of these, he is a harsh, compelling new voice' – Victoria Glendinning

☐ **The Stories of William Trevor** £5.95

'Trevor packs into each separate five or six thousand words more richness, more laughter, more ache, more multifarious human-ness than many good writers manage to get into a whole novel' – *Punch*

☐ **The Book of Laughter and Forgetting**
Milan Kundera £3.95

'A whirling dance of a book ... a masterpiece full of angels, terror, ostriches and love ... No question about it. The most important novel published in Britain this year' – Salman Rushdie

A CHOICE OF PENGUINS

☐ *Man and the Natural World* **Keith Thomas**   £4.95

Changing attitudes in England, 1500–1800. 'An encyclopedic study of man's relationship to animals and plants . . . a book to read again and again' – Paul Theroux, *Sunday Times* Books of the Year

☐ *Jean Rhys: Letters 1931–66*
   Edited by Francis Wyndham and Diana Melly   £3.95

'Eloquent and invaluable . . . her life emerges, and with it a portrait of an unexpectedly indomitable figure' – Marina Warner in the *Sunday Times*

☐ *The French Revolution* **Christopher Hibbert**   £4.50

'One of the best accounts of the Revolution that I know . . . Mr Hibbert is outstanding' – J. H. Plumb in the *Sunday Telegraph*

☐ *Isak Dinesen* **Judith Thurman**   £4.95

The acclaimed life of Karen Blixen, 'beautiful bride, disappointed wife, radiant lover, bereft and widowed woman, writer, sibyl, Scheherazade, child of Lucifer, Baroness; always a unique human being . . . an assiduously researched and finely narrated biography' – *Books & Bookmen*

☐ *The Amateur Naturalist*
   Gerald Durrell with Lee Durrell   £4.95

'Delight . . . on every page . . . packed with authoritative writing, learning without pomposity . . . it represents a real bargain' – *The Times Educational Supplement*. 'What treats are in store for the average British household' – *Daily Express*

☐ *When the Wind Blows* **Raymond Briggs**   £2.95

'A visual parable against nuclear war: all the more chilling for being in the form of a strip cartoon' – *Sunday Times*. 'The most eloquent anti-Bomb statement you are likely to read' – *Daily Mail*

PENGUIN TRAVEL BOOKS

☐ *Arabian Sands* **Wilfred Thesiger** £3.50

'In the tradition of Burton, Doughty, Lawrence, Philby and Thomas, it is, very likely, the book about Arabia to end all books about Arabia' – *Daily Telegraph*

☐ *The Flight of Ikaros* **Kevin Andrews** £3.50

'He also is in love with the country . . . but he sees the other side of that dazzling medal or moon . . . If you want some truth about Greece, here it is' – Louis MacNeice in the *Observer*

☐ *D. H. Lawrence and Italy* £4.95

In *Twilight in Italy, Sea and Sardinia* and *Etruscan Places,* Lawrence recorded his impressions while living, writing and travelling in 'one of the most beautiful countries in the world'.

☐ *Maiden Voyage* **Denton Welch** £3.50

Opening during his last term at public school, from which the author absconded, *Maiden Voyage* turns into a brilliantly idiosyncratic account of China in the 1930s.

☐ *The Grand Irish Tour* **Peter Somerville-Large** £4.95

The account of a year's journey round Ireland. 'Marvellous . . . describes to me afresh a landscape I thought I knew' – Edna O'Brien in the *Observer*

☐ *Slow Boats to China* **Gavin Young** £3.95

On an ancient steamer, a cargo dhow, a Filipino kumpit and twenty more agreeably cranky boats, Gavin Young sailed from Piraeus to Canton in seven crowded and colourful months. 'A pleasure to read' – Paul Theroux

PENGUIN TRAVEL BOOKS

☐ *The Kingdom by the Sea* **Paul Theroux** £2.50

1982, the year of the Falklands War and the Royal Baby, was the ideal time, Theroux found, to travel round the coast of Britain and surprise the British into talking about themselves. 'He describes it all brilliantly and honestly' – Anthony Burgess

☐ *One's Company* **Peter Fleming** £2.95

His journey to China as special correspondent to *The Times* in 1933. 'One reads him for literary delight . . . But, he is also an observer of penetrating intellect' – Vita Sackville West

☐ *The Traveller's Tree* **Patrick Leigh Fermor** £3.95

'A picture of the Indies more penetrating and original than any that has been presented before' – *Observer*

☐ *The Path to Rome* **Hilaire Belloc** £3.95

'The only book I ever wrote for love,' is how Belloc described the wonderful blend of anecdote, humour and reflection that makes up the story of his pilgrimage to Rome.

☐ *The Light Garden of the Angel King* **Peter Levi** £2.95

Afghanistan has been a wild rocky highway for nomads and merchants, Alexander the Great, Buddhist monks, great Moghul conquerors and the armies of the Raj. Here, quite brilliantly, Levi writes about their journeys and his own.

☐ *Among the Russians* **Colin Thubron** £2.95

'The Thubron approach to travelling has an integrity that belongs to another age' – Dervla Murphy in the *Irish Times*. 'A magnificent achievement' – Nikolai Tolstoy

PENGUIN TRAVEL BOOKS